Bad Business

BAD BUSINESS

The OPM Scandal
and the Seduction of
the Establishment

ROBERT P. GANDOSSY

Basic Books, Inc., Publishers   *New York*

Library of Congress Cataloging-in-Publication Data

Gandossy, Robert P.
  Bad business.

  Includes index.
  1. OPM Leasing Services. 2. Computer leases—
United States—Corrupt practices—Case studies.
I. Title.
HD9696.C640664 1985   364.1'68'0926   85–47556
ISBN 0–465–00570–5

To the memory of Carol Janet Gandossy

and Angelo A. Fusco

and to the future of Taylor Erin Gandossy

CONTENTS

Contents vii

ACKNOWLEDGMENTS

There are very few in-depth case studies of white-collar crime, particularly where large corporations were involved. Access to people and materials about such cases are understandably significant barriers to serious and even not so serious research. Comprehension of certain areas of business and law also pose substantial difficulties for any author. Anyone wishing to tread on this ground necessarily accumulates a great many debts. Such is the case here. My research led me across several disciplinary boundaries and into corporations under circumstances where few researchers have been allowed. The advice, counsel, and cooperation extended by a number of people is greatly appreciated. Without their help, this project could not have been completed.

I would first like to thank a valuable friend and advisor, Arthur F. Mathews of Wilmer, Cutler & Pickering. Arthur first introduced me to the OPM case in the fall of 1982 and, over the many months that followed, provided extremely useful insights and advice that few others are capable of providing. This project would simply not have been done were it not for his help, and for that I am forever grateful.

I am also thankful for having had the opportunity to get to know the OPM trustee, James P. Hassett. In many lengthy discussions, Jim patiently imparted his extensive business knowledge and his understanding of OPM and the players involved.

Stephen F. Black, the Wilmer, Cutler & Pickering partner who headed the trustees' investigation, took time out from his busy schedule to explain evidence and legal procedures on a number of occasions.

Throughout the two-year investigation, Steve served as a model of fairness and diligence and taught me a great deal about scientific objectivity.

This book, I think, paints a very dim picture of the legal profession. Whatever negative feelings I and others drew from this case, those feelings were overshadowed by the careful, thorough, and just efforts of the Wilmer, Cutler attorneys and legal assistants who worked on the case. All were extremely helpful to me. In addition to Stephen Black and Arthur Mathews, I'd like to thank attorneys Stephen P. Doyle, Richard Goodstein, and Kathy B. Weinman; and legal assistants Mitchell Barnett, Dale Brown, Kevin Lane, and Mary McKie. Stuart S. Poloner, General Counsel to OPM Leasing Services, was also helpful.

I would also like to thank Jack Finz, president of Manhattan Court Reporting, who generously donated a set of transcripts and exhibits for my personal use. Linda Dealy was also very helpful in making sure I got all the materials I needed.

A number of professional colleagues provided advice and counsel and valuable criticism. Stanton Wheeler of Yale University stands out among them. Stan encouraged me from the beginning and made himself available at almost any time to review a chapter or talk over an idea. Rosabeth Moss Kanter, also at Yale, was extremely supportive and responsive. Rosabeth's insights about people and organizations are unparalleled.

Mitchell Lewis Rothman of Hamline University School of Law has been a valued friend and advisor from start to finish. His contribution cannot be measured.

A number of colleagues at Goodmeasure, Inc., were extremely supportive and constructive in their advice. Allan R. Cohen was both enthusiastic and creative in providing comments and suggestions. Barry A. Stein provided support and valuable advice as did David V. Summers.

Other faculty members at Yale made important contributions. Geoffrey C. Hazard, Jr., provided significant insights and clarifications on the role of lawyers in situations such as these. Other faculty members who provided advice include: Daniel J. Freed, Irving Janis, Reinier Kraakman, Burke Marshall, Charles Perrow, and Walter Powell, who is now at MIT's Sloan School of Management. Albert J. Reiss, Jr., taught me a great deal about organizations and white-collar crime, and

I hope his influence is reflected in these pages. Richard Lovely, Kenneth Mann, George Miller, and Frank Romo were also extremely helpful.

David Goldblatt, Jennifer Leuba, Alan Lieberman, William Schwartz, David Segal, and Kathy Whipple shared their views on the case and clarified the roles of their clients. Monroe Freedman of Hofstra University Law School also provided important insights about the attorney's role. John Clifton, Myron S. Goodman, Joseph L. Hutner, Henry Peter Putzel III, and other witnesses also cooperated by describing their motivations and other facts about the case.

I would also like to thank a number of people at Basic Books and Harper & Row for their valued advice and careful editing of the manuscript. Martin Kessler deserves special thanks for his early interest in the book and for his patient advice while it was in the making. I thank Sabrina Soares and Anne Griswold for being wonderful editors and Sabrina for keeping everything on schedule, and Debra Kass Orenstein of Harper & Row's legal staff for her careful attention to the manuscript.

Mona Kotch deserves considerable thanks for yeoman's work in preparing the manuscript. Paul Loranger, Darlene Pinkerton, and Paula Antrum also deserve thanks for their help. And, finally, I'd like to thank my most valuable critic and supporter, Simone Gandossy, for encouragement and guidance where and when it was needed most.

Bad Business

1

An Introduction

ON THURSDAY, February 19, 1981, Myron Goodman and Mordecai Weissman, the two owners and chief executive officers of OPM Leasing Services, Inc., and Craig Barany, Weissman's assistant, boarded an early afternoon flight bound from Los Angeles to New York. As the plane taxied from the gate, the stewardess asked Goodman to come to the front of the plane. All three went forward. The airline had received a message from OPM's New York office asking that Goodman not take that flight home but that he should get off the plane and call New York immediately. Goodman and Weissman left the plane, leaving Barany. Inside the terminal, Goodman found Gary Simon, OPM's general counsel for corporate affairs in New York, on the phone. Simon told Goodman that grand jury subpoenas had been issued to OPM and to several of its officers and that the subpoenas appeared to be related to Rockwell International lease transactions. Goodman nearly collapsed. At that moment, he knew the massive fraud he had engineered was over. His struggle to prevent OPM's financial collapse had ended; his multimillion dollar enterprise was gone.

In less than ten years, OPM had become one of the biggest

computer leasing companies in the world. Except for the U.S. Government, OPM was the largest single purchaser of IBM-manufactured computer equipment. Its clients included corporate giants like AT&T, American Express, Rockwell, Occidental Petroleum, and even the People's Republic of China. Nearly a billion dollars in loans for the purchase of computer equipment was supplied by blue-chippers like Manufacturers Hanover Trust Company and Metropolitan Life Insurance Company, and the transactions were arranged by the prestigious Wall Street investment banking firms of Goldman, Sachs & Company and Lehman Brothers Kuhn Loeb.

By 1980, just nine years after Myron Goodman and Mordecai Weissman began their partnership in Brooklyn, New York, the former neighborhood business employed over 100 people and had offices in thirteen U.S. cities and five more in Europe. In 1972, they had moved their headquarters from atop a candy store in Brooklyn to Wall Street, and in 1980, they moved to plush quarters at 71 Broadway in Manhattan's financial district, where they occupied three floors. Such rapid success brought many benefits to Goodman and Weissman—they even had helicopters to transport them to and from work. But that's not all.

Both Goodman and Weissman amassed personal fortunes within a comparatively short time. By 1976, each had earned nearly a half a million dollars a year, in addition to other perks, such as chauffeur-driven limousines, a corporate aircraft, and officers' loan accounts, which grew to $10.5 million by 1980. They moved out of their Brooklyn neighborhood and into expensive houses in exclusive Lawrence, Long Island. Goodman's huge white house—the former Wardwell estate,* known as "The Castle" around Lawrence—was equipped with its own disco room complete with mirrors, a game room with pinball machines, a ballet room, a soda fountain, and a hospital room, where Myron recuperated from his various ailments.

What appeared to be a prime example of an American rags-to-riches story, however, ended suddenly. Or, at least, that's how it seemed. In March 1980, OPM pleaded guilty in a New Orleans federal court to twenty-two counts of check-kiting—drawing checks from one bank and depositing them in another, even when funds were not

---

*Former home of the Edward R. Wardwell family. Wardwell was one of the founding partners of the New York law firm, Davis, Polk, Wardwell, Gardiner, and Reed, now called Davis, Polk, and Wardwell.

available to cover the checks in the first bank. OPM was fined the maximum penalty of $110,000. Only one year later, OPM filed for protection from its creditors under Chapter 11 of the Federal Bankruptcy Act. At the same time, OPM was accused of fraud amounting to over $200 million by nineteen financial institutions and several of their customers. Another $100 million was owed to others stemming from the bankruptcy.

On December 17, 1981, five OPM officers—Allen Ganz, Mannes Friedman, Stephen Lichtman, Jeffry Resnick, and Martin Shulman— pleaded guilty to charges of mail fraud, wire fraud, and making false statements. Myron Goodman pleaded guilty to one count of conspiracy, one count of mail fraud, and fourteen counts of wire fraud. Mordecai Weissman pleaded guilty to one count of conspiracy, seven counts of wire fraud, and one count of making false statements to a bank. On Monday, December 20, 1982, in a crowded federal courtroom in lower Manhattan, Goodman was sentenced to twelve years in prison. Weissman was sentenced to ten years. Less than a month later, they began serving their time at Allenwood Federal Prison Camp in Montgomery, Pennsylvania. All the other coconspirators received prison terms, except Resnick, who played a relatively minor role in the crimes. In addition to the convictions of seven OPM employees, a half-dozen employees of other corporations, including IBM and Fireman's Fund Insurance Company, pleaded guilty to tax evasion, a charge stemming from illegal payments made by Goodman and Weissman in return for corporate secrets and lease contracts. Another ten employees of other companies were known to have received bribes, but were never prosecuted. Moreover, the fraud and the subsequent bankruptcy were followed by a profusion of finger pointing and by scores of civil suits filed by OPM's investment bankers, lawyers, auditors, lenders, and lessees.

For nearly ten years, OPM managed to appear prosperous to the outside world. It had all the accouterments of a successful company— prestigious investment bankers, a valued location, Fortune 100 clients, a growing New York City law firm to handle its legal matters, a nationally known accounting firm to audit its books, financial statements showing growth and profit, offices throughout the world, and on and on. These accouterments helped Goodman and Weissman make OPM appear legitimate, to look like a prosperous and growing enterprise and contributed to their snowballing success. More significantly, the images of Goodman, Weissman—and of OPM—made it easier to carry out their crimes. Few people were willing to raise questions about a company that associated with such an exclusive group of people and customers—and a company that provided such good deals. According to a statement made by federal district court Judge Charles S. Haight, Jr., in sentencing Goodman and Weissman on December 20, 1982, behind the "sham appearance of prosperity"[1] hid a corrupt corporation that was insolvent from its very inception.

"Only by financing fraudulent leases and paying commercial bribes did OPM avoid early bankruptcy," said James P. Hassett, the appointed bankruptcy trustee of OPM.[2] As early as 1972, Goodman and Weissman had begun to obtain money fraudulently from lending institutions. They financed the same pieces of equipment with two or three banks, they bribed employees of clients, they laundered funds, and they prepared false financial statements. Forgery was among their many crimes.

Between 1972 and 1977, Goodman and Weissman obtained fraudulent loans amounting to $15 to $20 million. Had they been discovered at that time, these frauds would have constituted a major crime, but it was later—from the end of 1978 until the scheme collapsed in February 1981—that most of the frauds were committed. During that period, OPM obtained over $196 million from nineteen lending institutions through misrepresentation. Goodman and Weissman and their team of coconspirators provided fraudulent computer lease agreements with Rockwell—the large aerospace and defense manufacturer—to major banks and insurance companies in exchange for multimillion dollar loans to purchase the computer equipment. In sentencing Goodman and Weissman, federal district court Judge Charles S. Haight, Jr., said that "for ten years OPM perpetrated a series of commercial frauds which in length of time and amounts stolen from their victims are without parallel in the recent annals of this court."[3] Indeed, both the *New York Times* and the *Wall Street Journal* have called the OPM fraud one of the largest ever committed in the United States.[4]

The OPM tale is troublesome. It is troublesome because it raises numerous questions about the public's ability to detect and control corporate misconduct. It is troublesome because acts like these undermine the very foundation of our economy. In a letter to Judge Haight, Trustee Hassett wrote:

> I believe that efficient commerce relies on the assumption that individuals—particularly senior corporate executives—are honest. Without such an assumption, conducting business would become excessively cumbersome . . . it is my view that more consideration ought to be given to the increase in white collar crimes and, in particular, the consequences to our society when senior management abuses the trust that their position grants them. If not deterred by the courts, business practices may become so cumbersome and restrictive as to further weaken our ability to provide the goods and services that have made our nation a model for the world.[5]

Goodman and Weissman committed many criminal acts over a nine-year period. Why weren't their illegal activities discovered earlier? How were they able to wheel and deal with the nation's elite corporations without anyone detecting the vast number of crimes they were perpetrating? Where were the controls that were designed to protect against such fraud? Where were OPM's auditors? Or their lawyers? Or their investment bankers and others in the financial community? Or OPM's own employees? Why didn't any of these people see the illicit practices?

Many did. But they failed to take the steps necessary to prevent further crimes; they simply closed their eyes to the massive fraud going on around them. OPM's lawyers, for instance, knew about Goodman's and Weissman's criminal ways for years. Moreover, nine months before the multimillion dollar Rockwell fraud was exposed, Goodman had made a partial confession to his legal counsel. But the lawyers did little to prevent the future occurrence of fraud. Following Goodman's disclosure to his attorneys, he managed to close nearly $100 million in fraudulent deals. Worse yet, the lawyers helped close those deals. Several partners from OPM's outside accounting firm also knew about OPM's frauds as early as 1975, but they continued to work for the company and failed to alert others about the possible dangers of doing business with OPM. Inside the leasing company, numerous employees, many of them vice-presidents, learned of the crimes but did nothing to stop them. Some even aided Goodman and Weissman in their criminal scheme.

The OPM case is not an isolated event. Over the past several years, the business press has reported numerous scandals: National Student Marketing, Great Salad Oil, Equity Funding, and Home Stake are all major frauds that have shocked the business community. At least, temporarily. And, in recent years, a number of bank failures— due, in part, to a series of questionable loans—have led us to question the decisions made by some of the nation's leading banks. Lawyers and accountants, too, have received their share of criticism for their failure to protect the public against corporate misconduct. Why would responsible people, many of them with fiduciary obligations, ignore such serious crimes? What is it about the relationships among the participants? Does greed alone explain the behavior of those involved? Why don't responsible people act to end the crimes?

There are no simple answers to these questions. Human behavior is complex, and explanations as to why we do the things we do cannot be found in tidy packages. Three factors were prominent in the OPM debacle. First, people trusted Goodman and Weissman, and they believed that illicit activity would have been discovered by one of the many associates and employees of the firm. But many of these people worked in virtual isolation from each other, rarely communicating or sharing information and knowledge about OPM's affairs. Second, Goodman and Weissman created an image of respectability and upright citizenship for themselves and for their company, which affected what people saw. In a sense, the image they created served as a weapon that disarmed the company's victims. Third, a number of individuals who worked for and with OPM were loyal to and dependent on the leasing company, which influenced their perceptions and their ability to control Goodman and Weissman. But none of these factors alone can explain what occurred. Interactively, though, they resulted in incredible lack of perception and action on the part of those involved with OPM.

In telling the OPM story, I will make clear how these factors influenced the behavior of both individuals and organizations. As the narrative develops, I will take a step back from the story and provide some substantive content as to why people and organizations behaved the way they did. But before turning to the tale, a little more needs to be said about the three factors that led to the extraordinary blindness and paralysis that resulted in ten years of inaction.

Trust and Isolation

Whenever we enter the economic market, whether it is to seek employment, to purchase a product, or to strike a business deal, we are confident that the terms of the transaction are exactly as they appear. We rely on the words and actions of the other parties involved. What these people say and do are moral and legal assurances to us that they are what they seem; that is, devoid of fraud and material misrepresentation. We are comforted by the belief that our laws and regulations protect us against unscrupulous business practices, and we believe that violators will be discovered quickly and dealt with appropriately. We have confidence that the commercial activity of our everyday life operates in this manner. Without such confidence, the economy could never have evolved as it has.

But this confidence—or trust—is not always well-placed, as the OPM case illustrates so well, and participants in modern economies are often unable to determine who can be trusted and who cannot. Participants are not omnipresent. They can't be sure that their business associates have remained within the bounds of the law. They trust that they have. In part, this trust is derived from a reliance on others—including the government—to police commercial activity.

Government regulators, however, are too understaffed and underfinanced to effectively control the behavior of those they regulate. For the most part, they are reactive enforcers; they rely on reports of misconduct made by others. Thus, our trust in the system also stems from the network of professionals who monitor and report on other businesses and commercial transactions. We establish elaborate mechanisms through the use of lawyers, accountants, bankers, regulators, and other professionals to reduce the risk associated with business. Nearly all commercial activity and the financial transactions supporting them are now completed in assembly line fashion. A vast army of specialists work in concert, contributing pieces to a whole, each depending on predecessors in the line to do their part in a timely manner. The use of such experts provides comfort that the enterprise or business transaction is reasonably free from risk.

In the case of OPM, numerous specialists contributed to the company's operation. Lehman Brothers Kuhn Loeb, the firm's investment banker, arranged financing for the multimillion dollar deals. Dozens of banks, insurance companies, pension funds, and equity participants provided the money needed to purchase the computer equipment that was subsequently leased to Fortune 500 clients. Fox & Company, OPM's outside auditor, provided financial statements that reflected OPM's ability to meet its obligations. Rashba & Pokart, another accounting firm, provided bookkeeping services. For a time, Coopers & Lybrand served as consultants to OPM. Lawyers for OPM, the lenders, and OPM's customers executed lease and finance documents protecting the interests of their respective clients. OPM itself employed over 100 people, including accountants and lawyers. Each of these independent institutions relied on the presence, if not the expertise and diligence, of others involved; they derived comfort from the prestige and the number of professionals associated with OPM. But the very structure that gave them comfort provided a structure to conceal the fraud.

Each of these specialist organizations concentrated on a set of narrow concerns. The concerns that occupied the time of Lehman's representatives were of little interest to people at Rockwell and others who leased computers from OPM, and vice versa. Because of this division of responsibility, information about OPM was diffused among a number of actors. Lenders were aware of late payments and bounced checks—both signals of the fraud; others often were not. OPM's lawyers, accountants, and even Lehman learned about OPM's criminal violations, but others did not. Few professionals were in a position to piece all the evidence together; no one saw the big picture. Moreover, Goodman and Weissman restricted the flow of communication between the various parties. Rockwell representatives, for instance, were not allowed to contact Lehman, the lenders, or OPM's lawyers without first obtaining Goodman's permission. Lehman and OPM's legal counsel, too, were warned not to communicate with Rockwell or with each other. Where these professionals were not bound by Goodman's instructions, confidentiality norms prevented the free flow of information between parties of interest. OPM's lawyers and auditors, for example, learned about improprieties but felt compelled by professional standards to remain silent.

We must also realize that this network of actors not only diffused information about OPM, making it difficult for people to understand what was happening, but it also made it easier for people to look the other way, to shift the responsibility for investigating or for blowing the whistle to someone else.

The OPM Weapon

OPM began as a legitimate enterprise. Over the course of its history, the company engaged in thousands of legitimate transactions —many times the number of fraudulent deals. The contacts Goodman and Weissman developed and nurtured and the structures and procedures they implemented were not always designed to deceive, but rather were attempts to generate licit business. But the image they built and the associations they established were important factors in allowing the crimes to continue, once they began.

Any discussion of OPM's image must begin with its principals, because the image of the organization is difficult to separate from the images of Goodman and Weissman. Young, hardworking, and ambitious, they symbolized the entrepreneurial spirit that is deeply embedded in American folklore. They were not Horatio Alger heroes, but they began with little and within a few years, they had a long roster of Fortune 100 clients—this while they were still in their mid-twenties. Small wonder they were able to attract attention.

Goodman and Weissman appeared trustworthy. Both were Orthodox Jews, and over the years, they developed strong reputations for charitable contributions to Jewish causes. Some people said that Goodman, in particular, wore his religion on his sleeve; he was certainly aware that his orthodoxy conveyed a feeling of trust and upright citizenship, deflecting any suspicions people may have had. Moreover, Goodman used members of the Jewish community to perpetrate his frauds, and they may have placed more faith in him and given him a freer rein—perhaps, subconsciously—than they would have given non-Jews.

This is an extremely controversial aspect of this case, but it need not be. Every day we associate with people who think and act as we do. People with common religious affiliations, educational training, ethnicity, race, social class, age, and so on, tend to associate with one another. At work, too, managers tend to hire people like themselves, those they see as being "their kind." Social similarities reduce uncertainties and promote trusting relationships; there is a common tie, a communion that lessens the perceived risk of doing business. Thus, it would not be surprising to learn that many of the key actors in this case, who happened to be Jewish, treated Goodman differently than they might have treated others. They may not have checked as thoroughly or they may have failed to ask for confirmations or ask the right questions for fear of offending Goodman.

There were other reasons for trusting Goodman and Weissman, of course. Goodman, for example, was naive and boyish, uncharacteristic of the stereotypic, smooth-talking, flawless con man. Being ordinary, however, worked in his favor—no one suspected him of being able to commit a massive fraud. The trail of the swindle—the bounced checks, missed payments, even the check-kiting—was easily passed off as being inadvertent errors or as inexperience.

Most people do not suspect such crimes even with the evidence staring them in the face. After all, frauds and embezzlements are relatively rare events and are simply overlooked by many who come across them. Indeed, most of us—with the possible exception of lawyers and accountants—never encounter such crimes other than through the media. If business people are by their nature unsuspecting and trusting, there was no reason to alter these attitudes when they first came into contact with Goodman and OPM.

Like most executives, Goodman and Weissman were concerned about OPM's corporate image, and they did several things to elevate their standing with outsiders. First, they associated with elite, well-known corporations, correctly believing that by doing so, outsiders would see them as bigger and better than they actually were. In their first few years, they hired Big Eight accounting firms and, later, venerable investment banking houses to arrange credit. They didn't employ such firms merely to obtain improved service but simply to establish legitimacy in the marketplace.

Whenever possible, they exploited their elite associations. They frequently placed tombstone advertisements in the *Wall Street Journal,* the *New York Times,* and the *Financial Times* when Goldman, Sachs or Lehman placed an OPM note. And, in meetings and correspondence with prospective lessees and lenders, Goodman was quick to mention OPM's relationship with Goldman, Sachs and with Lehman.

Second, Goodman and Weissman moved their offices from Brooklyn to Wall Street to improve their image. As Goodman later testified:

> We had or were planning to open offices outside of New York and we felt that, being a small company, if we were on Wall Street, psychologically people outside of New York would think we are a big company. It worked, because people did do business with us because of it.[6]

Third, they became majority owners of the First National Bank of Jefferson Parish in Gretna, Louisiana, outside New Orleans, for similar reasons. Weissman believed the bank would add a degree of respectability to OPM. Fourth, Goodman wanted to have a lawyer, Andrew Reinhard, on OPM's board of directors for the same reason. He thought it would be prestigious to have an attorney on the board.

But images have certain limitations; after all, the organization's image worked precisely because certain firms with which OPM associated had respectability and that respectability had been *earned*. Thus, OPM used such elite organizations only when Goodman and Weissman knew that this strategy could keep such firms from knowing what OPM was up to or from acting if they did know. Goodman and Weissman apparently believed it would have been difficult to conceal their activities from top New York City law firms and auditors since they chose smaller, less prestigious firms for those functions.

Dependence and Loyalty

Even though the structure of OPM prevented people from learning about its illegal operations, some people were aware of, and certainly others suspected, improper behavior. Why didn't these people investigate further? Why didn't they take steps to end the crimes or, at least, sever their relationship with OPM?

Individuals often try to avoid hearing and seeing things that adversely affect them. We have all faced situations in which we have learned something we did not really want to know. Such knowledge may cause pain or grief. It may force us to do something we don't care to do. Or it may create more work for us. In such circumstances, we may shield ourselves from being told or made to see. The young child who covers his ears as he watches his mother's reaction to the mess he's made is a comical yet appropriate example of this phenomenon. Terminally ill patients often don't want to be told that they are about to die. They frequently go to great lengths to evade conversations with doctors or nurses or anyone else who might tell them their prognosis. Even when they are provided with information about their illnesses, patients often block it out. Doctors report that 20 percent of the terminally ill patients who are told that death is near have no memory of the news several days later.[7] They know, but they don't want to know.

In corporate life, the boss doesn't want to hear bad news—that profits are down; that the department's pet project is a failure; or that the firm's most important client is committing substantial crimes and, if caught, it might lead to the client's downfall and the company's reputation along with it. We all have heard kill-the-messenger stories. Somehow, we tell ourselves, these things will go away in time. Knowing but not *really* knowing protects us all—for the time being.

Sometimes the bearers of bad news help us adjust to the unwanted situation. They may talk euphemistically or they may skirt the issue, using ambiguous language, failing to clearly state what the problem is.* By doing so, they avoid the stigma of being an informant and of being held culpable at a later time for having known about the problem. At the same time, such techniques allow listeners the freedom to do what they want with the information. Or they may settle for knowing half the truth because partial knowledge gets them off the hook, for then they are neither culpable nor inadequate for their failure to act.[8]

This knowing-but-not-knowing phenomenon occurred quite regularly among those who dealt with OPM. And a number of mixed messages were communicated by the parties involved. What was it about the situation that provided an incentive for people to ignore signs of misconduct?

---

*It is not uncommon for language to be used to neutralize the effects of the reality we attempt to convey. "Pacification" is used to describe killings and assassinations; "body counts" is used instead of "kills"; "technical violations" is used to describe fraud and embezzlement; "resignation" masks firings; and so on. During the Watergate hearings, theft and break-ins, forgery and other crimes were referred to as "pranks" and "dirty tricks."

Many people—and the organizations they worked for—became dependent on OPM. The economic downturn during the 1970s sent many companies scurrying to cut costs and increase revenues. Goodman and Weissman were able to capitalize on the competitive and financial pressures faced by other firms. They didn't have to be deliberately exploitive. Leasing becomes a favorable alternative to purchasing when firms can get tax advantages, and when capital is tight, companies can obtain state-of-the-art equipment without laying out too much cash. And OPM's leasing deals were generally better than those of any others in the business. Several representatives of companies that leased computers from OPM gradually came to rely on its good rates and used OPM almost exclusively. Before long, their own company's contingent liability on the leased equipment—if OPM defaulted—became substantial; their ability to control OPM had become severely constrained.

Others, too, became dependent on their association with OPM. Goodman and Weissman paid high fees to their lawyers, investment bankers, and accountants during a period when stable revenue streams were crucial to these professional firms. Lenders also became reliant on OPM. Interest rates were spiraling, and bankers were losing money on the "spread"—the difference between what they paid in interest to depositors and what they received in interest on borrowed money—particularly on long-term loans. Financial institutions were looking for short-term credits whose interest rates were more closely tied to inflationary trends. The OPM notes were a good source of inflation insurance—or so the lenders thought.

OPM's own employees were loyal and became dependent on Goodman and Weissman. Many of the company's executives were young and inexperienced. Dozens were relatives of the principals. But all were well paid and had a great deal of responsibility. Few could have found comparable opportunities elsewhere.

Under such conditions of loyalty and dependence—and diffused, segmented responsibility—people frequently interpret events in favorable ways, particularly if the evidence is equivocal. People may observe or learn about minor deviations, but they see them as being too small to call to anyone's attention. Further, explanations for offensive conduct are more readily accepted; we are easily convinced to take a vow of silence to protect a person to whom we owe a debt or to whom we are loyal in return for an assurance that it won't happen again. Because of their loyalty and dependence, people's courses of action become restricted. Individuals fear pushing too hard for reform; after all, they might lose their jobs or an important client.

In circumstances such as these, individuals invoke a wide range of mechanisms to justify averting their eyes and stopping their ears to the wrongs they observe or are told about. Inaction is the result.

Individuals may claim lack of responsibility for doing anything about misconduct they observe. Cries of "that's not my responsibility" or "I have nothing to do with that, so-and-so handles that" are familiar sounds in corporate corridors, and everywhere else for that matter. Although such buck-passing statements might be legitimate—reflecting real obligations and duties—they may also be mechanisms used by the individual and organization to remain at arm's length from suspected improper behavior. There is evidence suggesting that responsibility-ducking of this kind may be a function of the number of participants engaged in or observing a specific activity. The more participants there are—and there were many in the OPM case—the easier it is to shift responsibility to someone else. Accountability for action—or the lack of it—is more diffused and ambiguous,[9] making it easy for someone to say "so-and-so will take care of it."

Sometimes individuals invoke ethical prescriptions for their failure to report crimes they uncover in the course of their work. Under certain conditions, for example, lawyers and accountants are bound by the ethical codes of their respective professions not to reveal criminal acts committed by their clients. There are times, however, when the use of such codes are nothing more than ethical pretensions—shields that allow lawyers and accountants the freedom to continue serving unlawful clients who pay them large fees. In some cases, the privilege of silence may be invoked to mask a previous wrong committed by the lawyer or accountant.

OPM's lawyers, who were well aware of the crimes committed by Goodman and Weissman, chose to withhold that knowledge from others, thereby allowing the frauds to continue for months. The lawyers claimed that the information about the frauds was privileged communication between a client and legal counsel. But a number of questions arise. Was Goodman the client or was OPM—the company? If the client was the organizational entity, it is the lawyer's duty to serve the company—OPM, not Goodman. Notwithstanding that particular issue, one can question whether the rules of confidentiality always hold. Are there circumstances in which exceptions can or should be made? The law firm's decision is one that continues to be debated by the American Bar Association and by a congressional committee investigating legal ethics in the United States today.

Finally, there are occasions when wrongdoing is discovered and communicated—but it is communicated to the wrong person. Nothing gets done in the end. There are times when people become aware of criminal activity and are bribed to keep quiet. In other situations, less obvious forms of payment may be used to attain the same end, such as the promise of a promotion or favoritism in the future, making the detecting and reporting of corporate crime problematic. Some of these factors were at play in the OPM scandal and help explain why the fraud went on for so long. Many people simply did not know. Others knew or suspected but failed to dig deeper or to ask the right questions to confirm or dispel their suspicions. Some people were bribed to look the other way. Others—unaware of the massive fraud—received such good deals that they refrained from asking too many questions or from pushing too far on the things that bothered them; they did not want to upset the applecart. The general feeling was "Why look for trouble when I'm getting mine?"

2

In the Beginning

IN JULY 1970, Mordecai Weissman, a twenty-three-year-old former New York City elementary schoolteacher, opened the doors of OPM Leasing across from Erasmus High School on Church Avenue in Brooklyn, New York. Weissman originally wanted to call the company "Leasing Services Division," but—he claimed—because its initials were "LSD," the New York secretary of state rejected the name; in fact, the name was rejected because a subsidiary of another company already had the name. Weissman then chose the initials of "Other People's Money," unaware, at the time, of the two books of that title, one written by Louis Brandeis in 1914, the other by the sociologist Donald Cressey in 1953.

Later that year, Weissman's brother-in-law, Myron Goodman, only a year older than Weissman, joined OPM as a director and executive vice-president. A law school dropout, Goodman had been working for Chase Manhattan Bank, spending some time in its London office. Passed over for the promotions he thought he deserved—he claimed he didn't get promotions because he was an Orthodox Jew—Goodman was eager to be on his own.

The two men were considered a perfect team: both were Orthodox Jews who grew up together in the Williamsburg section of Brooklyn—their mothers even took them for walks together while the babies were still in their carriages; both attended Brooklyn College at the same time; and both eventually married sisters—Lydia and Carol Ganz. They had a loyal, dedicated relationship, one that could only be built over a long period of time. To this day, after all that has happened to them, Goodman will do anything for Weissman.

Although they traveled extensively, often in different directions, they conferred daily. Even their responsibilities were compatible. Weissman was the supersalesman type—the prototypical outside man —easygoing, friendly, and a genius when it came to marketing. Goodman, on the other hand, was the perfect inside man—interested in managing the fledgling company.

Weissman's interpersonal skills had a great deal to do with OPM's rapid growth. He worked hard to please clients, once paying off a contractor in Florida who was interfering with the installation of a client's computer equipment. He also had a certain charm that Goodman lacked. Weissman made it his business to get along with people and to nurture his contacts. Over time, however, he developed a distant relationship with the company he founded; he was rarely available. Some people assumed he was carrying out his longtime dream of retiring in his mid-thirties. He enjoyed exotic vacations—like going on a safari in Africa and mountain climbing in Hawaii. For Weissman, OPM was a means to an end; it allowed him to pay for his extravagant lifestyle.

Weissman was absent from OPM so much in the later years that many people believed the company was being run by Goodman alone. Insiders knew differently. Despite the division of labor and Weissman's vacations, several key employees said everything was done jointly by the two partners.

Goodman had many more rough spots than Weissman. In fact, some considered him socially incompetent. He also knew little about the leasing business, but Weissman, who had a bit more experience in leasing, was a big help. In OPM's early years, Goodman befriended an equipment salesman, Mike Iracondo, who taught him the social graces. Iracondo, who later went to work for OPM, said Goodman was awkward, lacking social skills, and uncomfortable in public, all of which stemmed from the sheltered life he led. Sheltered indeed. Iracondo took Goodman to his first nonkosher restaurant when Goodman was in his mid-twenties.

Goodman's personality was also a bit more complicated than Weissman's. Actually, he was a puzzle to many of those around him, and in testimony provided in OPM's bankruptcy proceedings, he was described as "erratic," "unusual," an "effete snob," and "from another world." Others said he was a "nice person" and "well-liked in the community." Still others said he was trustworthy—there was never any reason not to trust Goodman, people claimed. And because of his strong religious beliefs, his integrity was rarely questioned; his beliefs were so strong they were obvious to anyone who knew him or who visited OPM's offices. Both Goodman and Weissman were devoted Orthodox Jews who practiced Jewish dietary laws and refrained from work and travel on the Sabbath. A mezuzah hung on every office door at OPM. There were daily *mincha* prayer meetings held in OPM's conference room, and on Fridays work ended early for OPM's Orthodox Jews so they could arrive home early on the Sabbath eve. Weissman's faith was so strong that he left OPM in 1973 to fight in the Israeli war in the Middle East.

Goodman was also a man of great intensity. Everyone spoke of the force with which he attacked both his work and his play. Despite serious medical problems, so severe that he was equipped with a pacemaker while he was still in his early thirties,* his heart condition did not slow him down. Goodman once broke his leg sliding hard into second base during a recreational softball game. For his aggressive play, he was given a three-foot-high trophy by his investment bankers, Lehman Brothers Kuhn Loeb.

At work, Goodman was considered a workaholic, often having his chauffeur or helicopter pick him up at half-past four in the morning, stirring complaints from a number of his neighbors who objected to the noise of the helicopter passing overhead at that hour. To put a stop to it, the village passed an ordinance barring helicopter landings within its confines. Goodman persisted in taking his helicopter jaunts despite warnings from village officials. Finally, criminal charges brought by the village against Goodman ended his helicopter rides, but not before he

---

*Goodman had his first pacemaker installed on July 7, 1977. In 1982, he learned that the pacemaker was defective and was being recalled. He subsequently had a second pacemaker installed.

considered having the aircraft equipped with pontoons so it could land in nearby Long Island Sound, outside the village boundary. The pontoons proved too expensive, even for Goodman's taste, so he gave up the helicopter and went back to being chauffeured.

When Goodman wasn't working at the office, he cleared his desk and took his work home with him—thirteen suitcases worth of paper —every night. The stacks of paper on Goodman's desk were so voluminous they often buried his huge trapezoidal desk under foot-high stacks. He would pack the bags each evening before heading home, and his chauffeur would lug all thirteen suitcases down to the limousine. The next morning, the chauffeur would retrieve Goodman and the bags, and Goodman would place the documents in the precise location they had occupied the day before.

Along with the documents, Goodman carried a smaller bag containing thousands of dollars in cash. Always prepared to buy off anyone who might endanger him, Goodman believed muggers would be satisfied with the loot and not harm him or demand his other bags.

Despite his company's phenomenal growth, Goodman continued to maintain control over all of OPM's operations, a practice that is not unusual for young entrepreneurs and that often leads to their downfall. Goodman interviewed *all* job applicants, right down to the lowliest employee. He even opened all the mail delivered to OPM before it was circulated to the addressees. If he happened to be out of town, the mail sat in a pile until he returned or it was forwarded to him wherever he happened to be. While Goodman was on a three-week trip to China in February 1980, all of OPM's mail was sent to the Orient.

Consistent with his despotic rule, Goodman was known for his violent outbursts—everyone who worked for him talked about them. Allen Ganz, Goodman's brother-in-law and head of OPM's finance department, was often a target of his tantrums. Once Goodman heard his in-law make a remark that was critical of him. Goodman, according to Ganz,

> . . . stormed into my office and rearranged it and almost rearranged me. . . . I picture him slamming the door open and slamming me. I am on all fours, so to speak. I back off and he comes by me. We had the plaques—tombstones, I unfortunately had a lot of them on my desk. So he proceeded to take them and hurl them at the desk and at me, and

he took me and threw me to the side, just rearranged everything, threw everything on the floor. That is when he started getting into just saying everything under the sun. It was a very scary situation.[1]

Goodman's secretaries often bore the brunt of his rage, and few stuck around for the next episode. Goodman employed seventeen secretaries in less than four years. Even outside the office, the slightest incident could spark an irrational response. On one occasion, following an on-the-field tirade during a softball game, Goodman wrote a three-page letter to the commissioner of the Young Israel Softball League, protesting calls made by an umpire who, he said, "exhibited an undue amount of favoritism and subsequently led to our loss of psychological control."[2]

Myron's pen could burn paper. He often wrote scathing letters to his employees, frequently his most senior people, calling them everything in the book. In one memorandum to several OPM executives, Goodman wrote:

> If [a certain transaction fails to close on time] someone's head will be very, very smoothly severed from the remaining parts of their body. That person being the same person to lastly almost ha[ve] another part of his anatomy removed. I.E. Mr. Allen Ganz.[3]

No matter how vicious his letters were, however, he always ended them with "Best personal regards, Myron."

But despite his sometimes tyrannical behavior, Goodman was also known for his extreme generosity. He gave away millions to charitable organizations, particularly to those with Jewish affiliations. One secretary said the phone would ring off the hook around the Jewish holidays with people requesting donations; moreover, his correspondence files were filled with requests for contributions, few of which were ever turned down. Several examples illustrate Goodman's compassion. Once he saw an elderly woman searching for something to eat out of a garbage can in front of Bernstein's Delicatessen on Essex Street, on New York's Lower East Side. Feeling sorry for her, he made sure she received social aid and was placed in a nursing home. During Jewish holidays—Hanukkah, Rosh Hashanah, Yom Kippur— he provided her with whatever she needed. Another time, Goodman read in the *New York Post* about a young man who was stricken with cancer of the brain and needed money to get from New York to Chicago where he was to receive treatment. Goodman sent him a $5,000 check.

From 1977 through 1981, Goodman and Weissman—but mostly Goodman—donated nearly $3.5 million to charitable organizations, including almost $1 million in 1980 to Yeshiva University. The million to Yeshiva University was part of a $10 million pledge Goodman had made—the largest pledge the nearly 100-year-old institution ever received. Commenting on the commitment, Goodman said:

> I'm a firm believer in God. We do God's work. We are put here to do what he wants. God wanted me to do this. My thought processes were not really my own here. I'm here for a purpose.[4]

Shortly after his pledge was made, Yeshiva University's board of trustees elected Goodman a member—the youngest board member ever to serve—an honor he was quite proud of. At about the same time, the board elected Weissman to the board of trustees of an affiliated theological seminary. Representatives of Yeshiva University deny any connection between the pledge and the appointments.

But Goodman was more generous to members of his and Weissman's families than he was to anyone else. No fewer than seventeen OPM employees were relatives of Goodman and Weissman, yet some of them never came to work. Dubbed "phantom employees" by Trustee James P. Hassett, several OPM workers testified that a number of relatives of Goodman and Weissman were on the payroll, but few people could state what it was they did or even if they had ever been on the premises. Weissman's mother, Lillian, for instance, apparently never did any work for the company, but in 1980, she was paid a salary of $20,000; between 1978 and 1980, she received over $35,000; and in 1979, she received $112,000 to purchase a house.

Weissman's sister, Rifka Ruditsky, and his brother Herbert, also benefited from the generosity of Goodman and Weissman. Late in the year of OPM's birth, Weissman hired Rifka as his secretary. In 1976 or 1977, she stopped working for OPM, but never left the payroll. In 1976, she received a total of $13,800 from OPM's holding company, CALI Trading International, Ltd.,* and from 1977 until

---

*CALI Trading International, Ltd. was established in 1975. The only operations that were material to CALI were OPM's. "CALI" was drawn from the names of the wives of Weissman and Goodman—Carol and Lydia, whose nickname was Lila.

February 1981, she received $275 every two weeks, a total of over $61,000.

Herbert helped Weissman obtain OPM's first lease—providing air-conditioning equipment for the San Carlos Hotel on East 50 Street in Manhattan. For his help in getting OPM off the ground, Herbert Weissman was to receive a 5 percent interest in the company. He never obtained that interest—for which he was probably better off—but between 1976 and 1980, he operated an equipment leasing company, Fundways Ltd., out of OPM's accounting department, and during that period, OPM paid Fundways and Herbert Weissman $447,295 in "commissions."*

In addition to employees who worked for OPM, more relatives were employed by firms that derived a significant amount of business from the leasing company. Weissman's cousin, Marvin Weissman, for example, worked as an accountant for Rashba & Pokart, an accounting firm that did work for OPM for over six years. Rifka's husband, Howard Ruditsky, an attorney, was given a job with Singer Hutner Levine & Seeman, OPM's outside legal counsel. The law firm received from 60 to 80 percent of their billings from OPM, often amounting to well over $2 million a year. Henny Ganz, Goodman and Weissman's mother-in-law, worked for Reliable Travel, OPM's exclusive travel agent.

Relatives and friends were recipients of substantial loans and gifts as well. David Lesnick, Goodman's brother-in-law, who worked in OPM's marketing department, received $25,000 shortly before the leasing company's collapse. Howard Walfish, a friend of Weissman's, who was employed by OPM's contract department, received $26,000. In 1980, the two "philanthropists" had OPM buy a Jaguar sedan for Gary Simon, OPM's in-house general counsel. And Joel Klein, who headed OPM's equity department, accepted $43,000 within months of the bankruptcy.[5] Goodman claimed he discussed the Rockwell fraud with Klein in the spring of 1980.

All of this generosity was driven by Myron Goodman's enormous ego. He often bragged about "two Jews from Flatbush making it big," and he was determined to make it bigger. He dreamed of building a

*On March 4, 1983, the OPM trustee filed suit against Herbert Weissman and Fundways to recover the "commissions" that the trustee claimed were fraudulent conveyences. The matter is pending.

multinational empire, and as his empire grew, he became more and more dominant inside and outside OPM. He enjoyed his budding power and sense of importance. He once wrote letters to the owners of the New York Yankees, the Mets, the Nets, the Rangers, the Islanders, and other professional sports teams, offering to buy out the owners. He even made an offer to buy the Boston Red Sox, the Yankees' arch-rivals, hoping to trade its stars to the Yankees, making the Bronx Bombers stronger. He even wanted to buy Madison Square Garden because it bore his initials—MSG.

Despite such extremes in personality, Goodman was always able to convey a feeling of trustworthiness. He had a disarming quality about him. He was boyish, naive, and could be the perfect gentleman when it suited him. Within hours of meeting him, people felt as if they had known him all their lives. He was deferential, too. All of these qualities helped him to get away with the things he did. Despite his naiveté, he was able to convince those around him that everything was going to be all right and that he would take care of things even in the face of sometimes overwhelming odds. Equipped with 20/20 hindsight, some now say he had "acting talent," that he was a sophisticated con man; others claim he just got himself in too deep and did what anyone else would do: try to save himself and his company.

Why would prestigious investment banking houses, accounting firms, and Fortune 100 companies do business with such an eccentric personality? For one thing, Goodman was able to hide his eccentricities from a number of people; to others, these eccentricities didn't matter, as long as he continued to provide them with good business. For another thing, some people knew that the fluctuations in Goodman's personality were caused by the variety of drugs he was taking for his numerous ailments, most of which were caused by a condition called "sarcoidosis"—an excessive degeneration of scar tissue. Doctors had told Goodman that sarcoidosis contributed to a loss of hearing in his left ear, a problem with his vision appropriately diagnosed as "tunnel vision," and a decrease in his heart rate that had dropped to a dangerous thirty-four beats per minute, which led to his getting a pacemaker in 1977. For his various problems and the pain caused by them, Goodman took enormous quantities of codeine, and then tranquilizers to depress the effects of the narcotic. Early in 1981—just prior to OPM's collapse—Goodman had to be hospitalized for detoxification from the drugs he had been taking.

The Early Days

At first, OPM leased everything from chicken fryers to air conditioners to office equipment. OPM claimed it would have leased water to General Motors. But its patrons were hardly the size of the giant automaker, at least, not at that point. Its customers were mostly small businesses and individuals, but both Goodman and Weissman knew that this would soon change—they were too aggressive and innovative for OPM to remain small for long. Their innovations, however, were often illegal. They provided "services" their competitors could not, or, others have said, would not match. Some services included payoffs to various vendors and customers to win their business. Weissman had worked for another equipment leasing company for a short time before forming OPM and quickly learned that greasing a few hands was a key to making quick money, and these payments proved critical to OPM's growth. Payments recorded in OPM's cash disbursements journal for 1973 show checks written to individuals for several thousand dollars and checks to others for the purchase of automobiles; one person received $9,000 to purchase a Cadillac. Over the years, Goodman and Weissman paid over $600,000 to twelve employees of other firms.[6] Weissman was also alleged to have arranged prostitutes for employees of certain corporations, including at least one Fortune 500 company.[7]

Weissman used the payoffs to establish close ties with several representatives of thriving companies, hoping the customer's growth would also carry OPM. One of them was Basic Four International Systems, a subsidiary of MAI, a leading manufacturer of minicomputers. By making payments to Basic Four's salesmen, Weissman and OPM made great strides in the minicomputer field. By 1975, OPM had over 2,000 clients, most of whom were leasing minicomputers that ranged in cost from $40,000 to $200,000.

To improve its growth and nascent national image, OPM moved

its headquarters to Wall Street in April 1972. With such a prestigious address, the owners correctly believed that people would assume OPM was bigger than it was. Actually, the offices were cramped and unimpressive—appropriate for OPM's size—but, according to Goodman, the marketing ploy worked. People did believe OPM was much larger than it actually was.

The Problem of Rapid Growth

Rapid growth can cause difficulty for managers. Controls are often lacking, information systems are not in place, and employee responsibilities frequently overlap. All are classic problems of high growth and entrepreneurial enterprises, and all were profoundly apparent at OPM. Indeed, one employee said, "We always seemed to have two of everything."[8] That statement could not have been more prophetic.

One of the most serious problems for high-growth companies is financial management: the efficient administration of current assets and the planning for a profitable future. Many entrepreneurs, managing rapidly growing firms, give short shrift to fiscal control, believing a booming business has no need for restraint. But when markets become depressed or competition becomes intense, the importance of financial management becomes all too real, too late. Such was the case at OPM.

The company was always thinly capitalized and highly leveraged. Excessive payoffs—or "commission payments" as they were booked in OPM's ledgers—the premature opening of four branch offices, and a growing number of lessee defaults inevitably led to cash shortages, until Goodman and Weissman stumbled upon a solution to their cash flow difficulties—fraud, or what euphemistically became known as "double-discount," "double-hocking," or "dipsy-doodle" leases. Whatever it was called, it was fraud: the pledging of the same collateral to two or more banks without informing the lenders that the equipment was already encumbered. By fraudulently financing lease transactions, OPM obtained two or three times the cash it needed to purchase the equipment. Of course, it also incurred the liability of the fraudulent loans—obligations that mounted over time—but it temporarily delayed financial disaster.

In June 1972, a little less than a year after they began, Goodman and Weissman obtained their first fraudulent loan. Sig Smith and Company signed a lease with OPM, and Chase Manhattan agreed to finance it. But Sig Smith had problems with the software for the equipment and refused to sign the equipment acceptance form that Goodman and Weissman had to present to Chase Manhattan to receive the financing. The two owners couldn't afford a delay; they needed the cash to meet OPM's outstanding obligations, and since the only thing standing in the way was an executed equipment acceptance form, they decided to forge the necessary signature. As they did in many of the fraudulent deals that followed, Goodman crouched under a glass table holding a flashlight while Weissman traced the signature from the lease to the acceptance form. Chase Manhattan provided the loan.

Some time later, Sig Smith accepted the equipment and signed the equipment acceptance form. But OPM was still short of cash, so Weissman came up with the idea of financing the lease with a second lender. The second loan closed without a hitch. Goodman and Weissman had found a solution to negative cash flow, a solution that kept them in business for the next eight years.

The frauds were not part of a get-rich-quick scheme. Goodman saw the double discounts as temporary loans that the company would buy out when its cash flow improved, which it never really did. Goodman and Weissman continued to make poor business decisions, and they continued to resort to fraud to bail themselves out. But they weren't especially good at the fraud game, either. Fortunately for them, the people who were monitoring the transactions weren't particularly good at monitoring, either. The two grifters often misspelled equipment descriptions and even the names of the representatives whose signatures they forged; they made up prices; and they used a different typeface on IBM bills of sale from the one used by IBM. Goodman claimed that he and Weissman were not "professionals who would know how to forge something properly."[9] Yet, it took almost nine years for anyone to catch them.

But these frauds created more problems for OPM. They increased the company's obligations, and they created the more urgent problem of keeping the crimes hidden from OPM's outside auditors. Goodman and Weissman knew they would need "flexible" auditors; accountants who would be willing to bend a few rules and close their eyes to what Goodman and Weissman believed were minor improprieties. While some companies look for "flexibility" when selecting an outside auditor, for OPM it was a necessity.

The Search for Flexibility

In 1973, the families of Goodman and Weissman spent the summer in New York State's Catskill region, a popular Jewish resort area several hours north of New York City. Weissman's first cousin, Marvin, was also vacationing there. Marvin Weissman didn't know Mordy very well and hadn't met Goodman until that time. Marvin Weissman was a partner at Rashba & Pokart, a small New York City accounting firm. During the time they spent together, Marvin Weissman found Goodman persistently questioning him about accounting practices. Goodman and Weissman liked his answers, and although Goodman was bent on having a Big Eight firm continue auditing OPM's books for the prestige it offered,[10] Mordy convinced him otherwise.

In the fall of 1973, OPM hired Rashba & Pokart to audit the company's financial statements for the 1973 fiscal year. Goodman thought he had found the "flexibility" he wanted. Goodman testified that Marvin Weissman told him there would be "no surprises" when the audit was complete.[11] But if flexibility was what Goodman wanted, he picked the wrong man. Six years his senior, Marvin Weissman was not intimidated by Goodman's wealth and growing power.

Before he began his audit work, Marvin Weissman reviewed OPM's previous financial statements and took a cursory look at the company's books and records. What he saw surprised him. The company had never shown a profit. The six-month report prepared in 1971 by Horne Nadler & Company,[12] another small New York City accounting firm, showed a loss of $9,400—some people later said this was the high point of OPM's life. In late 1971, Horne Nadler & Company was replaced by the prestigious Peat, Marwick, Mitchell and Company. In March 1972, Peat, Marwick provided an unqualified opinion on OPM's first certified financial statements covering fiscal 1971, which showed a loss of over $27,000 and a negative net worth of $15,907. A subsequent audit by Touche Ross & Company resulted in a "going-concern" qualification. OPM's losses steadily grew to over $124,000 and the negative net worth to nearly $140,000. Like his predecessors, Marvin Weissman also found the company's books and records in very poor condition. By the time he had completed his own audit over the summer of 1974, Marvin Weissman concluded that the company was insolvent.

On August 5, Marvin Weissman submitted a "pencil draft" of OPM's financials for 1973 reporting losses of over $196,000 and a negative net worth of more than $335,000. Confirmations sent by the auditors to OPM's lessees and lenders uncovered $947,000 in lease receivables that were in default, Goodman claimed, and OPM was obligated to make the installments to remain in good standing with its creditors. If the truth were known, however, $700,000 of these lease receivables actually reflected fraudulent loans. But Marvin Weissman's primary concern about the company's financial condition stemmed from $500,000 in stockholders' loans—used by Goodman and Weissman to purchase their homes—loans made while OPM was insolvent. Marshall Zieses, another Rashba & Pokart accountant, found such loans "highly unusual." Here was a company with a history of losing money, Zieses said, yet they were taking large sums of money out for nonbusiness purposes. Marvin Weissman and Marshall Zieses believed OPM would be in "deep trouble" if things kept going in the direction they were headed.[13] Thus, another prophet was born in the OPM debacle.

Goodman hit the ceiling when he saw the draft statements. He said he was "more than upset," "slightly ill," and "almost livid" about footnotes Marvin Weissman wanted to insert and about the going-concern qualification. Goodman's tirade didn't persuade Marvin Weissman to alter his draft opinion. Determined that the drafts would never see the light of day, however, and always believing a good defense is a good offense, Goodman fired Rashba & Pokart on August 27 before it could issue its opinion.

Shortly after firing the accountants, Goodman did something odd —or at least something that seemed odd at the time. He asked Rashba & Pokart to submit a typed, executed copy of the draft financials. At around the same time, Chase Manhattan insisted that OPM submit audited financial statements before it would agree to extend more credit. Since they then had the Rashba & Pokart letterhead to work with, Goodman and Weissman went to OPM one Sunday in September and created statements that appeared more favorable to them. The phony financials were submitted to Chase Manhattan. Although the bogus statements presented a better picture than the pencil draft, glaring problems remained. An officer at the bank asked a number of questions about the financial report, although he never questioned its authenticity, and he wanted answers before he would lend OPM any more money.[14] Goodman took great pains to respond in writing to the banker's queries, and he eventually got the loans he wanted. But if Goodman learned anything from that experience, it was that he had to be careful about what was presented in statements and who saw them. Never again would outsiders—or insiders, for that matter—have access to OPM's financial statements. The image had to be preserved.

In the fall of 1974, Goodman realized Rashba & Pokart would not change its position on the qualified audit and footnotes, and rather than have no financials at all, Goodman agreed to have Rashba & Pokart issue its report—with some revisions—and rehired the firm to work for the company for the next year. Late that year, Rashba & Pokart issued certified financial statements for the year-end November 30, 1973. These financials also contained going-concern qualifications. It was the only certified audit ever done for OPM by Marvin Weissman's firm.

The Company Goes Big Time

In late 1972, Weissman was introduced to George Prussin, a marketing representative of Electronic Memories and Magnetics Corporation (EM&M), a firm that manufactured computer memory and peripheral equipment. Prussin had been in the business for about seven years and had numerous contacts with Fortune 100 clients, contacts Weissman valued. Weissman struck a deal with Prussin: OPM would purchase products from EM&M and, in addition, would pay Prussin a "finder's fee" for contacts that materialized into lease agreements. The arrangement proved lucrative for both parties. Over the years, Prussin received a total of over $4.7 million from OPM in "commissions," and Sha-Li Leasing, the company Prussin formed some years later, received another $2.4 million. As for Weissman and OPM, Prussin provided an entree into major league leasing.

During the summer of 1974, Prussin introduced Weissman to Henry Weiss, a representative of Montefiore Hospital in the Bronx, who was responsible for acquiring the hospital's data processing equipment. Weiss liked Weissman. He saw him as a member of the "community" (an Orthodox Jew) as well as a source for charitable contributions and payoffs. Weiss was a fund-raiser for several Jewish organizations and suggested that "it would be nice" if Weissman donated money in exchange for Montefiore's business. Weissman also agreed to pay kick-backs directly to Weiss—a percentage of the equipment cost leased by the hospital, usually 3/4 to 1 percent. On August 29, Montefiore agreed to lease an IBM 370/145 from OPM. Over the next seven years, Weiss received over $60,000 from OPM. Sometimes the money was laundered through charitable organizations in Monsey, New York.[15]

Several months later, another Prussin contact led to more business and more payoffs for OPM. Prussin introduced Weissman to representatives of American Express and its subsidiary, Fireman's Fund Insurance Company. Weissman struck a deal with Josef Verner, a contract officer at Fireman's Fund, whereby the insurance company leased three IBM 370/168 mainframe computers from OPM in return for a "finder's fee" to Verner. Over the next five years, Verner received approximately $150,000 in finder's fees from OPM.*

The Fireman's Fund deal couldn't have come at a better time in Weissman's view. Lessee defaults and other cash flow difficulties had Weissman so discouraged he considered leaving the leasing business. But the large Fireman's Fund deal provided a source for optimism. With one foot in the door, Goodman and Weissman decided to concentrate on the more lucrative mainframe business. Both men believed more money could be made from leasing mainframes for several reasons. First, the lease terms were longer; second, customers who leased mainframes were generally larger corporations and, therefore, less of a credit risk than some of the small fly-by-night operations OPM ordinarily leased to; and third, the size of the leases meant fewer would be needed to produce an adequate income.

Like other computer-leasing companies, OPM bought computers

---

*The U.S. Attorney charged that Verner received $114,000 in illegal payments; in an interview with the OPM trustee's attorneys, however, he stated he received $150,000.

from manufacturers, primarily from IBM, and rented them to users, such as American Express, on long-term leases. Like other lessors, OPM put up little money of its own. Indeed, OPM literally meant "other people's money," which Weissman later denied in his testimony,[16] but the evidence suggests otherwise. For instance, Goodman and Weissman distributed copies of Judge Brandeis' book *Other People's Money* as a marketing ploy.

Another Prussin contact followed the pattern of the previous two. In late 1974, Prussin introduced Weissman to Martin Shulman, a data processing specialist at American Express. In March 1975, OPM leased two mainframes to American Express in exchange for payoffs to Shulman. Over the next four years, the thirty-two-year-old American Express employee received $120,000 to $300,000 from Prussin and Weissman. No one knows for certain how much Shulman actually received. He estimated he received $120,000; Weissman said he paid him $125,000 to $300,000; and a U.S. attorney general said Shulman received $140,000 in illegal payments.[17]

Shulman not only facilitated leasing transactions between OPM and American Express, but he also assisted Weissman and Goodman in their fraudulent scheme. Shulman signed leases and equipment acceptance forms when his company never intended to lease; he covered for Goodman and Weissman when banks called to check on certain transactions; and he misled auditors at American Express by replacing company records with those supplied by OPM. He proved to be a valuable ally. So valuable, in fact, that OPM hired him in 1978 and, soon after, his experience with fraud was put to good use: he became a member of OPM's fraud team.

The Discovery of Double Discounts

In June 1975, Goodman asked Rashba & Pokart to produce an unaudited financial statement for the 1974 fiscal year. No one seems to know why Goodman and Weissman wanted unaudited financials. But a discovery made by Marshall Zieses in the fall of that year provides some rationale for the unaudited financials..

While preparing the 1974 financials, Marshall Zieses followed the procedures he had established the previous year. He first prepared a schedule of all the OPM leases, which included the name of the lessee, the kind of equipment leased, the date of the loan, and the record of payment by the lessee to OPM and by OPM to the lender. After recording all of the items, Zieses had his assistant, Donna Cerniglia, total all of the columns. In theory, the totals should have agreed with the general ledger balances for those accounts recorded in OPM's books. They did not. But Zieses didn't become alarmed. Given the state of OPM's books, any number of things could have accounted for the discrepancies. Besides, he remembered he had had a similar problem the year before, and it had all worked out.

Zieses then checked his listing against a computer printout provided by the lenders, which indexed all the loans made to OPM. Since his schedule catalogued all the loans carried on OPM's books, any discrepancies in the two lists would identify the source of the problem. Zieses discovered a number of loans on the lender's printout that OPM didn't carry on its books. For example, he found three loans made to OPM on American Express leases that were listed by the banks, but only one loan was listed by OPM. He checked and double-checked OPM's books to try to find an explanation. He was told by someone—he doesn't remember who—that the materials he was looking for might be in OPM's safe. He went to the safe and found a loose-leaf binder that contained records of the two American Express loans as well as the other loans recorded by the lenders but not by OPM. Yet Zieses still wasn't suspicious—he didn't know what he was on to. He just added these items to his growing list of questions and then proceeded.

Zieses took the records he found in the safe and began listing by lessee the information they contained onto his lease schedule. He immediately noticed something odd. The newly found information was similar to the information already on the schedule—the lease terms were the same, the equipment costs were the same, the dates, the bank terms, and the lessees were all the same—except for one difference. Each was financed at a different bank. It seemed strange, Zieses thought, that a lessee would enter into two or three leases for the same kind of equipment on the same day but obtain financing from different banks. It was also strange that information on some of these leases was kept in OPM's safe, separate from the other records. But Zieses still didn't know what it all meant. Nor was he overly concerned.

Several weeks later, Zieses was working on OPM's accounts payable records and found invoices from computer suppliers that had been entered into OPM's books, but had never been paid. He couldn't understand how or why a vendor would allow the purchase of equipment but not insist on payment from OPM. Why wasn't OPM paying? Which leases did this equipment correspond to? After more checking, Zieses found, lo and behold, that the equipment OPM didn't pay for was being carried on the same American Express leases he had had a problem with earlier. Three American Express leases, three loans, three liabilities, but only one of the three was being paid by American Express. The other two were outstanding liabilities.

Only then did Zieses begin to think something was not quite right. He decided to do a little more digging to satisfy himself that there were actually three loans per lease. "I started checking through the documentation that OPM had documenting the record of payments by the lessee, and in going through this," Zieses said, "we would only see payments coming in on one lease . . . OPM themselves were making the other two."[18] Zieses further stated, "When I put that together with all the rest of what I had found, at least to me it became pretty obvious what had happened, that they had taken one lease, and however they managed to do it, somehow managed to obtain three loans against that lease, which obviously meant that only one of those three banks in fact had collateral for that loan."

Zieses documented what he had found and brought it to the attention of John Clifton, the CPA hired a year earlier by OPM from Touche Ross, at the insistence of Marvin Weissman. Zieses said he told Clifton what he had discovered, showed him the schedule, and told him that if he didn't get an adequate explanation, he was going to have to tell Marvin Weissman. Clifton seemed to know about the double- and triple-financed leases, Zieses recalled, because he made no attempt to dissuade him that what he had found was evidence of a fraud—he merely said, "You do what you feel you have to do."

Clifton testified he and Preston Baptist, an OPM bookkeeper and later vice-president, had discovered discrepancies in OPM's records around this time. He claimed he asked Goodman about them and that Goodman told him the leases may have been inadvertently financed, that OPM had a lot of transactions to do, and that they may have financed them by accident.

Zieses took his lease schedule, and he and Donna Cerniglia went into a vacant office, closed the door, and called Marvin Weissman at Rashba & Pokart's uptown office to tell him what he had discovered. Marvin Weissman was stunned. He asked whether Zieses had checked every avenue. Zieses said he had. "I'm going to have to confront Myron with this. I don't want to be embarrassed," Marvin Weissman told him. "Are you absolutely sure?" he asked. Zieses said he was sure. Marvin Weissman was "disgusted," annoyed. He asked Zieses to make a copy of the schedule and bring it back to Rashba & Pokart's office the next morning so they could go over it.

Toward the end of the day, Zieses gave the schedule to Cerniglia to copy. He remembered thinking he wanted the original and a Xerox to bring to Marvin Weissman the next day. When he got home that evening, he opened his briefcase and discovered he had the copy—the last time he saw the original was when he had given it to Cerniglia to duplicate. He thought it must still be in the machine; he had to get the original back. Zieses called Preston Baptist at home that evening and told him about the schedule and that he had to have it. Baptist said he would go down to the office and see if it was in the Xerox machine, which he did. He later called Zieses at home to tell him it was in the machine. That was the last time Zieses and Baptist discussed the schedule.

After Zieses and Marvin Weissman reviewed the schedule, Marvin Weissman met with Goodman and told him what his accountants had found. Goodman was "relatively nonchalant" about the whole thing, saying, "What are you guys getting upset about? It's no big deal. I'll pay it off. I can take care of it." Goodman said there had been cash flow problems, but he promised he would take care of the improper loans. Marvin Weissman believed him.

Marvin Weissman told John Clifton that this discovery was the reason Rashba & Pokart refused to do a certified audit for year-end 1974—which Marvin Weissman later denied in his testimony.[19] But Weissman did say that Rashba & Pokart accountants were put on notice to keep an eye out for double-discounted loans.

Marshall Zieses, Marvin Weissman, and John Clifton were naive at best, given OPM's record of losses, deficits, and negative cash flow. Where did they think Goodman was going to get the money to pay off the bad loans?

But under the circumstances, it was difficult for any of these people to pressure Goodman any further. After all, Goodman had said he would pay off the bad loans. And, more important, each of these individuals had a great deal to lose by rocking the boat much more than they already had—there were strong incentives for believing Goodman.

3

Rubbing Shoulders with Giants

Engaging Goldman, Sachs & Company

During OPM's early years—when it leased office equipment and minicomputers—financing was arranged in-house; but as Myron Goodman and Mordecai Weissman began their plunge into mainframe leasing, they saw the need to hire specialists—investment bankers—who could quickly arrange loans for OPM's growing number of transactions. The new deals required considerably more debt placement than did previous transactions; the maximum cost of a minicomputer was about $200,000, whereas a mainframe could cost several million. Besides, Goodman knew that contact with an important investment banker would enhance OPM's legitimacy in national markets.

In October 1975, Goodman and Weissman sought the assistance of Goldman, Sachs & Company, one of the most prestigious investment banking firms on Wall Street and perennially one of the top five underwriters on the Street. Goldman, Sachs, like other investment bankers in the 1970s, was undergoing a significant change.

Securities sales and trading had altered substantially—the volume and profitability of traditional public underwritings were being surpassed by other areas of the investment banking business, such as private placements, mergers and acquisitions, real estate transactions, and leasing. Many firms were unable to compete. Indeed, in 1973, investment bankers had their worst year since World War II—an aggregate loss of $50 million. Many investment banks closed their doors or merged with more stable houses. Goldman, Sachs, however, had adapted its business to meet the changing conditions and, therefore, was receptive to OPM's overtures.

On October 20, 1975, Myron Goodman and Andrew Reinhard, Myron's boyhood friend from Brooklyn and, at the time, an OPM director and a lawyer with Singer Hutner Levine & Seeman, OPM's outside legal counsel, met with representatives of Goldman, Sachs at its offices on Broad Street in lower Manhattan. Richard Santulli, a streetwise, fast-talking New Yorker, who represented Goldman, Sachs, remembers Goodman as "the nicest guy in the world," as well as the most religious—all of which gave Santulli an image of great reliability.[1] Santulli, who eventually had responsibility for the OPM account and later became head of the lease financing department at Goldman Sachs, liked what he saw and heard from Goodman. Before it took on OPM, however, the leasing company had to be checked out.

The underwriter was primarily concerned with the credit rating of OPM's lessees, not OPM, since it was the lessee's responsibility to pay the lenders who provided financing for each transaction. But Goldman, Sachs doesn't accept just any client who walks through its doors —after all, it does have a reputation to maintain. Representatives of Goldman, Sachs called several banks and lessees whose names were supplied by Goodman. All provided positive reports on OPM. Of the six people called by Goldman, Sachs, however, three were on the OPM "payroll": Martin Shulman of American Express, Henry Weiss of Montefiore Hospital, and Josef Verner of Fireman's Fund Insurance Company.[2] Shortly afterward, Goldman, Sachs began providing investment banking services to OPM on a transaction-by-transaction basis and continued doing so until March 1978. Over this period, Goldman, Sachs received nearly $2.4 million in fees from OPM and, according to Goodman, it became one of the investment banker's largest private placement customers.[3]

The NBNA Slush Fund

Throughout 1976, John Clifton and others who knew about the earlier frauds believed Goodman had turned over a new leaf. OPM had stopped leasing minicomputers. They were active in the mainframe computer business. Goldman, Sachs was its investment banker. Business was booming. Everything seemed to be going well. The accounting department was monitoring the buyouts of the fraudulent loans; every so often Goodman would ask them to release a check on one of the fraudulent loans and send it up to him. The accounting department assumed he was paying off the bad loans. They also assumed he had stopped committing fraud.[4] Both assumptions were wrong.

In September 1976, David Lesnick, another OPM employee, who also happened to be married to Goodman's sister, called John Clifton. Lesnick had received a call from an officer at the National Bank of North America (NBNA), who claimed an OPM account was overdrawn. Clifton wasn't aware of any OPM account at NBNA, nor were any of the other people in OPM's accounting department. Clifton quickly called a meeting with Goodman and Weissman about the secret account. Goodman did all the talking; Weissman said nothing. Goodman told Clifton, "I have two choices. Either I give you the books or I fire you, and here are the books. I want you to go down, record the transactions and close the bank account."[5] Clifton took the books and recorded the transactions. It was clear to him that the transactions were not legitimate; that Goodman had continued to double finance deals; that the NBNA account was a "slush fund" used to make payments on fraudulent loans. This time, at least, he knew the double financing was no accident because a special account had been opened, and the two principals were making payments from it. Subsequently, Goodman once again assured both Clifton and Marvin Weissman, who had been told about the slush fund by Clifton, that the fraudulent loans would be bought out and the account closed. Once again, John Clifton and Marvin Weissman believed Goodman.

The Search for Another Auditor

Around the time the slush fund was discovered, OPM was looking for new outside auditors to certify the OPM financials. Rashba & Pokart were considered too small to handle OPM, although it would stay on to provide accounting support. Besides, if OPM decided to go public, as Goodman hoped it would, investors might raise questions about Rashba & Pokart's "independence" since Marvin Weissman and Mordecai Weissman were cousins. Goodman also wanted an accounting firm that complemented OPM's budding national reputation, but he knew that the Big Eight firms would have required OPM's books to be in better shape than they were, so those firms were not even considered. In addition, Clifton testified:

> Myron's preference at that point was that he wanted to be, as he put it, a big fish in a little pond as opposed to being a little fish in a big pond. So, he wanted quite a bit of service and attention. So, it had to be a medium-sized firm, a firm a little below the "Big 8."[6]

Marvin Weissman recommended Elmer Fox, Westheimer and Company, later renamed Fox & Company, the eleventh largest accounting firm in the United States. He had done some work with Morton Berger, the partner in charge of Fox's New York office; in fact, Fox once considered purchasing Rashba & Pokart. Goodman told Marvin Weissman to call on the firm to see if it would be interested in the account. But both John Clifton and Marvin Weissman told Goodman they thought Fox should be told about prior double discounting by OPM. Goodman agreed. But he insisted that Fox would have to agree to "look aside," as Goodman put it, or, to put it another way, to ignore the fraudulent deals that were already on the books.

On October 26, 1976, Marvin Weissman met Morton Berger and Stephen Kutz, the audit coordinator for the New York region, at the Fox offices on Sixth Avenue in Manhattan. Marvin Weissman told them about OPM's history—how it had grown rapidly and was beginning to lease mainframe computers to some very large clients. He extolled the virtues of the two principals, Berger later recalled—two young, "very bright people," who were "dedicated," "very religious and charitable."[7] He also provided a brief history of the company's previous audits, but Berger didn't remember Marvin Weissman telling them about OPM's insolvency. Or about previous going-concern qualifications. Or about double-financed loans.

Marvin Weissman recalled a somewhat different discussion. He remembered telling Berger and Kutz about OPM's business, its rapid growth, and the size of the fees that could be expected. Marvin Weissman testified:

> [Kutz and Berger] were quite excited about the prospect of being engaged by OPM, especially after we told them the size of our fees [over $56,000 for the 1973 audit].

Marvin Weissman went on to tell Berger and Kutz about the going-concern qualifications, the negative net worth, and the fraudulent transactions:

> I told them that OPM had engaged in improper lease financings. I cannot recite to you the exact terminology used, if I had told them they had improperly double-discounted or double-financed or financed the lease more than once. But the substance is that they were informed.

He also told them

> that OPM was in the process of repaying the excess and we have a commitment from Myron Goodman that those would be cleaned up before the end of the year.[8]

Marvin testified that both Berger and Kutz said that as long as the loans were being cleaned up, they would not cause a problem.

Goodman attended several meetings that followed. He made clear to the Fox partners that the OPM engagement would be extremely lucrative, involving not only audit work, but consulting and tax services as well. Goodman believed the OPM account was important enough to Fox that they would agree to meet certain conditions, conditions that would make OPM's financial picture appear brighter. Another condition, of course, was their agreement to overlook the earlier frauds. Berger and Kutz denied being told about the frauds or agreeing to any stipulations.[9]

It is not entirely clear whether Fox was told about the early frauds, but certain pieces of testimony suggest it was informed. On November 2, 1976, Berger and Kutz met with Myron Goodman, John Clifton, Preston Baptist, Marvin Weissman, Andrew Reinhard, and Henry Singer, another law partner from Singer Hutner Levine & Seeman. Goodman had devised a cover story for the problem loans, a story he said was suggested by Marvin Weissman, who assured Goodman that the frauds had been discussed with Berger and Kutz, but, according to Goodman, Marvin Weissman made him promise never to mention the frauds in the presence of Fox. To accede to Marvin Weissman's wishes yet acknowledge the existence of certain problems, Goodman invented a story. Marvin Weissman denied fabricating the tale with Goodman.[10]

There are several possible explanations for this conflicting and confusing testimony. First, Marvin Weissman may not have told Fox. Perhaps he feared that he had failed to do the right thing earlier when the frauds were discovered and decided not to call attention to himself, but he knew he was ethically bound by the norms of the accounting profession to disclose what he knew to Fox—so he made it *appear* as though he had told Fox. Or perhaps he "halfway" told Fox—enough to satisfy himself, but not enough to signal Fox. The second possibility, and the more likely one, is that Marvin Weissman told Fox, but Goodman alone—or with Marvin Weissman—decided to use the cover story to hide the frauds from the others present who were still in the dark about OPM's misdeeds.

During the meeting, Goodman mentioned certain "problems" that were "embarrassing" to OPM.[11] Goodman told his audience about twenty-five to forty "defaults" made by lessees in the previous year amounting to $1 million. He said OPM kept the defaults hidden from lenders by making payments itself. OPM made the payments, Goodman said, because he didn't want the banks to know that some of OPM's customers were poor credit risks. Goodman asked whether such problems required disclosure on OPM's financial statements. Berger and Kutz said they weren't items that required disclosure, but they raised questions of credibility and internal control. Goodman assured his audience that the problems were being handled and wouldn't happen again. No mention was made of "double-discounted" or "phantom" leases. Berger was unequivocally certain about that.[12] Marvin Weissman didn't say anything. Clifton didn't say anything because he believed Marvin Weissman had already told Fox. Berger and Kutz didn't ask any questions about the "problems."

Three days after the meeting, Berger wrote a memo to the file.[13] He said OPM's problems "were not items of disclosure," but he was assured that they would not happen again. Berger went on to say that such problems raised questions about OPM's credibility and internal control and that the problems should be reviewed by Fox in an "adroit" manner.

Despite having no audit experience with leasing companies—an area of accounting that can be extremely complex—Fox was retained by OPM as its outside auditor in December 1976[14] and remained in that capacity until March 1981. Over the years, it collected over $1 million in fees from OPM, and the leasing company became one of its largest New York clients. Kutz headed the engagement for Fox. Although Berger says he relied on Kutz to investigate the full details of those "problem" transactions, he never followed up and never explicitly told him to do so—it wasn't necessary, Berger said, since Kutz was a seasoned auditor and knew what to do. Kutz said he never analyzed the problem transactions nor did he tell any other Fox employee to do so.[15]

Whether Kutz or other Fox accountants "analyzed" the problem loans or not, Marshall Zieses testified that they at least examined a schedule listing the double discounts. Shortly after accepting the OPM engagement, Kutz and Alan Phillips, a Fox staff accountant,* asked Zieses if they could review the double-discount schedule. Since Zieses had been told by Marvin Weissman to answer any questions raised by Fox about the double discounts, Zieses gave them the schedule. He later testified:

> They sat down at a table, looked it over. I didn't really stand over their shoulders to listen to what they were saying. They just looked it over, and after a period of time, gave it back to me, said thank you, and went about their business.[16]

Zieses also claimed he had several discussions with David Hanlon, another Fox accountant, and Phillips about the double discounts and that Phillips referred to the loans as "dipsy-doodle" leases.

Whether Fox knew about fraud or simply about "problems," the

---

*Several years later, Phillips left Fox and became OPM's assistant controller, and in 1979, he left OPM to join George Prussin's firm, Sha-Li Leasing.

OPM trustee correctly noted that the accounting firm "was on notice that OPM had a problem of some kind with certain of its leases and that Goodman was embarrassed about it. Berger properly determined that the matter warranted scrutiny. Kutz dropped the ball."[17]

OPM's business continued to flourish, and it made deep strides into the mainframe computer market in part because it made a number of aggressive, if not risky, business deals. It built volume by offering leases at lower rents for as long as seven years instead of the usual four years. Moreover, the early termination agreement, which Goodman says was a Weissman innovation, was attractive to lessees. So attractive, in fact, OPM's lease-related assets increased by an average of $100 million a year between 1975 and 1978. But as OPM grabbed a greater share of the market, its exposure to disaster increased exponentially. Through its early termination agreements, OPM agreed to reimburse the lessee the outstanding obligation to the lending institution if and when the lessee decided to give up the equipment. Should a significant number of lessees terminate at once, OPM stood to lose millions. That was a risk few other leasing companies would bear.

But OPM's growth was also due to the information that was exchanged by an IBM employee for cash provided by Goodman and Weissman. From late 1975 and into 1976, Richard Monks, a senior industry marketing representative for IBM, working out of IBM's White Plains, New York, office, received $50,000 in cash from Goodman and Weissman for providing them with blank bills of sale and confidential IBM customer lists.[18] These lists included the names of IBM's customers, a description of the customers' equipment, and the date, or projected date, of installation. Weissman used the information to solicit IBM customers to lease their computers from OPM. One of the companies on the lists was Rockwell International.

The Company Meets Rockwell

In 1973, Rockwell Manufacturing Company merged with North American Rockwell, forming one of the largest companies in the United States, Rockwell International. Following the merger, all corporate divisions were encouraged to tighten their belts, for procedures are often altered and deadwood is chopped away when companies are joined. One of the areas that received fiscal scrutiny was Rockwell's method of acquiring data processing equipment. Over the previous decade, the huge aerospace and defense company had increasingly used computers to aid in the design and manufacture of products and to improve the productivity of their managers through the use of automated office systems and sophisticated telecommunications networks. The company had become one of the largest users of data processing equipment in the country. In 1971, the company began consolidating the computer function and, following the merger, Rockwell's corporate finance department requested a study of more cost-effective methods of computer acquisition. To conduct the study, it called on a fifty-one-year-old electrical engineer, Sidney L. Hasin.

An eleven-year veteran of North American Rockwell, Hasin was a star who had fallen. After six years with Rockwell, having made his mark as an expert on information systems, Hasin was made president of North American Rockwell Information Systems Company (NARISCO). The Brooklyn-born engineer had responsibility for over 400 employees and for field offices throughout the country. But NARISCO failed to meet the expectations the parent company had set, and Hasin was replaced within two years. Despite facing a demotion and cut in salary, Hasin chose to stay with Rockwell; he knew he could make his way back up the corporate ladder.

In 1971, Hasin was placed in charge of studying Rockwell's long-range data processing plans, and in 1973, when the corporate staff wanted to know how to reduce computer acquisition costs, he was the logical choice to look into the matter.

Following several months of interviews with representatives of computer manufacturing and computer leasing companies, Hasin reported to the vice-president of finance that the company could save 30 to 45 percent in computer acquisition costs if it leased equipment from third-party leasing companies instead of leasing or purchasing directly from IBM. Further, Hasin argued, leasing provided "off-balance sheet" financing for major computer acquisitions. Debt financing for lease transactions would not be carried as a liability on the balance sheet, he reasoned, but debt financing of a capital purchase would. Hasin strongly advocated that Rockwell replace its obsolete computer equipment, using tax-leveraged leases offered by the growing number of computer lessors. Shortly afterward, Rockwell began such a program, leading it down a road it has probably since regretted.

For the next two years, Hasin negotiated most of Rockwell's computer leases with Itel Corporation, the large but now defunct leasing company based in San Francisco. Although Hasin claims he followed Rockwell's procurement policies—all but small items were sent out for bid[19]—Itel nearly always came up the winner. Because it was the largest lessor around at the time, it was able to keep its costs below those of competitors. Over that period of time, Hasin negotiated what he considered were favorable terms on long-term leases for nine IBM 370/168 computers with lessors other than OPM. He estimated that Rockwell saved over $13 million on these leases. He didn't mind that the leases were long term. Despite the inevitable possibility of technical obsolescence for the machines, Hasin believed the secondary market for that equipment provided a sufficiently strong sublease base to offset most, if not all, of Rockwell's remaining obligations. "In effect," Trustee James P. Hassett wrote, "Rockwell obtained reduced annual costs for computing equipment by making a long-term financial commitment to the 370 series."[20]

It was understandable that Rockwell executives agreed with Hasin's reasoning. These were difficult times for Rockwell. Following the merger in 1973, Rockwell's profits increased as the company continued its early work on the space shuttle and the B–1 bomber. But cost estimates on the B–1 bomber project jumped six times the original figures, and it was in trouble on Capitol Hill. And by the end of 1974, inflation had cut deeply into Rockwell's profits—profits dropped 36 percent in the fourth quarter alone.

Of course, the recession didn't help matters. Nor did Rockwell's purchase of Admiral Television and Appliance Corporation in April 1974. Rockwell hoped to turn the marginally profitable television and appliance maker around, but facing the sharpest decline the appliance industry had confronted in years, Admiral only contributed losses.

Admiral was Rockwell's third major acquisition in less than two years, and Rockwell's balance sheet and the cost of the accumulated debt had begun to take its toll. Long-term debt rose from $374 million in 1974 to $599 million in 1975; short-term debt rose from $102 million to $484 million. Interest expense skyrocketed from $27 million in 1973 to $70 million in 1974. Rockwell noted in its 1974 annual report that it had a "limited capacity" to borrow long-term funds, and analysts feared significant problems for the aerospace company because it would have to borrow heavily if and when the B–1 bomber project was approved.[21]

In early 1975, Rockwell, hoping to cut costs, laid off hundreds of employees in plants across the United States. In a little more than a year, they had released 4,000 of the 11,000 workers assigned to the B–1 project alone. By the fall of 1975, the company had taken other steps to reduce its short-term debt. It concentrated on new financing methods, such as leasing, and it sold several subsidiaries.

In the early part of 1976, Hasin was rewarded for his efforts and money-saving ideas: he was named director of the newly created Computer Planning and Controls Department (CPC) within the Information Systems Center (ISC) at Rockwell's facility in Downey, California.

The ISC operated as a separate unit, maintaining its own financial and operating objectives, and was designed to provide computing and telecommunications services to all Rockwell divisions. As part of the ISC, the Computer Planning and Controls Department (CPC) had responsibility for acquiring and managing Rockwell's leased equipment portfolio. CPC officials provided forecasts of Rockwell's computer needs; determined whether it was more economical for Rockwell to lease or purchase equipment; solicited suppliers to submit competitive bids; awarded the bids; and prepared, executed, transmitted, and maintained financing documents necessary to lease and insure the equipment. The CPC also assisted other corporate entities, helping them identify needs and prepare Appropriation Requests (AR), justifying acquisitions to Hasin's superiors: Larry G. Manly, the ISC general manager; Maury R. Dahn, vice-president of the ISC; Robert C. Petersen, director of procurement for Rockwell's western region; and Robert A. DePalma, vice-president of finance at Rockwell's corporate headquarters in Pittsburgh. Depending on the size of the acquisition, some or all of these individuals had to approve the lease or purchase of equipment; all items over $500,000, for example, had to be approved by DePalma.[22] It was Hasin's job to keep his superiors informed about acquisitions in the pipeline and to obtain their approval whenever necessary. However, none of Hasin's superiors had any formal computer training; he was the most senior Rockwell employee in the computer planning and acquisition process with technical expertise in computer hardware.

Thus, it was Hasin's job to ensure that Rockwell's divisions had access to the most advanced computer equipment available and, of course, at the least possible cost. For large acquisitions, it was also Hasin's responsibility to ensure that the acquisition of equipment, whether through lease or direct purchase, met Rockwell's rigorous bidding policies. He prepared the requests for bids, mailed them to lessors or vendors, and opened the returned bids in the presence of others. Hasin would then recommend the manufacturer or lessor to receive the award. It was really a one-man show, but others—Dahn, Petersen, and DePalma—were required to sign off on Hasin's recommendations. Hasin had so much responsibility that for some time after OPM had begun leasing to Rockwell, Myron Goodman thought Hasin alone ran data processing at Rockwell.

Forecasting computer needs for Rockwell was a tricky business. Much of Rockwell's work is defense-related and, thus, business swings coincide with political temperaments. Throughout 1976, Rockwell forecasts indicated a significant increase in the company's computer capacity because of the space shuttle and B–1 bomber projects. Since Rockwell was working on projects that were on the cutting edge of technological innovation, it was important to keep pace with the rapidly changing computer technology.[23] This was not an easy task, but it too was part of Hasin's job.

In the spring of 1976, Mordecai Weissman called the new director of the CPC and asked if OPM could be placed on Rockwell's bidders' list. Hasin thought he already had enough bidders and declined, but Weissman persisted and asked for a few minutes of Hasin's time on Weissman's next visit to California. Hasin agreed.

Soon afterward, Myron Goodman called on Hasin at the ISC headquarters in Downey, California. They hit it off immediately. Goodman seemed pleasant and knowledgeable, Hasin recalled, and was quite interested in submitting bids to Rockwell. Myron told Hasin about OPM's growth and how he was determined to make OPM a multinational corporation and to beat out Itel, its stiffest competitor. He told Hasin about some of the company's other clients, such as American Express and Fireman's Fund. He also told him about the company's investment bankers, Goldman, Sachs. Hasin was impressed with Goodman's straightforward manner, and after Goodman left, he called the references Goodman had provided and everything checked out to his satisfaction. He decided to put OPM on Rockwell's bidders' list—after all, the competition between OPM and Itel could only benefit Rockwell, or so he thought.

Over the summer and fall of 1976, Hasin and an outside consultant, McKinsey & Company, undertook a study of Rockwell's long-term computer needs. Projections showed dramatic increases in computer needs stemming from the revived but controversial B–1 and space shuttle projects, and Hasin thought it was important to have that capacity available when the projects began to roll full steam. At the time, Rockwell had over 16,000 people working on the B–52 replacement. Recommendations were made to add still another IBM 370/168, plus two Attached Processors, in 1977—bringing a total of six IBM 370/168s and a Control Data Corporation 175–16 (CDC 175) scientific computer within the portfolio of the ISC. OPM successfully bid for the CDC 175 and an earlier IBM 370/168. The IBM machines alone provided more than 7.5 times the computer power of the original equipment at Downey in 1971. The second recommendation made by the study group was to consolidate the western computer center within the ISC at a larger facility in Seal Beach, California. Rockwell's corporate management committee approved the multimillion dollar consolidation in February 1977.

Hasin had already begun his climb back up the Rockwell ladder. He had control over what was becoming an important Rockwell operation—computer forecasting and acquisition. Although he went out on a limb to change the firm's computer acquisition methods from purchase to lease, he had already saved millions of dollars and had been recognized for these savings. He also had a lessor on the hook who was determined to become Rockwell's exclusive source of computer equipment. He knew Rockwell's name lent prestige to the New York-based leasing company, and Hasin believed the relationship could save Rockwell even more money. He was on his way. And now his center was being moved—at his recommendation—to a larger, more modern facility.

The move wouldn't be easy. A number of things can go wrong when three IBM 370/168 computer systems are turned off, packed into forty moving vans, moved twenty miles down crowded Lakewood Boulevard, set up, and turned on again. Valuable computer time is lost even if there are no problems. Hasin, however, designed a plan whereby

Rockwell would set up a parallel operation at Seal Beach, leaving the original equipment in place. The new equipment, which became known as the "swing machines," or the "G," "H," and "I" machines (all pieces of Rockwell computer equipment had a letter designation) would be installed at Seal Beach—there would be no lost computer time; the Downey machines would be turned off at the same time the Seal Beach machines would be turned on. Following the move, Rockwell would simply sublease the Downey machines and leave the swing machines in place at Seal Beach.

In March 1977, some time prior to the proposed move, IBM announced the introduction of its advanced 3033 mainframe computer, an announcement that usually means the new technology would be available for delivery in about a year. The 3033s were far more powerful than the 158s and 168s and could be purchased and operated at less cost. Keeping with the CPC's dual objectives of maintaining state-of-the-art computer technology at the lowest cost, Hasin knew he had to obtain the new models and get rid of the obsolete 158 and 168 models shortly after the 3033s were made available. He had to convince a lessor to immediately lease three mainframe computers to Rockwell, but the lessor had to allow Rockwell to terminate the lease in less than one year when the 3033s came on line, at no cost to them. If this wasn't enough—after all, most early terminations were available (if they were available at all) after three years, not one—Hasin also needed to keep the rental payments low. In other words, he wanted a standard lease written for seven or eight years to keep the lease payments low, but he also wanted the option to get out of the lease in less than one year. All this on equipment that everyone in the industry knew would soon be obsolete and thus almost impossible to sublease. But he realized he had a hungry leasing company in his hip pocket.

In September 1977, Hasin negotiated leases with Myron Goodman in which OPM agreed to lump-sum buyouts after five months on the G and H machines and nine months on the I machine, provided Rockwell gave OPM sixty days' notice of its intention to cancel. The leases were written as though they were standard eight-year leases, which kept the monthly payments low. These were unheard-of terms in the leasing industry. Rockwell's payments were low since these were typical eight-year leases, yet it had no long-term commitment—OPM would buy Rockwell out. OPM would be forced to make a multimillion dollar payment to Rockwell upon termination, at which time Rockwell was obligated to pay the creditors. OPM would then take possession of what was certain to be obsolete computer equipment, which they would try to sublease. In a memo, Hasin wrote that the leases with OPM represented savings to Rockwell of $760,000 over the bid of the nearest competitor, Itel, and savings of nearly $2.5 million, compared to the equivalent IBM rental over the project period.[24]

Goodman took the gamble, Hasin says, because he believed Rockwell would keep the machines longer than the required period, and he wanted to obtain Rockwell's goodwill. Hasin was asked if Goodman understood that Rockwell intended to terminate the leases at the earliest opportunity, and he responded, "It was my understanding that they could read and, therefore, they understood what they were signing when they signed it."[25] Goodman was gambling that IBM wouldn't be able to deliver the machines to Rockwell within a year since there was already a long queue for the new technology. In spite of Goodman's optimism, Hasin thought the terms of the leases were not very favorable to OPM. He couldn't have been more correct. But what he didn't know was how those terms would eventually haunt Rockwell and him personally.

Shortly after the award for the swing machines was made to OPM, Goodman met with Hasin in Hasin's office in Seal Beach and said that he was pleased with the award but that given his liability—the million dollar buyouts—he would prefer a guaranteed sublease arrangement whereby OPM would take possession of the equipment, sublease it, and make monthly installments to Rockwell—instead of the lump-sum buyout—for the equivalent amount that Rockwell owed lenders. Either way, Goodman said, Rockwell would be relieved of its obligation to make further payments on the equipment. Hasin told Goodman he would bring his proposal to the attention of the appropriate people when the time came.

On November 12, 1977, the G, H, and I machines were installed at Seal Beach. The remainder of the equipment at Downey was moved during the Christmas holidays. Rockwell's total obligation on the swing machines was $13 million. Of course, whenever Rockwell decided to terminate the leases on these machines, OPM was obligated to pay Rockwell an amount equal to the outstanding debt on the equipment. Given Rockwell's dependence on OPM, there was some concern by

Rockwell executives about OPM's ability to meet those obligations when Rockwell decided to terminate the leases. But Hasin defended OPM. Based on OPM's "growth and viability," he said, and Rockwell's review of OPM's financial statements, he believed OPM would meet its commitments. A *Business Week* article that appeared on February 27, 1978, which was critical of OPM's "crazy deals," did not heighten Hasin's concern about OPM's viability or its ability to pay Rockwell.[26] In fact, Hasin said, the article lessened his concern because he thought the report was "stupid."

But it was Rockwell, not OPM, that was committed to the lenders on those leases. The banks didn't care what side arrangements were made between OPM and Rockwell as long as they got paid by Rockwell as the financing documents stipulated. For this reason, Rockwell should have been more concerned about OPM's ability to pay.

Growing Pains

OPM Looks for Acquisitions

Each time IBM releases new equipment, the value of a computer lessor's leasing portfolio immediately declines. Lessees can terminate obsolete equipment, forcing lessors to remarket the equipment at a substantial loss. IBM watchers spend thousands of dollars monitoring the computer giant trying to avoid surprises. But IBM is careful about leaks and the timing of its announcements; most are planned to catch competitors off guard. Several of the computer giant's announcements led directly to the downfall of OPM and of Goodman and Weissman.

Minutes after IBM announced the introduction of the 3033 mainframe (the same technology that concerned Sidney L. Hasin) on the New York Stock Exchange tape on Friday, March 25, 1977, Goodman was told of the news by a friend, and he "almost passed out"—he knew instantly what that meant.

OPM had gambled on the IBM 370 series, leasing the equipment at very favorable terms to its customers. Long lease periods, early termination agreements, and low monthly payments were the OPM standards. OPM could survive these deals (barely) as long as there wasn't a rush to terminate the contracts. But with IBM's announcement on its new advanced equipment, Goodman knew the rush was not far off.

After the Sabbath, Goodman and Weissman met and tried to assess the impact of the IBM announcement and to find a way to minimize the damage. They quickly realized the company would face severe cash shortages for the next several years. Despite the financial drain, Goodman and Weissman believed they could gain protection from IBM by diversifying, even though they lacked the capital to establish new ventures. But that didn't concern them—after all, the lack of cash hadn't stopped them yet.

Throughout 1976–77, OPM, like other lessors, sought freedom from IBM's technology cycle by exploring the purchase of several corporations, including a toilet paper company in Connecticut, a travel agency, and a dress manufacturer in the garment district of New York City. During the summer of 1977, Goodman and Weissman unsuccessfully attempted a hostile takeover of Century Factors, a commercial finance and factoring business located on Fifth Avenue in Manhattan. They continued to look for other targets. Late that year, Henry Singer, a partner in Singer Hutner Levine & Seeman told the two owners of OPM that he knew of several brokers who were trying to sell 52 percent of the stock from the First National Bank of Jefferson Parish (FNJ) in Gretna, Louisiana, just outside New Orleans. Singer sold Goodman on the bank purchase by asking him if he would like to be "Chairman of the Board of the 468th largest bank in the United States." From that moment, Goodman knew the purchase would be made. But it wasn't only ego that led Goodman and Weissman to acquire the stock. Weissman believed the bank "would add a degree of respectability to OPM,"[1] and as a practical matter, Goodman reasoned, OPM could obtain the numerous short-term loans it needed from its own bank.

Goldman, Sachs & Company opposed the purchase for three reasons. First, Goldman, Sachs thought that OPM had a computer leasing business to run and lacked the management expertise to operate a bank. After all, Goodman and Weissman knew nothing about the banking industry, one of the most heavily regulated industries in the United States. Second, the purchase required a considerable amount of cash, and Goldman, Sachs believed if OPM had that kind of money, it would be better spent at OPM. Goldman, Sachs' Richard Santulli said he was also concerned about the impact on OPM of IBM's announcement; could it survive the shock? Third, Santulli thought New Orleans was not the right place for two Jewish men from New York City to own a bank.[2]

Encouraged by their legal counsel, however, Goodman and Weissman persisted, causing a split with Goldman, Sachs. In a letter dated March 13, 1978,[3] Peter Sacerdote of Goldman, Sachs terminated the relationship with OPM. Later, always with the final word, Goodman insisted he ended the association, not Goldman, Sachs. He claimed that OPM did not get the attention of senior people at Goldman, Sachs despite being one of its largest private placement customers; that Goldman, Sachs was too slow in placing OPM debt; and that some OPM and Goldman, Sachs personnel did not get along.

By the time Sacerdote wrote his letter, OPM had already taken steps to replace the investment bankers. In the previous month, Joseph L. Hutner, one of the senior partners at the Singer Hutner law firm, contacted a friend at another one of Wall Street's venerable investment banking houses, Lehman Brothers Kuhn Loeb. Hutner was eager for OPM to find another investment banker because he didn't get along with Sacerdote.

Established in 1850, Lehman Brothers* is well respected for its integrity, philosophy, and aggressiveness, according to the late Joseph Wechsberg, who wrote about the company. Wechsberg claimed Lehman always had a reputation for consistently making money in a big way. Indeed, *Fortune* called Lehman Brothers "one of the biggest profitmakers—many believe the biggest—in the business."[4] Such an emphasis on profitability, of course, filters down to each employee. Lehman's own "Descriptive Memorandum" reads: "The common characteristic of Lehman Brothers Kuhn Loeb's approach to all markets is the emphasis on productivity in terms of revenue generated per employee. . . . The firm's emphasis will remain on dollar value per employee."[5]

At the time OPM approached Lehman, the underwriter was located at 1 William Street† in a triangular eleven-story building with a four-story annex attached. The structure combines the dignity one associates with the tradition of the investment banker and the fast-paced world of high finance. Employees move at a quick pace and speak

---

*Lehman Brothers merged with Kuhn Loeb in 1977.
†The firm has since moved to Water Street, also in lower Manhattan.

loudly, much more so than employees of, say, a London merchant bank, which is more austere, according to Wechsberg. But the partners' room on the third floor has "ancestral paintings and a fireplace, deep rugs and paneling . . . the large oval walnut table in the main dining room on the eighth floor seats the entire partnership . . . there are also small, private dining rooms."[6] Partners are served by a staff of ten, including a famous chef who prepares the meals. "On the top floor is a gymnasium," Wechsberg continued, "where the partners are kneaded into condition by an able masseuse. Rows of slippers are on the floor, each with a name."[7]

Such amenities are compatible with the firm's general reputation and with how members of the firm view themselves—insiders and outsiders believe Lehman is a notch better than most investment banking houses. They always have. In 1950, for example, the government brought an antitrust suit against Lehman and sixteen other underwriters. Counsel for Lehman convincingly argued that

> Lehman Brothers' special attitudes form a continuity of character that is impossible to confuse with the modes of business of the other sixteen defendant firms. The investment banking activity of the firm is but a part of its completely independently conceived relation to industry.[8]

The activities in civic and national affairs of some of Lehman's past and present partners support this claim. Emmanuel Lehman performed important missions for the South in the nineteenth century. Herbert Lehman was governor of New York and, later, a member of the United States Senate. His brother Irving was chief justice of the New York State Court of Appeals. Another Lehman associate, Alex Sachs, presented the views of Albert Einstein to Franklin D. Roosevelt, and stirred the president's interest in nuclear fission as early as 1939. John M. Hancock, another Lehman partner, with Bernard M. Baruch drafted the first United Nations plan to control the atom. Peter G. Peterson, the chairman of Lehman during the years Lehman worked with OPM, was the secretary of commerce in the Nixon administration.[9] George W. Ball, once a managing partner at Lehman, was formerly the ambassador to the United Nations and undersecretary of state in both the Kennedy and the Johnson administrations. He retired in 1982. James R. Schlesinger, a senior advisor for Lehman, was formerly the secretary of energy under President Jimmy Carter and secretary of defense under President Richard M. Nixon and President Gerald R. Ford.

For these reasons, Lehman is careful about whom it associates with. "It is less worried by financial losses than by loss of reputation," Wechsberg wrote.[10] The firm "feels it can afford some mistakes but not many." Lehman's partners know the firm's sponsorship can make or break a company, and many companies like OPM will try to get close to them for that reason. One partner stated, "Our sponsorship often becomes more important to the company than its past records. If Lehman Brothers approves of a company," he continued, "Wall Street will almost automatically fall in line."[11] Within Lehman employees steer away from anything that might taint the firm's reputation. Memories of the government's antitrust action and other litigation linger and, according to Wechsberg, there is a "widespread aversion to putting anything in writing. Everybody is constantly aware of the uncomfortable commitment of the written word." Wechsberg quotes, "Don't write a memorandum that might someday become a source of conflict."[12]

When David Sacks,* a lawyer and chief administrative officer of Lehman, received a call from Joe Hutner telling him he had a client who was looking for an investment banker, Sacks was interested but cautious. Although Lehman continued to be careful about whom they associated with, times were changing. Competition on the Street was fierce. Over the previous thirty years, 130 securities firms had either vanished or merged with more stable houses.[13] Lehman itself was losing business and was on the verge of extinction in the early 1970s, according to the *Wall Street Journal.* [14] Twenty years earlier, Lehman might not have been interested in a small company such as OPM, but as Sacks listened to Hutner talk about his rapidly growing client, he liked what he heard and decided he wanted to hear more.

On the morning of February 28, 1978, Hutner, Marvin Weissman, and Goodman, who as usual arrived late, met with Sacks at Lehman's offices on William Street. Although Goodman considered Lehman a step down from Goldman, Sachs, he didn't feel it was that

---

*Sacks is now Of Counsel to the New York City law firm of Simpson Thacher & Bartlett.

far down, and he was determined to sell the firm on OPM. He knew how important Lehman was for OPM's image. He told Sacks that OPM was a reasonably "small-potatoes outfit" when it first went to Goldman, Sachs, but it was taken under the wing of the late Gustav Levy, then the senior partner at that firm. OPM had become the second largest purchaser of IBM-manufactured equipment—the General Services Administration (the procurement agency for the U.S. government) was the largest—Goodman told him, and had clients such as American Express and Rockwell International. The split with Goldman, Sachs, Goodman claimed, was caused primarily by the lack of attention given OPM by senior people at Goldman, Sachs. Since Gustav Levy's death in November 1976, Goodman stated, there was a lack of sympathy "to a couple of Orthodox Jews from Brooklyn";[15] and, Goodman went on, Goldman, Sachs had objected to the bank purchase, so he decided it was best to terminate the relationship.

Several meetings were held between representatives of OPM and Lehman. Lehman remained wary. It, too, had reservations about the bank purchase but believed OPM had legitimate business reasons for going ahead with the deal. The *Business Week* article questioning OPM's business practices also raised eyebrows. Lehman also wondered why Goldman, Sachs would let a large client slip through its fingers, but Lehman would never call Goldman, Sachs and ask why—that was taboo for Wall Streeters. Sacks also wondered why OPM didn't perform investment banking functions in-house, but he and others at Lehman reasoned that OPM was not about to take a step down from Goldman, Sachs and, therefore, wanted a comparable investment banking house to perform these services. Furthermore, Sacks thought there was a "bit of an ego trip involved" in having prestigious investment banking houses working for Goodman. Sacks believed it was another one of the status symbols of success.[16]

Alan Batkin, managing director of the investment banking division at Lehman, provided information on OPM to Lehman's banking planning committee—now the commitments committee—which had final approval on whether or not to accept OPM as a client. Batkin, who eventually headed the OPM team from Lehman, saw three advantages to having OPM as a client and reported them to the committee. First, Batkin claimed, Lehman would be placing debt for OPM involving large blue-chip corporations. The debt would be repaid through the assignment of "hell-or-high-water" lease obligations of these corporations, Batkin argued. It was the credit standing of the lessee that was important to Lehman and the lending institutions, not the credit of OPM. So Batkin perceived little risk in getting the notes paid off.

Second, Batkin and others at Lehman saw OPM as a rapidly growing company that would generate large fees to Lehman. Part of the investment banker's philosophy, testified Lewis L. Glucksman, president and chief operating officer of Lehman, "is to work small companies and see if you can make them into bigger companies."[17] Lehman is famous for being able to turn small companies into big ones; Litton Industries is one of dozens of examples, Glucksman stated. In 1953, when Charles "Tex" Thornton, vice-president and general manager of Hughes Aircraft Company, left Hughes, he took several executives and scientists with him to strike out on their own with Litton, a small electronics firm. Thornton contacted another Texan, Joseph A. Thomas, a partner of Lehman and known as "the deal person," to help raise money for the fledgling company. Thomas met a lot of resistance from other Lehman partners before the underwriter decided to help raise $1.5 million for Thornton. Lehman itself purchased 75,000 shares of common stock for prices ranging from ten cents to a dollar a share. Last year, Litton was ranked as the seventy-fourth largest corporation in America, according to *Fortune,* and had nearly $5 billion in sales and employed nearly 70,000 people.[18] Considering that Lehman purchased some of its shares for ten cents, most people would consider it a worthy investment. Some people thought the same thing could be done with OPM. Third, Batkin believed contacts might be made with OPM lessees that might stimulate other business for Lehman.

Batkin also was personally impressed with Goodman and Weissman. Two young entrepreneurs—Goodman and Weissman—dealing with some of the largest corporations in the world were bound to make an impression. Batkin and others at Lehman checked the references supplied by OPM. They spoke to OPM's accountants (Stephen Kutz and Marvin Weissman) and to its lawyers; they spoke to several lessees, including American Express and Sidney L. Hasin at Rockwell. All reports were positive; there was never any mention of double discounts. Everyone said Goodman and Weissman were "people you could trust, people of the highest integrity, and people who relied a great deal on living up to their word." Goodman, in particular, was viewed by Batkin as an emotional person who exhibited a very sincere belief in God, a belief that was expressed with a great deal of fervor.[19]

One week after the split with Goldman, Sachs, Lehman became OPM's investment bankers. Despite having little knowledge of the leasing industry and no experience in the computer business, thirty-four-year-old Alan Batkin headed the Lehman team.

Over the next three years, Lehman received $2.5 million in fees from OPM.[20] If fees-per-employee was an important criterion for recognition around Lehman, Batkin and the others responsible for bringing OPM on board must have been doing very well. Lehman's own figures show that in late 1978, OPM generated $339 per hour in fees.

Lehman's sponsorship of OPM began almost immediately. In the spring of 1978, OPM held a number of marketing seminars throughout the country to counter the adverse reaction to the *Business Week* article that had appeared in late February. The article reported that IBM's price reductions on some 370 models a year earlier led many customers to wonder whether OPM's contingent liability on leased equipment placed the company in jeopardy. The seminars were held to show customers that OPM was still in operation and that it did not offer "crazy" deals. Representatives from Lehman spoke at these seminars. Having members of its prestigious investment banking firm standing alongside Goodman probably quelled a number of rumors then circulating.

But Lehman wasn't properly prepared for dealing with OPM. It knew little about the computer business, and it knew less about OPM's financial picture. It wasn't aware of OPM's obligations to Rockwell. Although Lehman had reviewed CALI Trading International, Ltd.,* and financial statements prepared by Fox, these statements were deceiving; these, too, involved some creative accounting and made OPM look better than it actually was.

---

*The holding company for OPM.

The Swing to Positive

Since it had been founded in 1970, OPM had lost money at an accelerated pace. Losing about $30,000 in its first year of operation and $277,000 four years later is not quite the path to riches. The company's negative net worth plummeted from under $16,000 in 1971 to over $650,000 in 1975. Two accounting firms qualified their audits of the company's financial statements over that brief period. When the figures didn't come out the way OPM wanted, it changed auditors. In five years, OPM had gone through three accounting firms.

In 1976, Fox became OPM's auditors, with Rashba & Pokart supplying support. Rashba & Pokart's draft statements for the year ending November 30, 1976, showed that OPM was in desperate trouble. OPM's losses had descended to almost $2.25 million, and its negative net worth to just under $3 million. But some time after Rashba & Pokart completed its drafts, Fox certified financials for the same fiscal year—only extending it by one month—revealing a positive net worth of almost three quarters of a million dollars and a profit of over $1.6 million. OPM's "swing to positive" was nothing short of miraculous.

Stephen Kutz headed the OPM audit team for Fox. He was considered a superstar at Fox. With fifteen years experience as an auditor—ten with the Big Eight firm of Price Waterhouse—Kutz headed the audit review department for the New York office and held the title of audit coordinator. He also had responsibility for audit control, and he served as national associate director of auditing and accounting for Fox's eastern region. In addition, he served on the auditing standards executive committee of the American Institute of Certified Public Accountants. Despite such an impressive background, Kutz had no experience with a computer leasing company. He probably had never had any experience with someone like Myron Goodman, either.

The OPM account was important to Kutz—as it was to Fox—and his skills and flexibility as an auditor were severely tested. He found the company's books and records in shocking condition. Considerable work had to be done to make OPM even auditable. Moreover, during the course of the engagement, Fox auditors discovered a number of weaknesses in OPM's procedures for internal control. For example, Fox discovered that Goodman had a "mail rule"—only *he* opened OPM's mail—but Kutz didn't consider such a rule a "badge of fraud," as a relatively recent court ruling had.[21] Fox also found that OPM issued blank checks to Goodman and Weissman. And the accounting firm was unable to locate a number of documents—particularly invoices— that would have confirmed certain equipment costs.

Despite such problems and despite being warned before Fox took on the engagement, Kutz did not extend the scope of the audit to determine whether more serious problems existed. In fact, according to Goodman and others, Kutz didn't even maintain control over confirmation requests—letters that provide external validation of OPM's books and records—sent to OPM's lessees and financing institutions. Before the confirmation letters were sent, Goodman and Weissman removed letters where frauds might have been detected. Goodman testified that Kutz had never asked him why he wanted to review the confirmations—it was one of Goodman's conditions for keeping Fox as OPM's auditor. Goodman testified: "[It] was not . . . something that you stopped and discussed for 20 hours a week. It was a fact of life. It was a fait accompli . . . that's the way it was going to be."[22]

Confirmations were rarely sent without Goodman seeing them. Once, a Fox accountant inadvertently sent a confirmation letter without Goodman's approval, and Goodman learned about it some time later. He was furious. He screamed at John Clifton and at the Fox accountants. Alan Phillips recalled the incident:

> Mr. Goodman came downstairs . . . he was rather indignant . . . and he came into the Fox room and started screaming that somebody . . . forged a signature and sent a confirmation out. He claimed, "I didn't want this confirmation sent out." . . . He was screaming . . . he didn't want the confirmation out, why did we send it out.[23]

Kutz was later informed, but none of the Fox accountants or Clifton were suspicious of Goodman's tirade.

When Goodman first saw the Rashba & Pokart draft financials in the spring of 1977, showing a $2.25 million loss and a $3 million negative net worth, he was shocked. He couldn't believe it. "Myron was always saying he was making a profit," Clifton claimed. "It was just that the accountants didn't understand." He "was convinced that with all the transactions he did, there had to be a profit."[24] And he was determined to have the financials show it.

The first thing Goodman did was to stretch the fiscal year. If OPM didn't show a profit in twelve months, perhaps thirteen months would do it, particularly since a number of deals closed that December and Goodman thought they would paint a better picture. He was wrong. In early May, Kutz submitted the new financials to Goodman, and the figures were more bleak for the thirteen months than they had been for the old fiscal year. Goodman was enraged. He told his accountants "to get back to the grindstone and try to figure out a way to show a profit."[25]

On May 10, Kutz called together the team of accountants, Myron Goodman, and Andrew Reinhard of Singer Hutner and told them about a method that could be used to show a profit. On certain equity transactions, he said, OPM could recognize income immediately rather than amortizing the income over the life of the lease as they had been doing. The possibility that the leases could be terminated, causing the equipment to lose value and be subsequently re-leased at a lower rental, was apparently irrelevant to Kutz. The idea was to show a profit, and if Kutz didn't play ball with Goodman, he knew he'd be looking for another client. Everyone was relieved that a solution had been found.

On May 27, Fox issued an unqualified opinion on OPM's financial statements for the thirteen months ending December 31, 1976. OPM's first certified financials since 1973 showed a net income of nearly $1.7 million and a positive net worth of over $724,000. It may have taken OPM years to build the deficit and the negative net worth that the earlier Rashba & Pokart draft had shown, but it took Kutz only a few days to swing the company from the red to the black. Goodman, obviously, had found the flexibility he was looking for.

For the next two years, the Kutz magic worked on OPM's financial statements. But the Kutz method[26] did not conform to generally accepted accounting principles, according to Philip Lint of Price Waterhouse, the accounting firm brought in by trustee James P. Hassett to look at OPM's books. The problem with the Kutz method, according to Price Waterhouse, "was that it currently recognized income that was in fact contingent."[27] In 1977, CALI financials certified by Fox show an increase in net income of over 40 percent to almost $2.4

million and an increase in net worth to more than $3 million. Price Waterhouse claimed that without the Kutz method, the OPM losing streak begun in July 1970 would have continued, to a tune of over $10 million and a negative net worth of nearly $13.7 million. The "ever upward" trend continued in 1978. CALI's certified financials reflected a net income of almost $2 million and a net worth of over $4.2 million. Using generally accepted accounting principles (i.e., minus the Kutz method), says Price Waterhouse, CALI's statements would have shown a staggering net loss of over $17.8 million and a negative net worth of nearly $31.5 million.

5

Small Time to Big Time

AS OPM's financial position became more and more precarious, Goodman and Weissman were forced to raise the stakes of their fraudulent practices. Three factors allowed them to get away with the things they did. First, both Goodman and Weissman, but mostly Goodman, built a loyal and dependent following both inside and outside OPM— a group of people who were indebted to the pair and willing to close their eyes to their criminal ways or to make allowances for their behavior and, in some cases, to actually aid them in their scheme. Second, OPM's manufactured image—the lawyers, the investment bankers, the auditors, the accouterments of success—made it difficult for outsiders to see what was really happening. Third, the physical distance between the parties involved in OPM's transactions and the unclear differentiation of roles and responsibilities made it difficult for individuals to really know about suspect activities, and even when they did, it was easy to shift responsibility away from themselves and onto others. In the following chapter and throughout the rest of the book, I will make clear how each of these factors played a part in allowing the fraud to go on for several more years.

Hasin Takes It Easy on OPM

Despite the year's ominous start—changing investment bankers, being criticized in a national business magazine, and the Rockwell International obligation—Goodman and Weissman purchased 52 percent of the common stock of the First National Bank of Jefferson Parish (FNJ) in July 1978 for $9.8 million. More than $3.5 million was borrowed from OPM by Goodman and Weissman; the remainder was borrowed from the Louisiana National Bank. But the bank purchase was only the beginning of the drain on OPM's finances.

On July 27, Rockwell notified OPM of its intention to terminate the leases on the G and H machines; it later terminated the I machine as well. Rockwell's rental payments on the G machine would end on September 1, and the lease payments on the H and I machines on January 26, 1979. By January 26, OPM had to make a lump-sum payment of approximately $10 million to the large aerospace company to satisfy the early termination agreement between the two companies. In addition, OPM agreed to buy out Rockwell's obligation on a large Control Data Corporation scientific computer, the CDC 175, on October 23, 1978; Goodman did so to win the award on a new CDC 176 intended to replace the 175. Aware that the payment would hurt OPM, Goodman again went to Sidney L. Hasin to ask if Rockwell would consider a guaranteed sublease rather than the lump-sum buyout. Hasin took Goodman's proposal to his superiors, and it was promptly rejected.

At the time of the terminations, Hasin knew that the residual values on the 168s had declined about 20 percent since the date the award was made to OPM—20 percent in less than a year—and he knew that the deals couldn't possibly have been profitable to OPM. There was no way OPM could sublease the machines at a profit or even at a rate to break even. In fact, Hasin estimated that OPM lost $3 million on the buyouts. He was also aware that OPM had made several delinquent payments in late 1978 and early 1979, and he became concerned about OPM's financial condition.[1]

Hasin had reason to be concerned. The CDC 175 alone sat idle for over a year while OPM tried to find a company willing to lease the outdated machine. Meanwhile, OPM had to make payments of nearly

$42,000 a month on the equipment. Goodman and Stephen Lichtman, an OPM vice-president and member of Goodman's entourage, spoke to Hasin about OPM's cash drain. Goodman said OPM suffered heavy losses in late 1978 and early 1979 and the buyouts were difficult for him to manage. Although Hasin was concerned about OPM's ability to meet its commitments, he denied that OPM's default on these obligations would have been a personal reflection on him. He decided, however, to "take it easy on OPM," to give them a few breaks on future deals. Hasin insists the decision was made by him and by Maury Dahn, his boss, not him alone.[2] And take it easy they did.

From July 1978 through February 1979, a period in which OPM's cash flow problems were acute, OPM obtained a number of fraudulent loans with the apparent aid of Sidney Hasin. I say apparent because it is not clear whether Hasin knew the loans were obtained fraudulently. No one really knows for certain since testimony on this matter is conflicting—Goodman was able to induce Hasin to process some documentation for computer equipment at Rockwell, which Goodman then used to obtain the fraudulent loans on Equipment Schedule 81 and "The Bridges to Nowhere."

Equipment Schedule 81

The Tulsa computing center became part of Rockwell's Information Systems Center (ISC) in April 1978 and, at the time, it had been leasing a 370/158 from Itel Corporation, which would have expired in October 1978. Hasin wanted to extend the Itel lease if he could bargain the price down since the value of the 158s had declined over the previous several months. During the summer, Hasin's assistant, Bernard Wilner, began the paperwork—the Appropriation Request (AR)—so the lease extension could be made fairly easily.

Some time in July, Hasin learned from Hank Hahn, an Itel salesman, that Itel had no intention of coming down on the price because it didn't believe Rockwell was prepared to rip the machine out and put another one in. Itel's position created an urgent situation, according to Hasin, since it would have been difficult to obtain a 370/158 from another source because the market was so tight. The urgency justified another sole source to OPM, Hasin said, but he didn't bother to clear it or even to discuss it with his superiors or with anyone from purchasing. Once he received a firm bid from OPM, Hasin claimed he went back to Hahn to give Itel another chance, but Itel wouldn't budge, believing all along that Rockwell was bluffing. Hasin decided to go with the OPM offer, which, incidentally, was $11,000 a month below Itel's offer, something Hasin couldn't explain.[3]

At the same time, Goodman needed cash to meet another obligation and asked Hasin to proceed with the Tulsa lease even though the AR had not been approved and to get Rockwell's director of purchasing for the western region, Robert Petersen, to sign the agreement.

On July 27, Equipment Schedule 81 covering the 370/158 was signed—the very day Rockwell notified OPM of the terminations on the swing machines. There was no approved AR for Equipment Schedule 81. In fact, the only draft of the AR that would have covered Equipment Schedule 81 was sent by Wilner to Hasin on July 28, one day after the schedule was signed. Three days prior to the signing of the schedule, despite the lack of an approved AR, Hasin wrote Petersen, who was required to sign the equipment schedule, that the schedule "has been reviewed at ISC, is consistent with Approved Appropriation Requests, and is recommended for your signature." Hasin knew that this wasn't true and he knew he lacked the authority to advise Petersen to sign the schedule without an approved AR, but he did it "to get the job done."[4]

Prior to the signing of Equipment Schedule 81, Hasin learned that a projected increase in the computer needs at the Tulsa center required an Attached Processor (AP) on the 370/158, but instead of notifying Goodman of that fact right away, he claimed he waited until after Equipment Schedule 81 was signed. He didn't halt the execution of Equipment Schedule 81 to get the 370/158 and the AP on the same schedule because he didn't want to lose the 158 at the agreed price. Of course, had Hasin halted Equipment Schedule 81, Goodman would have been unable to get the cash he needed. After Equipment Schedule 81 was signed and after Hasin told Goodman of Tulsa's need for the Attached Processor, Goodman arranged to ship a complete 158 AP system to Tulsa. Hasin claimed he said, "Then, I assume you are going to take us out of the other one" and Goodman responded, "yes."[5]

Although he had never been told for certain, Hasin assumed Equipment Schedule 81 had already been funded. He also assumed that if it had been funded, OPM would cancel or buy out the financing related to that equipment.

The entire 370/158 AP was put on Equipment Schedule 83. Hasin never told anyone at Rockwell that Equipment Schedule 81 was being canceled or that Schedule 83 was replacing 81. Nor did he ask Rockwell's legal department what documents he should receive from OPM to ensure the schedule was, indeed, canceled. And, although he expected cancellation documents on Equipment Schedule 81, he never received them. Asked why he never followed up on the matter with Goodman, Hasin said, "I forgot."[6]

Equipment Schedule 81 was transmitted to OPM on July 27. The same day, Lehman Brothers Kuhn Loeb placed an OPM note with the National Bank of North America (NBNA) for $1,439,029—about half the amount of OPM's loss caused by the early termination of the G, H, and I machines. To expedite the closing and transmission of documents, Rockwell telecopied an amendment to the NBNA closing documents. The amendment was signed by Sidney L. Hasin. On the day after Christmas 1978, months after Equipment Schedule 81 was purportedly canceled by Hasin, OPM bought out the NBNA loan and permanently financed Equipment Schedule 81 with the Philadelphia Savings Fund Society (PSFS). Hasin signed the equipment acceptance form on the "forgotten" equipment. The form was a critical document in these transactions, indicating the machines were installed and ready for use, and it also triggered Rockwell's obligation to pay rent.

The Bridges to Nowhere

Equipment Schedule 81 wasn't an isolated event. From November 1978 through February 1979, thirteen equipment schedules were executed by Rockwell. They were all bridge-financed following review and approval by Hasin. None of the schedules had an approved Appropriation Request. Several equipment schedules represented identical equipment destined for the same location—duplication that Hasin himself said Rockwell did not need. He further stated, "It appears less than logical that we would have entered into these transactions as of the same date."[7] There was never any equipment purchased with the proceeds of the loans obtained by OPM nor was there any equipment related to the schedule ever installed at Rockwell. Forged bills of sale —allegedly, unbeknownst to Hasin—were used at the closings for these deals.

Hasin recalled little about these bridge loans until he was presented with documented evidence that bore his mark. The following items were discovered in his files: drafts of the schedules that either contained Hasin's signature or other notations in his handwriting; letters from Hasin to Petersen recommending the procurement officer's signature on the schedules; Hasin's notes of a meeting with Goodman regarding the schedules; and copies of closing documents related to the schedules.

Facing such evidence, Hasin conceded that much of the equipment on these schedules was ultimately leased on subsequent schedules, and the earlier ones, like Equipment Schedule 81, were supposed to be canceled; he remembered a conversation he had with Goodman about canceling them and preparing new ones. "When they financed a new schedule," Hasin said, "they would move or buy out or whatever the old schedule. But obviously, we didn't follow up on that properly."[8]

Although the conclusions of the OPM trustee, James P. Hassett, left little doubt that Hasin knowingly contributed to a fraudulent financing on Equipment Schedule 81, the Hassett report was more equivocal on the "bridges to nowhere." Goodman testified that he didn't "think Sid [Hasin] ever really understood what a bridge financing was."[9] Since an equipment acceptance form wasn't signed, Rockwell had no obligation.* To Hasin, processing the equipment schedules before they were actually needed was "like a purchase order." He merely thought he was doing OPM a favor by allowing it time to line up the capital. His favors, however, permitted OPM to commit fraud since the bridge financings OPM obtained were based on nonexistent equipment. The effect of the bridges to nowhere was to provide approximately $4 million in loans to OPM over a three-month period of

---

*An equipment acceptance form was required only for permanent financings.

time. Essentially, Hasin facilitated a short-term loan to OPM while the leasing company's cash flow problems were severe. But Hasin's sloppiness and willingness to sign whatever Goodman placed before him, also allowed Goodman the opportunity to accumulate signature pages that he and others used for later frauds. And his negligence dug a deeper hole for Rockwell. On May 1, 1979, the bridges to nowhere were bought out with proceeds from a "phantom loan" financed by the Philadelphia Savings Fund Society for $7,750,980.

In the literature on interorganizational relationships, dependence is often discussed in terms of one organization's reliance on another for a valued resource or service.[10] And the more powerful organization can cause weaker ones to behave in certain ways. But what is frequently overlooked is that the organization may not be dependent on a particular relationship, but the individual who links the two organizations, the person who controls the strings, might be and, thus, the *organization* may act as though it were dependent. A company the size of Rockwell was hardly reliant on the deals OPM provided. These were significant transactions, worth millions, but not enough to hurt Rockwell if OPM defaulted on its obligation. But they were substantial enough to hurt Sidney Hasin. He had pushed leasing at Rockwell. He had moved fast and taken total control, actions that eventually rankled others in the large aerospace company. He was also trying very hard to again climb the Rockwell ladder, and he knew he could not do it without a company such as OPM. This is not to say that Hasin "knew" about Goodman's crimes; the evidence is equivocal about that. It does mean that his dependence on the leasing company colored his perceptions and caused him to behave in ways that benefited OPM while, at the same time, led Rockwell deeper and deeper into the quagmire.

Goodman Kites Checks to Raise More Cash

The cash raised from Equipment Schedule 81 and from the bridges to nowhere was not nearly enough to satisfy OPM's obligations. Early terminations on the leasing company's portfolio of IBM 370/168 and 158 machines from Rockwell and other lessees continued to tap

OPM's resources reducing them to a desperate level. To obtain more cash, Goodman began to float checks, or engage in what is called "check-kiting"—drawing checks from one bank and depositing them in another, even though funds were not available in the first bank.[11] Actually, for years Goodman had been in the habit of releasing checks to pay banks or manufacturers with revenue anticipated from deals that would close in several days. Money was always in the account by the time the issued checks cleared. But in late 1978, OPM experienced a number of problems closing deals. These difficulties combined with the Rockwell buyouts left the balances in OPM's checking accounts overdrawn for days at a time. On March 22, 1979, officials from the First National Bank of Jefferson Parish reported OPM to the comptroller of the currency.* An investigation into OPM's banking policies was conducted throughout the next year.

Days after the investigation began, Goodman returned from London and told representatives at Lehman about the "check matter," as he called it. Lehman was quite taken aback since that was not the type of conduct it expected of a client. Lehman's operating committee, made up of its three highest ranking officers—Lewis Glucksman, David Sacks, and Harvey Krueger—met with Goodman to discuss whether the firm would remain as OPM's investment bankers. Glucksman later said, "I was trying to determine to my satisfaction whether or not this was an action, a regrettable action by a young man who was running a big business and who may have made a mistake; or by someone whose pattern was such that I should be careful about or worried about."[12]

Goodman was "petrified" that Lehman would resign and was very solemn when he met the three members of the operating committee. Glucksman, the cigar-chomping, street fighter from Lehman, struck fear into Goodman. Goodman admitted he had done something wrong. OPM had experienced a temporary cash shortage, and he "swore that this would never happen again, and there wouldn't be any more surprises, and he had made a mistake, and he was sorry for it," Alan Batkin remembered later being told by members of the committee.[13] Goodman was "extremely apologetic," "very contrite," and "emotional." He even broke down in tears at one point. "Gullible though we may have been," Sacks testified, "we really believed that

---

*The office of the comptroller of the currency, a part of the U.S. Treasury Department, regulates and examines the operations of national banks.

Myron Goodman was remorseful about what he had done and, in fact, . . . he burst out into tears at one point during this meeting. He was unable to control himself or was one superb actor, take your choice." Glucksman recalled, "It seemed they [OPM] were involved in a situation that wasn't going to be repeated. A mistake was made by a young man."[14]

Lehman decided to keep OPM as a client. It was convinced the check matter had been an "isolated event," and the kiting was not considered indicative of Goodman's behavior, Batkin stated. "It was aberrant behavior limited to this event," he testified.[15] Goodman was told that Lehman would "play it down," that they "wouldn't make a major issue about it." Of course, money probably had some influence on Lehman's decision. OPM generated a great deal of revenue for Lehman. In fact, OPM was one of Lehman's "largest Corporate Finance clients."[16] But there was more to it than money. Goodman was believable. He was believable, according to Glucksman, "because the precepts of a deeply religious man would suggest a certain type of activity in which promises not to do something . . . would give you a feeling of comfort."[17]

Indeed, Lehman was comforted. No one at Lehman ever called the comptroller of the currency, the U.S. attorney's office in New Orleans, or the First National Bank of Jefferson Parish to discuss the investigation or the charges. And, although Lehman considered the event serious, it did not believe the check-kiting investigation mattered to other lenders because the lenders were not relying directly on OPM to receive payment for the equipment. So, while Lehman continued to solicit creditors on OPM transactions, it never told the creditors about the check-kiting investigation. All except one bank, the First National Bank of St. Paul (FNBSP).

Interim Financings: The First National Bank of St. Paul

When purchasing used computer equipment, lessors generally pay the entire cost of the equipment before the machines are moved to the site of the lessee. For such transactions, and occasionally for the purchase of new equipment, OPM and other lessors relied on interim or "bridge" loans. Such loans are arranged for a short time, usually sixty to ninety days, until permanent financing can be obtained. Once permanent financing is arranged, the bridge loan is paid off. There is one other difference between the two kinds of loans. Bridge lenders rely on the leasing company, in this case, OPM, to repay the loan. Permanent lenders rely on the lessee. Therefore, bridge lenders had more of an interest in OPM's financial picture than did other creditors.

In 1978, OPM was finding it difficult to obtain permanent financing. Capital was scarce and lenders hesitated investing more money into computer leasing, particularly following the IBM announcement in March 1977 and the published reports about the financial troubles of Itel. Moreover, OPM's business volume strained the company's normal lending sources, and they were forced to look to less familiar institutions.

From 1978 to 1980, despite having to pay higher interest rates than were demanded for permanent financing, OPM frequently resorted to bridge financing to purchase equipment until permanent financing was arranged. OPM's primary bridge lender was the First National Bank of St. Paul (FNBSP)* in Minnesota, one of the 100 largest commercial banks in the United States, with total assets of greater than $2.5 billion. During the late summer or early fall of 1978, Glucksman, president of Lehman, called his friend of some fifteen years, Clarence Frame, then president of the FNBSP and now vice-chairman of First Bank Systems, a holding company that owns the FNBSP, to discuss the possibility of the FNBSP making bridge loans to OPM with Lehman acting as the investment banker for OPM. The St. Paul bank agreed to make bridge loans to OPM in August 1978 before it even met anyone from the company. But, it now contends, and it thought was clear from the beginning, that Lehman had to be involved; it claimed its primary relationship was with Lehman, not OPM. It was the belief of Jeffrey Werner, a vice-president and department head of the commercial banking group at the St. Paul bank, that Lehman would act as the bank's "eyes and ears" to ensure that OPM was a legitimate and profitable company. Werner understood that Lehman would be performing "due dili-

*Now called The First Bank St. Paul.

gence"* on OPM-FNBSP transactions. After all, Werner reasoned, Lehman was in contact with OPM on a daily basis, it was placing OPM's long-term debt, and it often traveled around the country on behalf of OPM. Lehman would know what was going on. Without Lehman's involvement, Werner claimed, the FNBSP would not have made any deals with OPM.[18]

But the St. Paul bank was also eager to lend its dollars at the favorable rates offered on OPM transactions. At a time when interest rates were going through the roof, the bank was trying to avoid committing its capital for long terms at fixed rates. The FNBSP built its portfolio by lending to the major food processing, grain trading, and high-tech companies in that region, and it had become the third largest bank in Minnesota. As short-term interest rates climbed in the 1970s, however, these companies began raising capital at less cost in the commercial paper market. To sustain its growth and profitability, the FNBSP had to expand its market, both internationally and in other regions of the country. When a call came in from a firm like Lehman, the St. Paul bankers were not about to ask a lot of questions.[19] Since OPM didn't quibble about interest percentage points, it was an even more attractive risk. The transactions also appeared relatively safe to the FNBSP. Although the notes were the obligation of OPM, they were secured by a first security interest in the equipment. In addition, the FNBSP believed that as long as OPM continued to lease to blue-chip clients, permanent financing would always be available, and the proceeds would be used to buy out the bridge loans.

On March 22 or 23, 1979, only seven months after OPM obtained its first loan from the FNBSP, the comptroller of the currency contacted the FNBSP and advised it about the check matter involving OPM. Since the St. Paul bank handled certain OPM accounts, it was told by the comptroller to examine all OPM transactions to see if the scheme extended to its bank. The operations department at the FNBSP checked all OPM accounts and transactions and found no evidence of wrongdoing.

Glucksman called Frame several days later to tell him that OPM

---

*Due diligence is a vague legal concept that has evolved from numerous court decisions. *Black's Law Dictionary* defines due diligence as "such a measure of prudence, activity or assiduity as is properly exercised by a prudent man."

was being investigated. "It is very normal for people who are involved in the credit business to share information about credit problems with each other," Glucksman later testified.[20] Glucksman was concerned since Lehman introduced the FNBSP to OPM, and he knew that the the FNBSP, as a bridge lender, relied on OPM and its principals to repay the loans. Glucksman said Frame wasn't surprised or excited since he already knew. The Lehman president remembered Frame saying, "Don't worry about us. We know how to look after ourselves. We are big boys."[21]

But inside the bank, another picture emerged. Meetings were held in late March and early April to determine whether the bank should make further loans to OPM. The bank subsequently decided to suspend lending and contacted Lehman informing them of the bank's decision. No contact was made with OPM until some time later when Lehman and the FNBSP requested a meeting with Goodman to discuss the check matter and OPM's financial statements for 1978. The meeting was held in St. Paul on May 14.

Jeffrey Werner and Diane Arnold, another vice-president from the FNBSP, Alan Batkin from Lehman, and Goodman met in a bank conference room. Goodman discussed the uncollected funds situation. He told the assembled group the FBI was investigating certain technical violations and that he assumed full responsibility for the matter. He said OPM had a short-term cash flow and that eight times from the fall of 1978 through March 1979, he had engaged in floating checks. He claimed this was all behind him now, that he had repented, and, furthermore, he had reached some kind of agreement with the comptroller of the currency, and the comptroller was apparently satisfied. Werner remembered Goodman saying:

> Nobody lost any money. It was a terrible thing to do. We realize it was a terrible thing to do. We're never going to do it again. It was a moment of lapse. If I had to do it again, I never would have done it. Having the bank there gave me the temptation to do it because we were in charge of the bank, and we're going to change our ways entirely.[22]

Batkin told Arnold and Werner that Lehman had decided the situation was exactly as Goodman said it was; that Lehman still believed OPM was a good firm, a firm worthy of its business; and that it had decided to continue its relationship with the leasing company.

The discussion then centered on the 1978 consolidated financial statements for CALI Trading International, Ltd., the holding company that owned OPM, which were circulated at the meeting. Goodman rarely allowed outsiders an opportunity to see OPM's financial statements, contending that OPM was a privately held company and that its finances were no one else's business.[23] This situation was apparently important enough to make one of his few exceptions. Arnold and Werner asked Goodman a number of questions about the statements, few of which he or Batkin were able to answer. One troubling problem was the enormous difference between OPM's equipment-related debt and the rental amount due on the leasing company's outstanding leases. Known as the "footnote 2/footnote 4 problem," the footnotes revealed a difference of almost $284 million in OPM's equipment-related debt and the minimum amount it could expect from the rental on outstanding leases. In other words, if all of OPM's leases were terminated early, they faced a shortfall of close to $284 million. Even if none of the leases were canceled, OPM would still owe over $76 million on its equipment purchases. That is, the difference between OPM's equipment-related debt and the *total* lease receivables—the total of all rentals assuming no cancellations— was still over $76 million. Goodman volunteered to have OPM accounting personnel come to St. Paul to discuss the statements some time in June.

On June 12, Arnold, Werner, Joel Peck from Lehman, Marvin Weissman, Goodman, and Alan Phillips, then with OPM, met in St. Paul to discuss the points raised at the May 24 meeting. Several accounting schedules were produced by OPM to explain items in the 1978 financials. But the statements proved unexplainable.[24] Werner's concerns centered on the footnote 2/footnote 4 problem as well as on the increased value of OPM's computer inventory, reflecting equipment that had either come off lease or equipment that had been terminated by lessees who wished to upgrade their equipment. In 1977, OPM's equipment inventory totaled about $2.5 million; by 1978, it had jumped to over $18 million. Such equipment does not generate income until it is re-leased, yet there may still be obligations to creditors. In the future, Goodman said, OPM would concentrate on remarketing the used equipment inventory and hold off on buying additional new equipment. This seemed like a reasonable strategy, but under the circumstances, Werner thought Goodman had little choice.

Werner and Arnold raised a number of questions about the financials that were not answered to their satisfaction. Goodman defended himself saying that he "was in business to make money, not produce accounting statements"—that if they would just pay attention to what he told them in terms of business instead of what they saw in accounting principles, everybody would be a lot happier. Werner was unpersuaded. Commenting on the size of the officers' loan accounts and charitable contributions, Werner's notes of the meeting state: "OPM is run as a Myron Goodman personal vehicle"; Arnold's notes state: "Every abuse in a privately held company has been done here." The bank officers also wrote that OPM "must have new business to survive."[25]

Following the meeting, Werner wrote a memo to Arnold and other senior managers at the St. Paul bank expressing his concern. Werner wrote:

> OPM as a closely held company has been run for the convenience of its two principals, Myron Goodman and Mordecai Weis[s]man. As such its statements reveal all the classic abuses to which such a company can be subjected. Advances to principals exceed net worth. Shareholder expenses are paid by the company but not segregated from true operating expenses. Transactions with affiliates controlled by the principals color the corporation's assets and liabilities. Profit and net worth generation are subordinate to volume and a style of business living which can only be classified as more than comfortable. Systems of control and financial reporting have, until the last 60 days, been nonexistent.[26]

Although far removed from OPM's inner circle, Werner seemed to have a better view of the company than did others. Despite his concerns, however, he recommended that the bank continue to make loans to OPM but suggested a $15 million ceiling, provided OPM met certain conditions—which were never met. And, even when the $15 million limit was reached, loans were sometimes made to Lehman Leasing—a subsidiary of Lehman—which would then lend money to OPM. Officers at the FNBSP were fully aware of the Lehman Leasing-OPM arrangement.

The Rockwell Fraud

When the check-kiting scheme ended and the cash from the bridges to nowhere and Equipment Schedule 81 had been long gone, Goodman still needed money, and he began to engage in fraud—fraud on a very large scale. Up until this point, Goodman and Weissman had double-hocked a few loans here and there, made some payoffs, and so forth, but compared to the crimes committed between 1979 and 1981, the early infractions were nickel-and-dime stuff. How did he carry out such frauds? After all, don't banks, lawyers, and lessees like Rockwell, establish elaborate mechanisms to prevent such crimes? Indeed they do. But Goodman knew what these mechanisms were, and he learned the ways around them. He saw which banks and law firms did their homework, which ones would check and which ones would not. He knew how Singer Hutner Levine & Seeman, Lehman, and Rockwell operated, and he knew he could get by them. He also believed he could conceal the fraud from OPM's accountants, Fox & Company. Goodman thought he was smarter than everyone else, and he was almost right. He also knew he could control the flow of information between all the parties involved.

Goodman had surrounded himself with lawyers, accountants, leading financial institutions, Fortune 100 clients, and one of the top investment banking firms in the country. Each of these organizations relied on the others to complete their deals with OPM. Lehman, for instance, relied in part on financial statements prepared by Fox for its continued involvement with OPM. Fox relied in part on the bookkeeping work done by Rashba & Pokart and by certain OPM employees. Singer Hutner depended on Lehman, on OPM's employees, and on the legal counsel to the banks, the lessees, and the vendor. The lenders relied a great deal on Lehman and the attorneys who represented them in these transactions. And on and on. Each of these institutions concentrated on a specific, sometimes narrow, part of these deals, rarely having a thorough understanding about what the other participants were actually doing; but they were all dependent on each other.

Goodman controlled the information that flowed from one participant to another. He didn't allow Rockwell to communicate with Lehman, or vice versa. Or Singer Hutner with Rockwell. Or any of them with the lenders. He claimed it had taken months, sometimes years, to establish relations with these institutions, and he did not want these relationships jeopardized by a curious lawyer or banker, not an uncommon concern of people in business. Therefore, each time one party wanted to communicate with another, Goodman served as the middleman, filtering out information that might trigger suspicion. And where his orders did not protect him, he knew that rules of professional ethics would—accountants, lawyers, and, to some extent, investment bankers would be reluctant to pass along to others information they obtained in a professional-client relationship. Goodman also knew these parties would do as he said—within reason; they had too much to lose if they did otherwise.

Unable to accept the mounting losses and negative cash flow, particularly in light of the volume of business they were doing, Goodman and Weissman saw the only way out of their predicament was to resort to using their only apparent skill: obtaining loans through fraudulent means. Whether it was ego or the fear that earlier crimes would be discovered, or both, other choices, such as declaring bankruptcy, weren't seriously considered.

On New Year's Day, 1979, Goodman and Weissman traveled from New York to Los Angeles and met at the Beverly Wilshire Hotel on Wilshire Boulevard to chart OPM's course for the coming months. It was an unusually tense meeting between the two longtime friends. Weissman's normally calm demeanor was lost under the mounting pressure. Goodman had never seen him so upset. Weissman said he had entered into a deal with George Prussin, sort of a payback for all the "help" Prussin had provided OPM over the years. Prussin claimed OPM owed him $2 million under the agreement. But Prussin also believed OPM was on the verge of collapse, Weissman said, and he agreed to accept three payments of $350,000 each.[27] Weissman disagreed with Prussin's $2 million claim, but thought there was "no choice" but to meet his demands "if [they] wanted to stay in business," according to Goodman's testimony.[28] Both Weissman and Goodman were uncomfortable with Prussin's demands, but believed they had to pay him to keep "his mouth shut."

Prussin's demand added to the torrent of obligations then facing OPM, and the stress was too much for Weissman. For some time he had feared OPM's cash flow difficulties would eventually lead to the discovery of the early frauds—frauds for which he was primarily responsible. He was so distraught he broke down and cried during the meeting and, in an extraordinary reversal of roles, Goodman had to calm him down. In the midst of all this, an earthquake tremor rocked the hotel. Weissman rushed to the door. But Goodman was more concerned about the documents he and Weissman had scattered around the room, and he began to gather them as Weissman shouted at him to leave the papers and get outside.

Once the earth stopped shaking, the two resumed their meeting. Weissman wanted out of OPM. He had always dreamed of going off to some island with a few million dollars stashed away; certainly, the timing couldn't have been better. The cash flow crunch was worse now than it had ever been, and Myron wanted control over the company. They both agreed Weissman would leave OPM before the end of 1979, perhaps by September. Goodman, generous as always, even agreed to pay Weissman $2 million to obtain sole control of the financially troubled company. But Weissman was leaving no stone unturned. They talked about buying out a fraudulent loan with the Bank of New York—one of the few remaining vestiges of Weissman's criminal activity—so that Weissman wouldn't be implicated in the event of an OPM bankruptcy.[29] But before Weissman could escape the OPM quagmire, his fraudulent touch would be needed one more time.

One month later, on a flight from San Francisco to New York, Goodman told Weissman that OPM's cash drain was leading them down the road to bankruptcy, a situation neither of them could afford in light of the fraudulent Bank of New York financing still on the books. Goodman said he was planning to fraudulently finance Rockwell leases to avoid the bankruptcy that had always threatened, but that was more ominous now than ever before. Goodman's deteriorating health had also entered his thinking. He may have had a sense of martyrdom —a willingness to save himself and Weissman from financial disaster —and from jail. Or, so he thought.

In early 1979, a new outbreak of sarcoidosis, the disease that had plagued him since 1971, again besieged him. He claimed he "lived every day in fear of death." He even obtained more life insurance and named Weissman the beneficiary. During their flight from the West Coast on February 1, Goodman implied[30] that he would do whatever he could to save the company and that Weissman could ease himself out of the picture. But since Goodman was such a bad typist, he asked Weissman to type a phony IBM invoice when they got back to New York so they could obtain a loan on a fraudulent Rockwell lease scheduled to close on February 9. Back at OPM, Weissman typed the phony invoice during the weekend. This was his last fraudulent act.

From that point onward, the Rockwell fraud was engineered by Myron Goodman. He decided when and how the frauds would be carried out. He organized the team of coconspirators who operated at his direction. He schemed, improvised, and patched up flaws in his plan, although the word "plan" gives Goodman too much credit. The frauds were meant to be only temporary, to provide the cash to keep the company afloat for the time being. There was no master plan. Thus, the "plan" was more haphazard and disorganized than the use of the word suggests.

During the next several years, Weissman stayed away from OPM. Employees said he was rarely seen at the company's offices. Yet he continued to draw his high salary and the perks he had grown accustomed to. He knew the company had been in desperate financial straits, but he never asked Goodman how he was managing to keep OPM afloat. There were even times when Goodman would ask his partner to leave the room while others discussed the fraud, but Weissman never asked why he had to leave. He knew. But apparently he believed that if he didn't participate or if he appeared ignorant of what was going on, he wouldn't be implicated. He later admitted "closing his eyes" to the frauds that kept OPM in business from 1979 until February 1981.[31]

Why Rockwell?

OPM obtained its first leasing contract with Rockwell in 1976. At some point after that date, OPM became the exclusive computer-leasing company for Rockwell. The relationship was beneficial for both parties: OPM took obsolete equipment off Rockwell's hands, saving the aerospace company millions of dollars, and OPM had virtually exclusive rights to lease equipment to the largest computer user in the United States—except for the U.S. Government.

Goodman alone handled the Rockwell account. No one else was allowed to communicate with Rockwell representatives without his approval. No one was to have access to the Rockwell files; Rockwell was his and only his. He didn't have to worry about anyone at OPM becoming suspicious; information to and from Rockwell—everything —first filtered through him.

Goodman knew Rockwell's operations intimately. He had developed a father-son relationship with Sidney Hasin, and he depended on Hasin's sense of loyalty and obligatory feelings toward Goodman and OPM to defend them against criticism from several senior managers at Rockwell who were concerned about Rockwell's growing dependence on OPM. Goodman frequently reminded Hasin that he "owed" OPM. And as his debts and reliance on OPM grew, Hasin became "OPM's man at Rockwell," according to Goodman.[32] Hasin recognized the interdependency and fidelity, too, once telling Goodman that he was OPM's only "comrade" at Rockwell. Myron also understood Rockwell's procedures and how key employees operated. For example, Goodman thought that Daniel Byrnes, the in-house Rockwell lawyer responsible for the firm's opinion letters and other lease documentation, was sloppy and unconcerned with paper work, often allowing OPM or his secretary to process the official documents.

In short, Goodman thought he "controlled Rockwell." In the event of a mishap, he believed Hasin would notify him or take care of the problem himself. Goodman also believed he could "talk around" the slipups—whatever they were. Moreover, Rockwell was a prime vehicle for the fraud because the company was a blue-chip credit, and banks would be quick to finance Rockwell-OPM deals without asking questions.

Goodman's calculations turned out to be accurate. Rockwell personnel were sloppy in handling its lease documentation, and Hasin remained loyal to OPM. But the size of the Rockwell fraud and the need to cover up occasional "glitches" in the scheme forced Goodman to recruit a team of young men from OPM who would work at his direction.

Goodman's Collaborators

Goodman was able to persuade or, in some cases, intimidate five young OPM officers to help him with the fraud scheme. All were in their late twenties or mid-thirties. All were well paid for their limited training and experience. And all were indebted to Goodman for providing them with jobs and salaries they couldn't find elsewhere.

They were each recruited singly, not as a group. Goodman appealed to their sense of loyalty, telling them if they didn't help—just this one time—the company would fail. He claimed that the fraudulent loans would be bought out as soon as the company's financial picture improved, that nobody would get hurt, and that he would take full responsibility if the frauds were discovered. Put that way, few could refuse his pleas for help, and once they became involved, it was easy to get them to help a second time. Before long, they were handling matters on their own. Some people said the team eventually knew more about the frauds than Goodman did.

The first person Goodman lured into the scheme was thirty-two-year-old Stephen Lichtman,[33] a former high school classmate of Weissman's, who served as Goodman's assistant since coming to OPM in March 1977. On Sunday evening, February 4, 1980, the same day Weissman typed the phony invoice, Goodman called Lichtman at home and told him he had something important to discuss with him and asked if Lichtman could ride into Manhattan with him the next morning. Knowing that meant Goodman's limousine would pick him up at 4:30 A.M., Lichtman was hesitant, but agreed. To Lichtman's surprise, the ride the following morning from Long Island to Manhattan passed in silence; Goodman mentioned nothing about the matter that had seemed so urgent the night before.

Only when they arrived at his office did Goodman tell Lichtman about "it." Goodman began telling Lichtman how poor OPM's cash flow was, something Lichtman already knew. He explained that OPM's future depended on "it" and that "Lichtman's willingness to do 'it' was indispensable." Lichtman wasn't sure what "it" meant until Goodman told him that OPM needed to buy out a Fireman's Fund Insurance Company deal with the financing from a Rockwell transaction. But the Rockwell deal wouldn't go through in time, Goodman explained, so they needed to finance a phony lease to cover the transaction with Fireman's Fund. Once the Rockwell deal was completed, Goodman made clear, the fictitious loan would be bought out. "It" turned out to be fraud, but it wasn't put in quite those terms. "It" would only be a short-term fraud, in any event. Lichtman paced back and forth in Goodman's spacious office. He reluctantly agreed to help.

Around the same time, Goodman recruited his and Weissman's brother-in-law, twenty-five-year-old Allen "Goodhands" Ganz. Like the motto of the insurance company, Ganz frequently said, "You're in good hands with Allen Ganz," and thus he was given the nickname "Goodhands." Subsequent events, however, have led people to wonder whether "Goodhands" related to Ganz's skill at forging documents to perpetrate the fraud rather than to the insurance motto. Ganz had already helped his in-laws commit crimes while working at OPM during his college days; he often served as a bagman, carrying OPM's commercial bribes to different parts of the city. When Ganz returned from vacation that first week in February, Lichtman, following Goodman's instruction, told him about the fraudulent financing that he and Goodman had just arranged.[34] He also said there would be others. Echoing Goodman's words to him, Lichtman said the company's poor financial condition made the frauds necessary to keep OPM going and to provide jobs and other benefits for OPM's employees and their families. The fraudulent loans were only temporary, he explained; Goodman would buy them out when things got better. But for now, he needed Ganz's help. Although he felt like a "mountain falling on . . . [his] head," Ganz agreed to participate. The day after Lichtman prepped him, Goodman asked Ganz to help on a fraudulent deal. Goodman assured him the loan would be bought out shortly. Ganz agreed to assist. The fraudulent loan is still on OPM's books.

The third and fourth team members were more volunteers than recruits, Goodman testified.[35] First, there was Mannes Friedman, a thirty-two-year-old former textile salesman. Friedman joined OPM in October 1978 without any experience in the leasing business and immediately became a member of Goodman's retinue. Friedman's ignorance of the leasing business was an advantage, according to Goodman, because it enabled him to train Friedman "his own way."[36] Unfortunately for Friedman, he was a willing student.

It wasn't long before Friedman became suspicious about certain

Rockwell leases. Lichtman, who also frequently traveled with Goodman, told the untutored Friedman about the fraudulent financing that
had occurred that February. It was a deal that was necessary to save
OPM, he said. Some time in mid-1979, Friedman confronted Goodman in a room at the Beverly Wilshire Hotel in Los Angeles. According
to Goodman, Friedman said:

> "Don't you think I know what is going on?"
>
> "I don't know what you are referring to," Goodman responded.
>
> Undaunted, Friedman said, "You know, doing deals that Sid
> doesn't know about and Rockwell doesn't know about and so on."
>
> "What's your point?"
>
> "Rather than me being an outsider," Friedman said, "I think you
> should know that I know all about it, and if I can do anything to help
> you let me know."[37]

Like Ganz, the fourth team member was a veteran of OPM's
criminal past. Thirty-six-year-old Martin Shulman, the senior player on
Goodman's team, was hired by OPM from American Express, where
he had received a substantial amount of cash from OPM in exchange
for facilitating OPM's frauds. When he came to OPM, he was placed
in charge of the operations department, but few people could figure out
what he did. Even Goodman said he "was a total waste as an employee"
and the only reason he was hired was because he helped OPM while
he had been with American Express.

In 1979, Shulman noticed Lichtman acting "funny," and he decided to approach Goodman. Goodman said he was "overfinancing"
equipment leases to Rockwell, but Rockwell was aware of the inflated
loans—it was a payback for OPM's losses on earlier Rockwell deals.
Shulman needed little convincing to join the team but, just in case,
Goodman reminded him of his exposure on the commercial bribes and
his complicity in the earlier American Express frauds. Shulman became
the team's most enthusiastic member, one person saying he "got off"
on the fraud. Goodman said that Shulman "volunteered that any time
I needed him, he would be more than glad to help."[38]

For the most part, these four—Lichtman, Ganz, Friedman, and
Shulman—handled the day-to-day management of the fraud. Each had
specific tasks to perform. Ganz, for example, managed the transactions

in such a way that none of the participants in the financings would contact or send the fraudulent documents to Rockwell. He also created many of the phony materials. Shulman was responsible for creating phony bills of sale and for an occasional impersonation of some official. Lichtman and Friedman moved the documents from OPM to Rockwell. All were extremely well paid for their talents. Between 1979 and 1981, Shulman's salary jumped from $55,000 a year to $77,500; Ganz's salary from $55,000 to $85,000; Lichtman's from $55,000 to $90,000; and Friedman's from $50,000 to $75,000. Ganz also received a "loan" for $90,000 to purchase a home in 1980. Lichtman received over $48,000 to purchase his home. And in 1980, OPM loaned Shulman $15,000.[39]

Some time in 1980, twenty-eight-year-old Jeffry Resnick became the fifth team member. Resnick worked as an assistant to Allen Ganz, who instructed him to create duplicate materials used in the frauds. At first, Resnick did not realize he had been creating two versions of the same lease—one for Rockwell and one for the lender—despite the vast differences in the values of the leases. Gradually he realized what was going on, but he didn't ask Ganz any questions. He continued to do as Ganz asked.

In January 1981, Resnick learned more about the fraud, but he limited his involvement to what he had previously been doing—he wanted no more responsibility. Resnick's role in the fraud was so small that Goodman and Weissman didn't even know he was involved at all until Resnick entered a guilty plea in federal court in December 1981.

The Mechanics of the Fraud

The Rockwell fraud evolved through several stages in the two-and-a-half years it was carried out. In the first phase, which included Equipment Schedule 81 and the bridges to nowhere, Goodman obtained fraudulent bridge loans on equipment Rockwell actually wanted. Myron induced Hasin to process the needed paperwork even though Rockwell officials had not approved the acquisitions; Goodman argued that Rockwell would need the equipment down the road anyway. The bridges to nowhere provided OPM with $3.8 million in short-term cash in late 1978 and early 1979; these loans were partially paid back with fraudulent permanent financings.

In February 1979, phase two began. Goodman, Lichtman, and Ganz created fictitious or "phantom" leases based on equipment Rockwell never intended to finance. For phantoms, the team had to arrange things so Rockwell never received any of the fraudulent documents. And they had to create fictitious Rockwell opinions of counsel and other materials to present at the closings. Both steps were easy. On February 9, the day the first phantom closed, Steve Lichtman instructed a Singer Hutner paralegal to deliver Rockwell's post-closing documents to OPM rather than to Rockwell, which was the usual procedure. The "new policy" was necessary because OPM wanted to monitor the flow of documents to Rockwell, Lichtman explained, and because OPM made such frequent trips out West that it would be just as easy to hand-deliver them. It all sounded reasonable enough, but the paralegal asked Lichtman to check with Andrew Reinhard, the Singer Hutner partner working on the closing. Lichtman did, and Reinhard, according to Goodman, responded, "No problem."[40]

For official Rockwell documents, the team—usually Allen Ganz —used the supply of Rockwell stationery that Goodman obtained from Verl Rosenow, a good friend of Sidney Hasin's and the head of OPM's marketing for the West Coast. Goodman testified that he was once searching Hasin's office while Rosenow was standing at the door. "What are you doing?" Rosenow asked. Goodman said he was looking for Rockwell stationery, and Rosenow said he'd get him a whole ream, which he did. By the way of explanation, Goodman told him that "it was good to have extra." Rosenow didn't inquire further. Ganz simply forged the signatures of Rockwell officials on the purloined stationery.

Other closing documents were provided by attaching surplus signature pages from legitimate Rockwell leases to the documents for the phantom leases. The fraud team didn't plan to accumulate original Rockwell signature pages. It just happened. When anyone on the team needed originals, he found that they were easy to get. Hasin, for example, liked to sign documents en masse. So, at the end of a long meeting, a member of the team would produce a stack of documents for Hasin's signature, and while he talked about other matters, he signed away. Another time, Goodman claimed he "lost" the Rockwell documents and, therefore, needed another set. The unsuspecting Hasin complied with Goodman's request.

Other closing documents were easily produced by members of the fraud team. Sometimes Ganz would white-out the date and equipment description on legitimate documents and type in the phony terms. At one point, Singer Hutner demanded original title documentation,[41] so Ganz doctored the IBM invoice forms Goodman and Weissman had obtained from Richard Monks, an IBM employee, in exchange for payoffs in 1975 and 1976. For the most part, no one was the wiser. But there were some close shaves.

Unlike Rockwell, IBM sent a representative to the closings, and on certain occasions OPM presented forged IBM documents at closings attended by an IBM employee. The fraudulent documents were often lumped with legitimate leases, however, so they wouldn't be so conspicuous. Lichtman once presented an IBM invoice marked "paid" and bearing the forged signature of the very IBM representative who showed up at the closing. Fortunately for Lichtman, the IBM rep just shuffled through the papers and didn't notice the counterfeit of his signature.

In late 1979, the fraud team worried about the risks of creating totally fictitious leases. Without any Rockwell counterpart to these leases, accidental discovery would have been difficult for Goodman to explain. If Rockwell and the lender each had a version of the lease, the different terms could be explained in some way, but if the lender had the only lease, Goodman and other team members would be hard put to provide a justification. So, in phase three, they began to alter legitimate Rockwell leases to reflect different equipment and higher rentals than Rockwell had bargained for. Rockwell forwarded legitimate lease and financing documents to OPM complete with necessary signatures. Ganz performed his handiwork, the altered documents were presented at the closings, and OPM obtained substantially greater loans than had they financed the legitimate Rockwell leases. The documents were switched before being sent back to Rockwell.

There were one major and many minor hitches in the scheme. For OPM to obtain permanent financing, it assigned the lessee's rental stream to the lending institution. At each closing, OPM presented a "consent and agreements" that was signed by a Rockwell official obligating Rockwell to pay the lending institution directly rather than

OPM. But Rockwell routinely paid OPM. There were no procedures at Rockwell to ensure that payments went directly to the banks. The accounting clerk who was responsible for making installments on the computer leases said she "never heard of" consent and agreements.[42] She followed OPM's direction as to where to send Rockwell's payments; Rockwell forwarded its payments to OPM, and OPM, in turn, paid the lender the inflated rental. The Hassett report concluded:

> The OPM team could not have conducted the fraud as it did if Rockwell had made its rental payments directly to the financing institutions on leases where the rental amount was fraudulently inflated. The amounts paid by Rockwell would have been smaller than the institutions believed they were entitled to receive. Efforts to resolve the discrepancy inevitably would have led to discovery of the fraud.[43]

Of course, had the *lenders* insisted on direct payment from Rockwell, Goodman would have faced a similar problem. But few did. And when they did, it was because OPM's payments on behalf of Rockwell were delinquent or because the checks bounced—not because Rockwell violated the direct-payment provision. Indeed, it was through the diligent efforts of a lawyer working for one of the lenders who insisted on direct payments from Rockwell that eventually led to the discovery of the fraud (see chapter 11). Had others done the same, the fraud could never have gone on.

Goodman often relied on the sloppiness of others to get away with the things he did.[44] Singer Hutner, for example, gave little thought to the changes in procedure requested by Lichtman that facilitated the frauds. In addition, representatives from Rockwell didn't attend closings because, for the most part, they saw the financing of deals as annoyances—all they wanted was the equipment. Lenders, too, failed to verify the terms of each deal. Instead, they relied on Lehman and on the prestigious legal counsel Lehman and OPM chose to represent them at the closing. Since Goodman paid the legal fees for lenders' closing counsel, he handpicked law firms that wouldn't "upset the apple cart."[45] Goodman wanted no part of the "belt-and-suspenders" type of lawyer, his term for a careful, conservative attorney. Some of the nation's leading law firms, such as Simpson Thacher & Bartlett, and White & Case of New York; Drinker Biddle & Reath of Philadelphia;

and Briggs & Morgan of St. Paul, fit what Goodman was looking for. Few sought to verify the terms of the lease with lessee and, thus, were frequently chosen by Goodman to represent lenders.

Although it may appear as though Goodman's team had all the angles covered for a smooth, efficient fraud operation, sloppiness and confusion were more characteristic of the team's methods. But Goodman and the others correctly perceived that many mistakes or signs of fraud would be overlooked or easily "explained away." Several flags of fraud were missed because few participants—investment bankers, lawyers, or lenders—had any knowledge about computers. In committing the fraud, for example, OPM obtained financing on an IBM Mass Storage Unit (MSU), an expensive piece of equipment that is capable of storing 236 billion bytes of information and serving four mainframes at one time. A company the size of Rockwell might be able to use one, possibly two MSUs. So few were needed in the United States that IBM stopped production of them in June 1980—after only 198 were manufactured. But from late 1979 until it ended in February 1981, OPM fraudulently financed over 30 percent of the Mass Storage Units ever produced—sixty-one in all—all allegedly headed for Rockwell. OPM even financed four of them in one day—all by the same bank, the FNBSP. None of the lawyers, investment bankers, or creditors who were familiar with these deals knew what a Mass Storage Unit was. Nor did they ever ask.

From late 1978 through February 1981, Goodman and others fraudulently induced nineteen different lending institutions to purchase sixty notes in forty-nine separate transactions, fraudulently obtaining over $190 million. The OPM trustee's investigation found that most of the money was used to keep OPM afloat, to make payments on earlier fraudulent loans, and to support the principals' extravagant lifestyles. For over two years nobody knew. Or if they did, they chose not to stop it.

The House of Cards Begins to Shake

Check-Kiting Indictments

On March 6, 1980, a federal grand jury in New Orleans returned a forty-three count indictment for check-kiting against OPM. According to Assistant U.S. Attorney Pauline Hardin, OPM eventually made good on all checks involved; the banks did not lose any money on the scheme. But Hardin claimed the checks were essentially "false statements because they purported to be of value but they were not."[1] Lying to a bank is a federal crime when the lie influences the actions of the bank.

The indictment charged that each of the forty-three counts, not eight as Goodman had reported to Lehman Brothers Kuhn Loeb, was based on $100,000 checks written by OPM and deposited at Irving Trust Company in New York City or at the First National Bank of Jefferson Parish. Twenty-eight checks were written against an account at Irving Trust and deposited at the First National Bank of Jefferson Parish between December 1, 1978, and February 26, 1979. The reverse was done on the remaining fifteen checks; these checks were written against an account at the Jefferson Parish bank and deposited at Irving Trust between December 1 and 22, 1978. For example, on December 1, OPM deposited four $100,000 checks in its Jefferson Parish account that were drawn from its Irving Trust account. The same day, OPM deposited four other $100,000 checks in the Irving Trust account drawn from the Jefferson Parish account. The false statements occurred when the checks were deposited since OPM knew that the accounts they were drawn on did not contain sufficient funds to cover them. In late March 1980, OPM pleaded guilty to the charges and was punished with the maximum fine of $110,000.

Articles in the *American Banker*—the banking industry's daily— on March 10 and April 15 represented the first public disclosures of the incident.[2] Anticipating inquiries from lenders about the matter, Andrew Reinhard wrote a response "guide" on March 26 to help people field questions about the incident from outsiders. The guide was also circulated to Lehman. OPM decided to plead guilty after twenty-one counts of the indictment were dismissed, Reinhard reasoned in the guide, believing it would be too costly to challenge the other counts.[3] Moreover, no individuals were charged.[4] The guide also stated, "Needless to say, this should be kept in the strictest confidence and should only be used as a reference in responding to requests from other sources."[5] Lehman stuck to the party line; outside of specific inquiries, it did not inform present or prospective lenders about the check matter.[6]

During the same month, Lehman was trying to place millions of dollars of OPM-Rockwell notes with John Hancock Mutual Life Insurance Company. Lehman never told officers at John Hancock about OPM's felony conviction. While Lehman was negotiating the deal with John Hancock, however, officials at John Hancock became aware of the indictment from other sources. Early in February 1980, Noel Barry of John Hancock was conducting a background check of OPM and called LeRoy McClellan, a vice-president of the Philadelphia Savings Fund Society (PSFS), the largest mutual savings bank in the United States and an important lender in OPM transactions. McClellan told Barry that OPM was slow paying at times but didn't add anything else. After McClellan learned about the check-kiting, he called Barry on March 12, to inform her. McClellan also called Joel Peck of Lehman to ask "Why the hell he hadn't called us." Sticking to the party line, Peck tried to tell McClellan that "it really wasn't all that serious." McClellan "disagreed strongly" and stated that kiting was "very serious." Within two weeks, the PSFS stopped making loans to OPM. After lending $279 million on OPM deals over the years, PSFS apparently had its fill of OPM's "slow pay" method, although it claimed it stopped lending to OPM because of "disintermediation"—too much money flowing out of the bank—and because it was "full up" with Rockwell debt.[7]

On learning about the kiting, John Hancock immediately confronted Lehman with its concealment and terminated the negotiations. A memo from Edward W. Kane of John Hancock to Nathaniel S. Collidge, a senior investment officer at John Hancock, dated March 13, 1980, related its position:

> [T]here is no way that Alan Batkin, Joel Peck, Stephen S. Wolitzer, Laura Weil or anyone else at Lehman with whom Noel and I were in contact could possibly have misinterpreted our desire to have been provided with full normal background information on OPM Leasing Services. . . . Yesterday, Noel and I spoke [after learning of the indictment] with Joel Peck who stated that he has been aware of a pending indictment against OPM for over one year . . . nothing in the brochure concerning OPM Leasing Services, Inc. gives any references to any Federal Grand Jury investigation nor have any discussions with Lehman brought to light the existence of a Grand Jury investigation.
>
> In my opinion, the representatives of Lehman Brothers have participated in what is clearly a material misrepresentation of fact and I consider them to have not acted in a professional manner. I believe that a concerted effort was made to hide the truth and, in this case, manifestation of an asset by silence is equally as harmful as fraudulent misrepresentation.[8]

Other potential lenders also withdrew from further negotiations with Lehman after hearing about the kiting. On April 1, 1980, the Bank of Tokyo Trust Company wrote Lehman and stated:

> It has very recently come to our attention that O.P.M. Leasing Services, Inc., is under criminal indictment by a Federal Grand Jury in New Orleans for alleged participation in a check-kiting scheme in violation of Federal law.

In view of the fact that these circumstances were not previously disclosed by you to this bank, we believe that this bank must carefully reconsider the possibility of its participation in the proposed transaction. In our opinion, a pending Federal Grand Jury indictment casts considerable doubt on the trustworthiness of O.P.M. Leasing Services, Inc., as a party with which to participate in business transactions.[9]

Soon afterward, the Bank of Tokyo dropped its involvement with Lehman and OPM.

Charles De Simone, a banker from the Society for Savings in Hartford, Connecticut, was entertained by Joel Peck and another Lehman associate on March 17, shortly after the article appeared in the *American Banker*. The banker was unaware of the conviction, and no one told him about it. At dinner that evening, the banker even donned a tie with the OPM logo. Needless to say, he was embarrassed about the whole situation once he learned about the kiting, and he called Joel Peck of Lehman and told him so.

Lehman continued to place OPM debt with other lenders who were either unaware of the check-kiting or, at least, didn't raise any questions about it. Lehman contended that activity within OPM was of no significance to lenders since lenders relied on lessees to pay off notes, not OPM. And, of course, Lehman could cite several banks, such as the First National Bank of Saint Paul (FNBSP) and Manufacturer's Hanover Trust Company, who did know about the kiting and continued to lend money on OPM transactions. However, this seemed like a feeble defense in light of what had taken place. Indeed, activities within OPM had considerable significance in these transactions.

Lehman Begins to Get Concerned

Throughout 1979, a number of incidents occurred at OPM that had Alan Batkin wondering what was going on. Nothing criminal, mind you, just concern about how the business was being run. And it wasn't a single event that caused him to worry—it was a series of events that bothered him. First, there was the check-kiting revelation in

March. Later that spring, Goodman was unable to produce the financial information Batkin had requested, which he interpreted as a sign of OPM's inadequate reporting systems, apparently insensitive to the possibility that Goodman might be trying to conceal the information he wanted. Batkin suggested to Lewis Glucksman and to David Sacks, who were now following OPM a bit more closely, that perhaps OPM should retain a consultant to help correct the situation. They both liked the idea. When Batkin suggested the idea to Goodman—who was obviously aware of the need to appease Lehman at this stage—he, too, was in favor of getting a consultant.

But at first, Goodman wanted Fox & Company to do the work, an idea quickly quashed by Batkin since he didn't have much faith in the accounting firm's ability to do what was needed.[10] Batkin persuaded Goodman that the company needed a fresh, objective observer. Batkin recommended Jack Coopersmith, the former chief financial officer of United Brands and a personal friend of several Lehman partners. Coopersmith met with Goodman and accepted a retainer of $5,000, but after one or two more visits to OPM, he declined the engagement, claiming his health problems would interfere with completion of the task.

By December OPM still had no consultant. Such things have a way of going unresolved until another crisis triggers another demand. On December 14, Goodman wrote Batkin complaining about how long it was taking Lehman to place OPM's debt. Batkin wrote Goodman back later that week and said, somewhat indignantly, that it was OPM's reputation not Lehman's that made it so difficult to place OPM's debt. He wrote, "There have been several instances where lenders have complained to us because they have been receiving late payments, or payments in the wrong form (e.g., payment by OPM rather than the Lessee) on OPM transactions. This, obviously, reduced the chances of these lenders participating in future transactions."[11]

Indeed, Lehman received numerous complaints. The next day, Stephen Wolitzer, who worked for Batkin, sent Goodman a list of eight of the most recent charges, all made by different lenders, nearly all of whom complained about receiving payments from OPM rather than from the lessee.

Although payments coming from the wrong party are often considered a red flag to those in the financial community,[12] Batkin wasn't suspicious. OPM was frequently entitled to the first lease payment made by the lessee as a commission payment of sorts, according to Batkin; OPM even sent out bills to the lessee to ensure that they were paid rather than to the bank. Subsequent payments were to be sent directly to the banks, Batkin testified, but mixups were not unusual. Batkin didn't explain why OPM would continue paying the lenders over long periods of time, even if occasional errors did occur.

Notwithstanding this explanation, Batkin must have been concerned about OPM. And when he learned later that month that the leasing company was unable to close its books for 1979, making it impossible to complete a financial audit, he knew that Lehman would have to insist that OPM retain a consulting firm. Glucksman wouldn't tolerate the lack of financials; part of Lehman's due-diligence obligation, he believed, was to review a client's financial condition.

Batkin believed it was important to get a consulting firm that he knew, that he could trust, and that he knew could provide a quick response because things seemed to be deteriorating rapidly. He proposed Lehman's own auditor and his former employer, Coopers & Lybrand, to Glucksman and to Sacks. They both liked the idea, and Glucksman suggested that Batkin call Louis Moscarello, a Coopers & Lybrand partner he had known for the past twenty years. Batkin had also known Moscarello when he had worked at the Big Eight firm.

Shortly afterward, Glucksman called Goodman into his office and told him that Lehman was going to "take the ball" on the management end of OPM and was going to find the "toughest, meanest accountant in the business—Louis Moscarello" to straighten out OPM. Glucksman, describing Moscarello to Goodman, said, "You're not going to like him," and "He is going to be tough and obnoxious." All of this Goodman later found to be true. But under the circumstances, he knew he had little choice. Batkin had already informed him—in substance anyway—that if he didn't accept the Coopers engagement, Lehman would terminate the relationship. Goodman said he didn't like being told what to do, but agreed to cooperate. Besides, Goodman was "afraid" of Glucksman. He later testified, "When Lew Glucksman said something, I listened."[13] Goodman realized he had to go along with Lehman. He knew he had to accede to Lehman's demands, even before he walked into Glucksman's office. His only hope was to buy time and to stonewall Coopers.

Such steps must have been difficult for Batkin and Lehman. Goodman and Batkin had developed a relaxed, if not close, business relationship over the previous few years. Goodman often arranged his business connections in that manner. He always found a way to make people feel indebted and loyal to him. He would bend over backward for people, exploiting their drive and ambition, and when he found himself in a jam—and that seemed to be occurring with greater frequency—he expected others to return his favors. Batkin and Lehman were no exceptions. Over the previous couple of years, Batkin enjoyed more than his share of rewards for the amount of money OPM generated for Lehman; fees-per-employee is important in the investment banking industry, and OPM provided a considerable amount to Lehman, as much as $339 per hour at one point. The company received over $1 million in fees from OPM in 1978 and nearly $1 million for 1979. At one time, OPM's weekly retainer for Lehman's services totaled $37,500. The leasing company was considered one of Lehman's largest private placement clients. Moreover, Lehman itself participated in several OPM deals as an equity investor. Lehman had to be careful with OPM or else Goodman would take his business elsewhere, something he was not afraid of reminding Batkin from time to time.

But nonetheless, things were getting out of hand. Something had to be done, and Batkin wasn't inclined to tolerate OPM's poor business practices much longer—large fees or not. In February 1979, OPM hired Phil Lisciandro at Lehman's insistence to help get OPM's financial management under control. Six months later, Goodman fired Lisciandro. Moreover, Goodman was continuing to open OPM branch offices throughout the country, although he had no idea how much money he was spending or how much he was bringing in. Throughout his testimony, Batkin insisted that OPM's operations had little to do with Lehman's debt placement, but he believed this situation was different. Lehman felt strongly that OPM obtain the necessary help. Batkin testified, "We were not comfortable working with a company where there clearly or appears to be some waste in method of operation, where the management is not getting information on which to base certain decisions and then information to test the judgment or the results of those decisions."[14] A firm like Coopers would make them fly right.

OPM Engages Coopers & Lybrand

Coopers is the largest of the Big Eight accounting firms, with its annual revenues approaching $1 billion a year. The firm employs nearly 25,000 people, including 2,000 partners scattered in ninety offices across the United States and 350 offices in ninety countries worldwide. Its clients include Ford Motor Company, Gulf Oil Corporation, Atlantic Richfield Company, Sun Company, and, of course, Lehman. And it was about to add OPM to that prestigious list.

On January 3, 1980, Louis Moscarello, a general practice partner with thirty-seven years experience at Coopers, received a call from Alan Batkin, who from time to time had worked for Moscarello when Batkin was a CPA in Coopers's New York office. Batkin told Moscarello about OPM and asked his former boss if he would be interested in helping the company develop and implement a financial reporting system. Although Moscarello had never heard of OPM, he reacted favorably to Batkin's request because it came from Lehman and "from a man like Lewis Glucksman." Moscarello also respected Batkin, calling him an "outstanding" employee while he had been with Coopers. He agreed to meet with Myron Goodman and John Clifton the following Monday morning.

The following Monday, Moscarello met Goodman; they agreed to complete a series of informal interviews with key employees to give them a general understanding of the problems—and Moscarello agreed to submit a proposal by January 17. Robert Lage, who would manage the project for Coopers, and Martin Zelbow, an MBA out of the Amos Tuck School at Dartmouth and, incidently, on his first assignment for Coopers,[15] conducted the interviews over a three-day period in mid-January.

Based on the interviews, Coopers learned that OPM's books and records were rarely completed on a timely basis; indeed, some lease accounting data hadn't been posted in a year. Coopers also found the 1979 financial statements could not be prepared because half of the 1979 lease-contract files were incomplete; and it discovered the company's management was basically a two-man operation characterized by "poor communication" and by "unreliable data flow." Further, Coopers reported to OPM and Lehman that the leasing company was a "chaotic, undisciplined [and] poorly controlled environment."[16]

That week, Goodman accepted Coopers' proposed study to improve the company's management information system. At no time did anyone from Lehman or OPM tell anyone from Coopers about OPM's bounced checks or cash flow problems. Nor did anyone raise the check-kiting problem. Nor did anyone ever question the integrity of Goodman or Weissman. Nor did anyone show Coopers any of OPM's previous financial statements or point out general problems in the computer leasing industry. Coopers would have to learn all of this on its own.

But the Big Eight firm did learn enough about OPM's cash flow problems in those early days to demand a $17,000 retainer for its services in addition to billing OPM every two weeks, precautions that it did not take with everyone.

Throughout the engagement, Coopers submitted weekly status reports to key OPM employees and to Lehman (Batkin, Glucksman, and Sacks) who, in turn, forwarded them to Jeffrey Werner of the FNBSP. Weekly progress meetings were held to discuss the reports and other difficulties Coopers was encountering. A number of people attended these sessions, including Goodman, Robert Lage, Martin Zelbow, Alan Batkin, John Clifton, Marvin Weissman, David Lesnick, Michael Weinberg (who was OPM's in-house tax counsel and a former employee of Coopers), Andrew Reinhard, and Stephen Kutz. Moscarello also attended several meetings. Thus, Coopers was the only organization that routinely dispersed information about OPM to interested parties.

Coopers's weekly reports served as a chronicle of its gradual realization that there was something terribly wrong at OPM. On February 15, 1980, Coopers again reported that the situation at OPM was "chaotic" and "undisciplined," and if Coopers was unable to implement controls soon, "it will be virtually impossible for any other firm or individual to gain control of this chaotic undisciplined situation without a far more painful and radical approach."[17] Moscarello later said that Coopers wanted all parties to know "how much more horrible the situation was than we had even anticipated," at least as bad as any he had ever seen.[18]

OPM's condition appeared worse still as Coopers addressed specific problems. Later that same month, Coopers reported that "after more than nine weeks on site, we are very concerned that the company's cash management is dangerously out of control." Coopers realized that OPM had over 200 incomplete lease-contract files and had inadequate control over its lease asset base; Coopers couldn't determine what equipment belonged to OPM or where it was located. Zelbow realized that the situation was more chaotic than his initial impressions led him to believe and that Coopers had understated the amount of work to be done.

At every step in his work, Zelbow faced delays. Some lag was inevitable, given the state of OPM's books and records and the inexperience of OPM's staff. But Zelbow also faced an uncooperative group of OPM employees—several members of "the team," particularly Martin Shulman and Allen Ganz frequently blocked his progress. Goodman himself seemed to go out of his way to stonewall Zelbow. On occasion, Goodman would chastise Zelbow for his zealous attempts to gather the information he needed. More than once, Goodman told Zelbow that "there were more important things to do" than to take the time to gather the materials he needed. Goodman's tyrannical behavior scared off several OPM employees, like Louis Dibari and Edward Hracs, who were collecting documents needed by Zelbow. Zelbow himself felt Goodman's wrath several times. "Mr. Goodman would lash out in anger to deflect my attempts to get this job done much more quickly." During a progress meeting in April, Zelbow told David Lesnick that OPM's mismanagement could lead to a bankruptcy that would be "very embarrassing to the entire Jewish community."[19] Lesnick carried Zelbow's remarks to Goodman, who burst into the conference room and went on an "unbelievable tirade" for more than two hours. Goodman was very animated as he screamed at Zelbow. Some time later, Goodman escalated his battle with Zelbow and even banished him from OPM's executive suite. Zelbow correctly sensed that Goodman

> did not want [financial statements] prepared, that it would have been to his benefit to delay rather than to have them prepared and finally for us to find some potentially bad news that there was for the world to see.[20]

But Zelbow did not suspect anything unusual at OPM. At least not for a while. He thought OPM was a "highly entrepreneurial" company "where the discipline" of providing management information "had not been instilled."[21] In such situations, the pervasive attitude is "when things are going so well, who needs bookkeeping?"

But Zelbow needed Goodman's cooperation. Shortly after the engagement began, it became apparent that most of the incomplete contract files were Rockwell International and American Express leases, which were under the personal control of Myron Goodman and Mordecai Weissman. This alone didn't disturb Zelbow, but he was beginning to worry about OPM's financial position and Goodman's apparent irrationality. At one point, Goodman called down to OPM's sixth floor where Zelbow was working and asked to see him right away. Zelbow went up to the executive suite, where he was kept waiting for some time until he was eventually called in. Goodman was sitting slumped in a chair at the end of a table. He appeared extremely tired. "He was just so worn out that I couldn't even get him to address or focus on whatever it was he wanted to talk to me about," Zelbow later said. Goodman did acknowledge his presence, Zelbow said, and he was trying to talk but he kept drifting off. Finally, when Zelbow realized Goodman was unable to communicate with him, he left his office and walked down the hall to OPM's library, where he found Stephen Lichtman. Zelbow told Lichtman that Goodman didn't appear well, and he suggested that Lichtman check on him.

Zelbow went back down to the sixth floor and called Lage and told him he had to speak to him right away. They agreed to meet when Zelbow returned to the office. Goodman's behavior made Zelbow's job more difficult and heightened his concerns about OPM. Goodman's irrational behavior, which Zelbow attributed to drugs, "was a continuing concern . . . we had a client who was a very sick man, emotionally and physically sick and tired, who had what appeared to be a troubled company."[22]

Troubled indeed. In February, at lunch with Kutz, Zelbow learned that OPM would show a loss and a negative net worth for 1979. Kutz told him, "I just don't know how Myron keeps on going."[23] Barely, according to Coopers' predictions. On March 21, a Coopers cash flow forecast projected shortfalls amounting to more than $1 million per week and a total deficit of over $14 million by the first week in April. Officials at Lehman, however, discounted these figures, claiming Coopers itself said the projections were based on unreliable information. Later, as the information became more dependable, however,

OPM's condition became dangerously apparent. Cash flow problems were so severe that Coopers reported that the only way OPM could raise funds was by placing new debt for equipment and diverting the revenue to pay off overdue and current obligations. Coopers realized this early in its engagement and later stated in the bankruptcy proceedings that OPM "in substance" was a "Ponzi scheme" since "the company was founded on the expectation that it must grow to continuously generate enough cash flow to meet its obligations."[24]

Zelbow's superiors didn't share his apprehensions, at least not at this point. Lage even criticized Zelbow for becoming embroiled with OPM's internal management problems and other matters that were beyond the scope of their engagement. Lage reminded Zelbow that they were "not OPM's auditors."

Goodman was thankful for that. He feared the "extremely competent" Zelbow, whom he referred to as a "younger Lou Moscarello," would discover the Rockwell frauds. Goodman used all the delay tactics he could muster to put Zelbow off. He even told Martin Shulman to help stall the persistent Zelbow. When this proved ineffective, Goodman sought to undercut Zelbow by complaining to Batkin about the young consultant's adverse effect on morale at OPM. Goodman also crabbed that Zelbow was too inexperienced to justify the fees Coopers charged. Batkin even spoke to someone at Coopers about Zelbow's behavior. In June, Goodman wrote Batkin, again complaining that Zelbow had "more than once insulted [and had] spoken down to" OPM employees. Goodman further stated that he hoped Coopers would withdraw "in the near future."[25] Indeed, Goodman sometimes thought that this was his only hope. For if Coopers got too close, he knew he'd have to fire the firm.

When Zelbow learned about OPM's check-kiting conviction in March, that alone did not heighten his concern for Goodman's integrity. He didn't consider it a very serious matter since check-kiting was "not unusual in the world of business" but was also "not a very smart thing to do." But he did admit, however, that he was more troubled about the integrity of OPM management than he had been with other clients he had worked for prior to coming to Coopers. As for Goodman, Zelbow testified, "I was . . . not totally confident in the man's personal integrity," and "I think it is fair to say I distrusted him."[26]

Around April, Zelbow was beginning to get curious about the

Rockwell leases. After fourteen weeks on site, many of the Rockwell lease contract files were still incomplete. Why the special handling? He wondered. He was also somewhat surprised about the large amount of cash flow generated by Rockwell. Kutz was interested in the Rockwell leases for the same reasons. He told Zelbow that he couldn't wait for the Rockwell files to be complete because he was personally going to audit every lease.

In April, Marvin Weissman and Rashba & Pokart, OPM's accountants over the previous six-and-a-half years, terminated its relationship with OPM citing "philosophical differences." Zelbow was "quite surprised" when he learned about the split. Marvin Weissman was the third key person to resign from OPM over a period of several months, all of whom had more than passing familiarity with OPM's finance and accounting records. In October 1979, Hoby Shapiro, OPM's vice-president and controller, resigned from that position, though he actually stayed with the company until the following January. The previous August, Alan Phillips, who headed OPM's accounting department, also resigned.

By the end of May, Zelbow worried about Coopers' exposure to civil suits in the event of OPM's insolvency. In a memo to Lage, later discussed with Coopers' legal counsel, Zelbow wrote, "Our client [OPM] is experiencing severe adverse business conditions and could during the course of the engagement, become insolvent or be petitioned into bankruptcy by one more more major creditors." Zelbow asked Lage:

1. In the event of insolvency, could our client find grounds to sue the firm?
2. While we have no measurement of the severity of the client's current financial condition, only symptoms, do we have any disclosure responsibilities? (This is a private company and is not an audit client.)
3. Should one or more key employees leave the client, could a case be made that the employee left the company due to our activities and that his leaving contributed to insolvency?
4. Since the client is dependent upon the sponsorship of an outside party, should that party discontinue its sponsorship as a result of our findings? Do we have any potential exposure?
5. Since some of the client's major creditors are audit clients of the firm, do we have any potential exposure?

6.   Is there any kind of legal exposure we should be prepared for?
7.   Am I unduly concerned?[27]

When John Clifton resigned from OPM, everyone became concerned.

Clifton's Resignation

John Clifton came to work for OPM in May 1974 directly from Touche Ross and Company, a Big Eight accounting firm that had previously audited OPM's books. At the time, OPM employed about ten people, most of them family members. Clifton probably knows more about OPM than any single person besides Goodman and Weissman. At twenty-eight, Clifton was hired as OPM's controller; he became a vice-president two years later and eventually became treasurer and chief operating officer. At certain times during his tenure at OPM, he was responsible for nearly every department within the company. He watched the company grow. He raised questions about some of Goodman's practices—like the frauds he discovered in 1975. But he didn't speak too loudly. Not for years. He was loyal to Goodman and Weissman and to OPM. To him, OPM was "more than a job."[28]

But in late 1978, Clifton discovered that Goodman provided an equity broker, Kent Klineman,[29] with financial statements that were different from those Clifton himself had prepared. Worried that Goodman may have violated federal securities laws by not providing certified financial statements to broker Klineman, Clifton sought the opinion of an attorney, William J. Davis of Shulman Berlin & Davis. OPM should submit certified financial statements to Klineman, Davis advised Clifton, and provide a rescission offer on any completed deals that were based on statements that were in error.

Clifton went back to Goodman and told him that he had spoken to counsel. Goodman wondered why Clifton hadn't come to him directly but agreed to do whatever had to be done to correct the situation. Klineman was sent the certified financials, but no rescission offer was made.

Goodman testified that Klineman knew the financials contained inflated assets, income, and net worth. Some time in 1973 or 1974, Klineman asked Goodman for OPM's financial statements and suggested that companies similar to OPM had a positive net worth. Goodman told Klineman that OPM's net worth was negative, to which Klineman responded: "You have to show me a positive net worth."[30] Myron did just that. Klineman denies encouraging Goodman to produce his own financials.

In the fall of 1979, Clifton was preparing interim financial statements for the FNBSP when it became apparent that Goodman and others—Stephen Lichtman and Allen Ganz—were withholding certain lease documentation involving Rockwell and American Express leases, making it impossible to close OPM's books. Around the middle of December, he told Lichtman that if there was something wrong with these leases, sooner or later it would be discovered. Lichtman told Clifton and Shapiro, who happened to be in Clifton's eighth-floor office at the time, that there was indeed a problem with these leases and that a Singer Hutner Levine & Seeman attorney told him he could go to jail for what he had done. He never mentioned the attorney's name. At this meeting or in subsequent discussions, Lichtman told Clifton that early in the year, Goodman had asked him for a favor. He wanted his assistance in obtaining phony loans on Rockwell transactions. Clifton testified:

> What Steve told me was that Myron had asked him to do him a favor, and that he had helped Myron and that his understanding was that Myron was supposed to do some bridge financings [of bogus Rockwell deals] which would enable him to get over a cash flow crunch for a short period of time, and that the transactions would be bought out relatively shortly from cash flow that he was anticipating from his backlog of leasing transactions. It was Steve's belief that once these transactions took place, that the bridges would be bought out and that would be the end of the matter.[31]

But, given the state of OPM's financial condition, Lichtman agonized that the phony transactions might never be bought out. He discovered his worst fears coming true during the summer of 1979. During a masquerade party at Goodman's home in July, Lichtman learned from Reinhard that the phony bridge loan was permanently financed, although Reinhard never indicated that he knew the loan was fraudulent. The day after the party, Lichtman, shaken by what he had involved himself in, spoke to Goodman and Weissman. At first, Weissman tried to "play dumb," but Lichtman told him to "knock it off," "you know perfectly well what I'm talking about."[32] Lichtman wanted to leave OPM, but they convinced him to stay on. Goodman even made a deal with him—just how, is not clear—to continue assisting on the phony bridge transactions. Goodman told Lichtman exactly how much cash he needed, and Lichtman produced enough phony transactions to generate the amount Goodman wanted and no more. Perhaps Lichtman thought that small, limited frauds were okay.

After learning all this from Lichtman, Clifton believed the fraud couldn't be that large. Although he remembered the earlier double discounts, he believed this situation was different—there were more people involved, legal opinions had to be obtained, and so forth—it couldn't be widespread. In fact, Clifton couldn't see how it was done at all. Nonetheless, he had to let Goodman know, without revealing what Lichtman had told him, that whatever it was that Goodman was doing, he wanted no part of it. In late December, Clifton met with Goodman and made that clear.

Over the next few months, Clifton tried in vain to get the information he needed from Goodman and from others. He didn't bother reporting what he knew to anyone else, such as Singer Hutner or the U.S. attorney, he said, because he really didn't have any information; he didn't know the scope of the problem. Besides, he didn't think the problem was that large. For some reason, perhaps wishful thinking, Clifton believed there would be some explanation for what Lichtman was telling him, that somewhere there existed documentation for the missing Rockwell leases.

But Shapiro had had enough. He had been concerned about OPM and Goodman ever since the check-kiting investigation began. Bounced checks and complaints from lenders added to his worry. There were times OPM couldn't even meet its payroll obligation. It was then that Shapiro decided he didn't want responsibility for what was taking place. So he resigned his controller's position in October, but Goodman also convinced him to stay on. Lichtman's confession to Shapiro in December confirmed his worst fears. He left the company shortly after the holidays. But he didn't bother reporting what he knew to anyone because "he really wanted nothing to do with it." Shapiro left Clifton holding the bag. "John was staying and I felt he would have to do what he had to do knowing that he was staying and knowing what he knew." Shapiro also failed to inform Fox and testified:

> Well, I'm sure a lot of people would have been interested to hear about it. But at the time, not knowing exactly what it was . . . and not knowing the specifics and that I was leaving, quite honestly . . . I didn't want to know anything, I just wanted to get out. And I felt the facts would come to light soon enough.[33]

In April, Lichtman told Clifton that Goodman was going to speak to Marvin Weissman about the problems Lichtman had been telling him about. Shortly afterward, Clifton learned that Marvin Weissman had resigned. He was becoming more and more uneasy with his predicament.

Goodman's Confession to Marvin Weissman

Marvin Weissman was well aware of OPM's cash flow problems. He had been attending the Coopers' progress meetings, and he had heard bits and pieces of conversation about the company's cash shortages and difficulties with the Rockwell leases. In April 1980, Goodman called Marvin Weissman to his office and confessed "that OPM was involved in illegal, improper or fraudulent transactions."[34] This time Marvin Weissman believed that the frauds were "substantial." Shocked at Goodman's revelations, Marvin Weissman told Goodman that Rashba & Pokart would have to resign. After all, they had been around a long time, and this was "strike three"— the double discounts, the kiting, and now more fraud. Marvin Weissman asked whether Mordy or Joe Hutner knew about the frauds. "No," Goodman responded. "Well, you better tell them both. You'd better make sure they find out," he ordered.[35]

Marvin Weissman and Goodman both decided to discuss the

situation with Reinhard since he was both an OPM director and a partner in the law firm that represented the company. Goodman called Reinhard and told him that Marvin Weissman was going to resign and wanted his advice.[36] According to Goodman, at first Reinhard said there was "no way" he'd meet with Marvin Weissman. After some coaxing, the Singer Hutner attorney relented. He agreed to meet with Weissman, provided they spoke in hypothetical terms. Reinhard did not want anyone to later accuse him of knowing about the fraud. Following the phone conversation, Weissman concluded that there was little doubt "Reinhard knew what was going on."[37]

Several days later, Marvin Weissman and Reinhard met for lunch in a Manhattan restaurant. Marvin Weissman stuck to the hypothetical ground rules but left little doubt whom he was talking about. He told Reinhard that Rashba & Pokart had a major client who was a repeat offender. Marvin Weissman said that he thought his firm should resign. Reinhard agreed, noting that it would be in the firm's best interest since "the client's communications with its accountants were not privileged like its communications with its lawyers."[38]

Although Reinhard pleaded his Fifth Amendment rights during the trustee's investigation, according to his attorneys, Reinhard knew that Marvin Weissman was talking about OPM. He later spoke to Goodman about his conversation with Marvin Weissman and Goodman told him that Marvin Weissman was "making a mountain out of a molehill" and suggested he ignore it.[39] Dutifully, Reinhard did as he was told. He even failed to tell his partners when subsequent events revealed that the molehill was truly a mountain.

Shortly after his meeting with Reinhard, Marvin Weissman met with other partners at Rashba & Pokart. Although OPM was the firm's largest client, it decided to resign. But it also decided not to reveal what it knew to anyone and instead chose to cite philosophical differences as the reason for the split. Marvin Weissman justified the misleading explanation in the following way:

> We were concerned that if we informed anybody that a fraud had occurred, we were not privy to any details, we were not [prepared] to prove that a fraud had occurred, and if a third party was so informed and had then damaged OPM, OPM could then turn around and sue us for . . . libel or slander. . . . And we didn't want, therefore, to be in such

a position, so we decided not to answer that we were informed that the company had committed a fraud.[40]

Rashba & Pokart resigned from the OPM engagement several days later without telling anyone the real reason for its action. Indeed, when Stephen Kutz and Morton Berger called Marvin Weissman and asked why he had resigned, Marvin Weissman said that Rashba & Pokart's services were no longer needed. When Berger asked whether there was anything wrong, Marvin Weissman said, "No."[41] The Rashba & Pokart partners did not consider whether or not they had a professional duty to disclose the frauds to OPM's board of directors: Andrew Reinhard and Mordecai Weissman.[42]

Clifton's Discovery and the Purloined Letter

John Clifton wasn't privy to the information Rashba & Pokart had, but he and his staff had been gathering materials since January to try to get a handle on the size of the fraudulent transactions. He hoped the fraud would be as little as $10 million so the phony transactions could be bought out with the sale of the Jefferson Parish bank stock. Then, on May 2, Dibari and Hracs, the two accountants who worked for Clifton, brought him some materials—invoices and bills of sale— they thought he ought to look at. It appeared as if OPM obtained financing for equipment that was never paid for. The company had millions of dollars coming in, but nothing went out.

Showing the materials to Clifton, they asked what they ought to do. Clifton told them not to worry, they had done what they were supposed to do, and he would take it from there. After they left his office, Clifton looked carefully at the documentation. He knew then that there wasn't anything that could explain the transactions and that what he probably had in his hands was evidence of "an out-and-out fraud." He became "a little frightened," and gathering up the documents, he went downstairs to a public telephone booth to call his attorney, William Davis.[43]

When Davis received the call from Clifton that Friday, he wasn't altogether surprised since his client had experienced legal problems with his employer before. (In addition to the Klineman incident, Clifton had also consulted Davis about the check-kiting matter.) But this time, Clifton sounded more troubled than before. He was "very grim," Davis said, as he expressed his "very deep concern" about what his staff had found. While preparing for the 1979 audit, Clifton said, two of his accountants, Hracs and Dibari, found some documents in Lichtman's office that weren't easy to come by. Clifton said the materials were in two folders that contained phony Rockwell leases, reworded bills of sale, and practice signature pages where someone had traced someone else's mark. Davis told Clifton to make a copy of the documents and to bring him both the copy and the original "smoking guns," as they came to be called.

Clifton and Davis met several times over the next few weeks. They both agreed the problem appeared serious; Davis advised Clifton to obtain as much documentation as possible so that someone unfamiliar with OPM could understand what had occurred.

Over the next month, Clifton and his staff—Dibari and Hracs—prepared a schedule documenting the fraud. They were only analyzing 1979 transactions since that was all the documentation they had access to, but it quickly became apparent to Clifton that he had uncovered "an absolute disaster." He "knew intuitively that selling the bank was not going to solve the problem."

Clifton and Goodman met on June 6 to discuss another matter. Clifton told Goodman what he had been documenting. He indicated that he was nearly finished and would be resigning soon. "I told him . . . that I would like to help him, but there was just no way that I could help him, and that for my sake and my family's sake, I just couldn't do it," Clifton later said.[44]

On June 10, Clifton met with Davis and showed him the completed schedule. There were massive amounts involved—$39 million in phony deals for 1979 alone. The company probably wouldn't survive another few weeks, Clifton revealed—they *couldn't* survive unless the frauds continued.

Davis told Clifton that the only way to protect himself from prosecution was to go to the U.S. attorney's office with the information he had. Clifton didn't want to do that; there had to be another way. Clifton explained that he "did not want to be the one who closed the

OPM doors." He later testified that Goodman had been too good to him. He had provided him with a good-paying job and given him a great deal of responsibility—things he knew he wouldn't have enjoyed elsewhere. Although Clifton once said he wanted to control his own destiny—that he didn't want to be one of Goodman's "captives"—he also felt indebted and loyal to the man. Goodman gave him "the opportunity to progress up the executive line from being just an accountant to gradually being a fairly high-up executive of a large company." Clifton continued:

> I looked at the relationship which I had with Myron during that entire period . . . and although most of what's on the record is negative, in my view the entire relationship was not negative. It was just, to me, it was just one of those situations where Myron had chosen a way to go which I didn't think was correct, and I just couldn't go along with it.[45]

Davis and Clifton talked for several hours about his alternatives. There was the possibility of resigning and doing nothing with the information Clifton had, but that was unpalatable to Davis. "That was unacceptable to me," Davis testified, "because I considered Myron Goodman to be a very dangerous person who, in view of his background and what had happened, could be counted on to do anything irrational." Davis explained: "Myron Goodman's background is a lot like mine. I come from a very Orthodox Jewish family . . . when I saw what John had turned up . . . I [knew] I was dealing with a person, namely, Mr. Goodman, who has some very strange abilities to ignore his background. . . . To my way of thinking, it was irreconcilable for a practicing Orthodox Jew to be engaged in these practices, and I therefore assumed he was irrational and operating under serious mental illness and he could do anything."[46]

They talked about telling Mordecai Weissman, but Clifton said Weissman tried to distance himself from these things and wouldn't want to hear about them. During the check-kiting incident a year earlier, Davis recalled Clifton saying, "Although Mordy often sought not to know, he knew."

Davis finally told Clifton that the only way he would avoid liability, other than going to the authorities, was to "drop the ball into the laps" of OPM's legal counsel, Singer Hutner, and see what it would do.

That way, Davis claimed, Clifton could fulfill his obligation not to knowingly conceal a felony while, at the same time, he did not have to "rat on his friends."

On June 10, 1980, Clifton told Goodman he had spoken to counsel and was stepping down. He also provided Goodman with a memo outlining problems he had uncovered involving forty-six Rockwell leases. Goodman's reaction was one of "resignation" and "depression." Clifton told him he didn't know whether he would have done what Goodman did. He went on to say that he would be sending a letter to Reinhard informing him of what he had found. While they spoke, the letter was being typed. Goodman told him to delay sending the letter—Goodman indicated he was doing everything in his power to protect people involved in this and he would like the opportunity to tell Reinhard personally. (This should not be interpreted as a statement of Reinhard's complicity in the fraud.) Clifton agreed to hold off sending the letter.

The next day, Clifton again met with Goodman, and they talked about severance pay. Goodman offered him $50,000. Clifton said he would have to speak with his attorney before accepting such a large amount. Davis later told Clifton that it was okay to accept the $50,000, which he did.

Following the advice of his legal counsel, on June 12, Clifton sent a hand-delivered letter outlining the fraud to Reinhard of Singer Hutner. He also enclosed the memo he had given Goodman. Clifton's letter to Reinhard said that the accounting department's review of Rockwell transactions raised "a number of issues . . . which I believe should be brought to your attention." The major issues raised by Clifton were:

1. Why isn't Rockwell making payment on the majority of transactions?
2. Why can't accounting verify payment for $26,700,000 of equipment which the IBM documents available in the files indicate are paid?[47]

Clifton also said that the enclosed documents "raise serious questions as to the authenticity and the source of the IBM title documents finally submitted in connection with financing."

The memo showed that Rockwell's obligations totaled $39,229,-123, requiring monthly payments by Rockwell in the amount of $640,-

473 to retire the debt. Yet OPM records showed that Rockwell was billed for only $124,267 per month; over $500,000 remained unpaid. Further, Clifton could not "verify in any accounting records" payments to IBM totaling $26.7 million for purchases of IBM equipment that had been financed for OPM-Rockwell transactions. And, finally, Clifton claimed "there is no record" of some equipment "ever being at Rockwell."

On Friday, June 13, Clifton went to Goodman's office and submitted his letter of resignation. Goodman pointed to a package on his desk. It was the material Clifton had sent to Reinhard. The package appeared unopened. Goodman said he had taken the package from Reinhard's desk. Goodman also told him that Singer Hutner wanted to explore the possibility of Clifton taking back the letter, that the firm was going to do some research to see whether he had to submit the package. Clifton was shocked that his letter had been intercepted but, trying to keep his composure, he said he would withdraw the letter if his attorney consented. He told Goodman he would have to discuss all this with his attorney, and he left Goodman's office to call Davis.

Davis was stunned to hear that Goodman had intercepted the package. Testifying about his conversation with Clifton, Davis said, "John said in a tone of great surprise mixed with exasperation, 'that he wants me to take the package back' . . . as only John can say it, kind of a high-pitched, eyes-squeezed exclamation." Clifton also told him that Goodman wanted to know if Davis would be willing to speak to Hutner. Davis said he would.

By June 1980, a number of OPM employees knew about the fraud. Hracs and Dibari had copies of Clifton's memo outlining the fraud. Joseph Datuin, OPM's controller, also had copies of the memo and had been kept informed of the foregoing events by Clifton. Preston Baptist, an OPM vice-president, also knew about the problems with the Rockwell loans. Baptist remembered Clifton telling him about duplicate leases; he wasn't specific, he recalled, but he was "very grave, and shaken."[48]

Clifton advised Datuin to resign in June, but Datuin stayed until November and would have accepted a position with OPM Data Services Company in California if the subsidiary were ever formed. Dibari and Hracs still worked for OPM several years after the company went bankrupt. During the summer of 1980, Hracs accepted a pay increase of $8,000 a year, retroactive to April; Goodman told him he was doing a good job. Preston Baptist also continued to work for OPM well after the company declared bankruptcy. None of these individuals ever contacted any governmental authority to reveal the information they had. And, of course, there was the team of Lichtman, Shulman, Ganz, and Mannes Friedman. (Resnick hadn't been brought on board as of June.) Other people—such as Samuel Ganz, Allen Ganz's father and Goodman's father-in-law; Joel Klein, the head of OPM's equity department; and Antoinette Pierre, Goodman's administrative assistant—probably knew about the frauds as well.[49]

Clifton was also concerned that he not mislead Fox, OPM's auditors. In March or April, Clifton told Kutz that there might be significant problems at OPM and that if they were major, Kutz would discover them. Clifton believed the frauds were so substantial that Kutz couldn't help detecting them, but he never did.

And then there is Mordecai Weissman. Before Clifton left OPM, Goodman had asked John to call Weissman. Weissman hadn't been around the office much, Clifton recalled, and he thought, "if Mordy wants to know about my resignation, he should call me." But since Goodman wanted him to call Weissman, he did. When Clifton reached him, Weissman said, "Hold on a second. Wait a minute. I've got somebody else on the other line, and I'll call you back." Clifton never heard from Weissman again.[50]

Knowing But Not Wanting to Know

The idea of Hutner calling him did not bother Davis.[51] His client had uncovered a massive fraud and to protect his client's interest, he'd be willing to listen to anyone, particularly in light of what had happened. The only way Davis could know what was going to happen next was to listen to what Hutner had to say. He didn't want to close any doors. But Davis was totally unprepared for what Hutner had to offer.

About four o'clock that Friday afternoon, Hutner arrived at Davis's midtown office. From the beginning, Davis recalled, Hutner conducted a "macabre dance around the issue." Hutner told him that

Reinhard hadn't seen the Clifton letter nor had he, and, furthermore, he didn't want to know what the letter contained—he insisted he not be told, Davis remembered.

Hutner went on to say that Goodman came to Singer Hutner's offices and admitted he had done "bad things he was not proud of."[52] But Hutner did not learn the specifics, and he didn't want to know. He proceeded to list the possible items that might have been described in the Clifton memo, such as problems with excessive charitable contributions, embezzlement, and, perhaps, fraudulent financial statements. Whatever the problem was, Hutner said, the law firm might be required to change the opinion letters it had issued on OPM transactions. Davis told him it had a firm obligation to retract these opinions now that it had reason to believe they were false. Davis also told Hutner, despite his insistence that he not be informed, that the wrongdoing would have to continue in order for OPM to survive.

The meeting took on an "air of unreality," Davis testified, as Hutner refused to address the issue. The contents of the Clifton memo became tangential to the whole process surrounding it. Everything Hutner stated was a possibility, not a fact. But Davis believed Hutner knew all along what the package contained. "I assumed that he had seen the contents of the package," Davis said, "because I found it difficult to believe that he would come in to me and talk about these matters with the intention of advising his most important client about them and not know what he was talking about."

Davis further testified that Hutner acted as if he didn't want to know what was going on.[53] Asked to explain this apparent contradiction—that he felt Hutner knew and, at the same time, he didn't want to know—Davis said, "You can know something and yet not want to know it at the same time. What he was doing in this meeting was going through a process in which he was asserting his lack of knowledge and doing what he could to protect himself from the knowledge."[54]

At length, Hutner tried to convince Davis to have Clifton withdraw or retrieve the letter. If Clifton had simply resigned following his discovery, that would have been enough, Hutner claimed, since Clifton wasn't involved in the wrongdoing. Clifton had no primary, secondary, or even misprision (an affirmative act of concealing a crime) liability for failing to reveal what he knew, Hutner told him. Davis was stunned by Hutner's suggestion and told him that what he said might be true, but Clifton *did* deliver the letter, and if he retrieved it in some way, that would be a violation of the misprision statute since it could be construed as an affirmative act of concealment to hide what he knew. Davis was not forceful in his argument, he later admitted, and it was something he regretted. Hutner suggested they study the subject before they made any decision. He volunteered the services of a Singer Hutner law partner, Eli Mattioli, to do the research during the weekend. Davis said he would also look at some cases and agreed to meet with Hutner and Mattioli on Monday.

The following Monday morning, Davis received copies of several legal cases[55] from Mattioli; he read them and decided they confirmed his view that Clifton could not take back the letter. Later that afternoon, Mattioli arrived at Davis's office, and then Hutner arrived. Davis told both attorneys that the cases Mattioli supplied supported his position that Clifton could not retrieve the letter. If the letter had never been sent, Davis argued, the Singer Hutner lawyers might have had a valid point about Clifton having no obligation to report what he knew. But the letter had been sent, and Davis was not going to advise his client to retract it.

At some point, Hutner sent Mattioli back to the Singer Hutner offices, and Hutner spoke with Davis for another fifteen minutes or so. Hutner told Davis that Singer Hutner might assert a "lack of knowledge" of the letter in the future. Davis replied that such a course would be difficult since Clifton had a record of the messenger slips showing that he had delivered a package to Reinhard on June 12. Then Davis realized Hutner meant that they would assert lack of knowledge about the contents of the letter. Davis thought the law firm would have difficulty defending this position as well. Davis later testified that

> the package was delivered to, at the very least, Andy Reinhard's desk and it was patently incredible to my way of thinking to believe it somehow had left his desk and had gotten into Myron Goodman's hands without anyone opening it and seeing what it was. I didn't believe it then and . I don't believe it now. I didn't believe any reasonable person would believe it and I was trying to bring that across to Joe Hutner. The fact he would admit the receipt of the package by Andy and deny anybody knew what was in it sounded ridiculous.[56]

In parting, Davis told Hutner that he had no present intention of advising Clifton to speak with the U.S. attorney, but circumstances might alter that advice. Davis did, however, advise Hutner to take Goodman to the U.S. attorney.

Davis was bothered by Hutner's apparent willingness to "stick his head in the sand" and ignore these problems. He felt this willingness to hide from the truth stemmed from Hutner's desire to maintain the very large fees he had received from OPM. He did not give Hutner a copy of the Clifton letter—which he had in his office—because he thought Hutner already knew what it contained and, Davis said, "I had visions of him clamping his hands over his ears and running out of the office. I didn't know what he was going to do. He didn't want to see a copy of the memo." Besides, even if he hadn't seen the memo, Davis believed he could get it from Goodman whenever he wanted to—Davis hadn't been told otherwise. If Hutner had control enough to get Goodman to return the memo to Clifton, surely Hutner could see it if he wished. But the question never came up. Neither Hutner nor Mattioli ever asked Davis for a copy of the letter.

Monday, June 16, was the last time Davis ever saw or heard from Hutner. Nor did he ever again hear from any other Singer Hutner attorney.

Persons often justify illegal and, perhaps, immoral conduct by invoking exceptions to the rules or by describing extraordinary circumstances, higher loyalties, or competing norms. Such "techniques of neutralization"[57] allow otherwise respectable and law-abiding citizens to commit and observe criminal acts without threatening the image they and others hold of them. Those who sit in judgment of such conduct, whether they are family members, business associates, fellow employees, or officials of the criminal justice system, are more or less persuaded by such rationales. The more intimate the relationship between the violator and the one who observes the behavior, the more likely the justifications for wrongful conduct will be accepted. Observers may even develop justifications of their own, excusing the impropriety, often without prompting from the deviant actor, as many defenders of OPM did. Reactions to OPM's check-kiting is such an example. At first, representatives at Lehman reacted strongly, but were "cooled out" by Goodman; he explained his conduct in such a way that it became more acceptable. Lehman, among others, went on to defend OPM or failed to mention the kiting to prospective lenders and clients. Others not so closely attached to OPM—like LeRoy McClellan at the PSFS and representatives at John Hancock—weren't so easily persuaded. Apparent acceptance or tolerance of the early frauds by Marvin Weissman, John Clifton, and others was also the result of some neutralization by these actors.

Of course, psychological processes play a part in the individual's filtering mechanism that determines what is acceptable and what is not. It is often said that people see what they want to see, that their psychological makeup, beliefs, and daily pressures predispose them to see things a certain way. The social psychologist, Leon Festinger, called this the theory of cognitive dissonance.[58] Following a decision to pursue a certain course of action, for instance, most people seek out information indicating that their judgments were correct while ignoring facts refuting that claim. Persons or organizations may have invested substantial resources pursuing a particular path. They may have too much to lose by exiting. They may have had to convince others to go along with their scheme. They become committed to a certain line and search for signals from their social worlds that show that their judgments were right. They strive for consonance in their attitudes, behaviors, and environments either by altering their original views or by selectively attending to cues from their social milieu, often misinterpreting or misperceiving social facts.

We know of certain instances, too, where monitors may position themselves so that they don't learn about improper conduct; such knowledge may require a readjustment of their views or an action on their part. A Kipling poem about a "shut-eyed sentry" describes such a situation: "But I'd shut my eyes in the sentry-box/so I didn't see nothin' wrong."[59] A less humorous example of this phenomenon comes from Albert Speer, one of Hitler's closest advisors. In his book, *Inside the Third Reich*, Speer described the forms of avoidance and rationalization he used to remain "unaware" of Nazi atrocities. Warned by a friend not to go to Auschwitz, Speer never asked why.

> I did not query him, I did not query Himmler, I did not query Hitler, I did not speak with personal friends. I did not investigate—for I did not want to know what was happening there . . . from fear of discovering

something which might have made me turn away from my course, I closed my eyes.[60]

Many people involved with OPM also closed their eyes. But the line between the avoidance of knowledge and ignorance is often indistinguishable. Or perhaps they convinced themselves that Myron Goodman's and Mordecai Weissman's conduct was acceptable. They did so because they had too much to lose by withdrawing or by blowing the whistle. Several people would have lost their jobs or a valuable client. They would have lost a friend, one who had done favors for them. They were able to convince themselves that everything would be all right. Besides, with so many others involved with OPM, it was easy to say to themselves: "It is not my responsibility."

The Aftermath of Clifton's Resignation

Lehman Brothers Kuhn Loeb

Despite gloomy reports throughout the late winter and early spring, Alan Batkin never doubted OPM's ability to survive. He believed the problem regarding incomplete lease files was being "chipped away," and he also believed OPM's balance sheet would remain in the black. When a Rockwell International representative called him in early March 1980, asking about OPM's financial condition, Batkin told him the company's 1979 financials were incomplete but he was confident "they will continue to reflect a positive net worth."[1]

But on April 14, Batkin received bad news. At lunch with Martin Zelbow, he was told OPM's 1979 financial statements "might be of some concern." Zelbow believed Batkin understood the seriousness of the situation. His contemporaneous memo to Louis Moscarello stated that Batkin fully understood OPM's condition and what the 1979 financials might show. Lehman was even taking steps to turn OPM around, Zelbow wrote. Batkin was preparing a list of conditions that OPM would have to meet in exchange for the investment banker's continued involvement. Contrary to what Zelbow wrote, Batkin claimed he never mentioned a set of conditions at this time and that he and Zelbow both agreed it was too early to know what the financials would reveal.

If Batkin chose to put aside the flood of warnings Coopers & Lybrand was putting before him, it was difficult for him to ignore the resignation of John Clifton, particularly since he already knew about the departures of Alan Phillips, Hoby Shapiro, and Marvin Weissman. In mid-June, Batkin was concerned enough to call Clifton to ask him why he had resigned. (Before calling Clifton, Batkin asked for and received Myron Goodman's permission.) Clifton gave Batkin a story about wanting to get back to public accounting and to work for a small accounting firm. Hinting at the real reasons for his resignation, however, he said he was worried about the amount of money Goodman gave to charities in light of the company's limited cash. He also provided some grim facts about OPM's future. He expected OPM to show a substantial loss for 1979, he told Batkin, at least $3 million. Seeking some kind of reassurance from Clifton, Batkin asked him if he thought OPM would continue to be a viable, successful company. Clifton told him he thought it would.

Some time after his conversation with Clifton, Batkin told Goodman he should consult with Singer Hutner Levine & Seeman about the propriety of obtaining loans from OPM during a period in which the company probably had a negative net worth. Batkin never checked with Goodman to see if he had followed his advice.

Although he insists he spoke with David Sacks about OPM's probable negative net worth, Batkin's weekly memo reporting on OPM to Lehman's senior managers never mentioned Clifton's prognosis; nothing was said about a projected $3 million loss—or any loss, for that matter. Nor did he notify Coopers of Clifton's forecast. Batkin didn't communicate this information to the First National Bank of St. Paul, either. Batkin did, however, tell Jeffrey Werner that Clifton had resigned, but added that Clifton was not a "critical man" since Coopers was involved with OPM. Coopers, on the other hand, was quite concerned that there was no one remaining at OPM familiar with the company's accounting systems or acquainted with lease accounting theory. Thus, Zelbow wrote, "No one within the company can be relied upon to implement revised procedures"[2] proposed by Coopers. Further, Coopers was concerned about the morale of the accounting department since the Clifton resignation.

Coopers & Lybrand

Until Clifton resigned, Zelbow hadn't worried about illegalities at OPM. Certainly, he thought the company might be insolvent and he didn't trust Goodman, but he hadn't seriously considered the possibility of criminal activity. In late May or early June, however, a number of events stimulated Zelbow's concern: adverse business conditions, a reduction in the number of new leases, tight cash flow, and the recent resignations of Hoby Shapiro, Marvin Weissman, and John Clifton. He couldn't pinpoint anything specific, he said, "just a series of things." Zelbow began to wonder whether Goodman, desperately wanting to keep his company afloat, may have been involved in some irregular activities. "I just could not understand how he was generating sufficient cash to keep his business going," Zelbow testified.[3]

Following Clifton's resignation, Zelbow asked Clifton why he had resigned. Clifton said he was tired and wanted to look for something else. Zelbow asked whether his resignation had anything to do with Rockwell. Clifton responded, "In part." He didn't elaborate, and Zelbow didn't pursue it because Clifton's response was so "close to the vest" that Zelbow thought it would be "fruitless."

In mid-June, Zelbow brought his concerns to the attention of his superiors—Louis Moscarello and Robert Lage. He was worried about possible illegalities at OPM, he said at a meeting in Moscarello's office, and he thought Coopers should withdraw from the engagement. Zelbow recalled saying, "We are in a situation where we have a client who is in a desperate situation. I cannot prove that the man is committing fraud, but we are in a situation where we have a very unusually high risk that our client is committing fraud."[4]

Moscarello reprimanded Zelbow for questioning Goodman's integrity. He said his allegations were simply opinions, all of which—to Moscarello—were unsupported by fact. "It was an opinion rather than a fact," Moscarello testified, "and that particular opinion was that there was a suspicion which ran to the integrity of Mr. Goodman because Mr. Goodman's company was believed to be in financial difficulties."[5] Asked about Clifton's resignation, Moscarello responded, "The man resigned. What about it?"

Moscarello didn't see any reason to withdraw from the engagement. "I see no reason why I should withdraw from an engagement unless somebody can show or give me facts that run to the integrity of management. Suspicions alone, uncorroborated, are not sufficient."[6]

In substance, Zelbow was told to go back to work, to concentrate on the systems design effort, and to keep his nose out of the company's finances. Quite simply, Moscarello told him he was being unduly concerned.

Singer Hutner Levine & Seeman

Since Goodman's confession to him in mid-April of 1980, Marvin Weissman had been after Goodman to tell Joseph Hutner about his crimes. He had been unsuccessful for nearly two months. Early Wednesday evening on June 11, Marvin Weissman called Goodman and demanded he come to his house, to call Hutner, and to confess. Marvin Weissman was tired of Goodman's stalling and told him:

> "You're going to come and we're going to have a meeting in my house this evening because if you don't come, I'm going to call Joe myself right now."
>
> "I don't come to people's houses," Goodman replied.
>
> Never one to back down from Goodman, Weissman responded, "But this time you're coming."[7]

A short time later, Goodman arrived at Marvin Weissman's home in Woodmere, New York. Goodman was quite upset about the prospects of calling Hutner. He was pleading with Marvin Weissman, arguing that Marvin was "putting him out of business" by forcing him to tell Hutner.[8] All of this fell on deaf ears, and Weissman insisted Goodman call Hutner. Finally, Goodman relented.

Early that evening, Hutner received a telephone call at his home in White Plains, New York, from Marvin Weissman, who was with Goodman. Marvin Weissman told him that Goodman wanted to speak to him about something important, but Goodman wanted to be sure that what he was going to say remain a privileged communication between Hutner and him. Marvin Weissman then handed the phone to Goodman and left the room so his presence would not jeopardize the privileged status of the conversation. Hutner remembered Goodman was sobbing, having a lot of trouble controlling his emotions. Goodman asked if Hutner had time to meet with him the following day to discuss a matter of importance. Hutner said he'd make time. But Hutner was concerned about Goodman's state of mind at the time and asked Goodman if he wanted to talk about it—whatever it was—over the phone. Goodman said he'd prefer to meet the next day, and he'd like to have Marvin Weissman and Andrew Reinhard present.

Later that evening, after Goodman had left his home, Marvin Weissman heard from Hutner again. Hutner called to find out what Goodman's conversation was about. Weissman testified that he told Hutner everything he knew about the frauds. Hutner doesn't recall the second conversation with Weissman.

The following morning, Hutner found Reinhard at the Singer Hutner offices and told him about the previous evening's conversation with Goodman and about the proposed meeting later that day. Hutner recalled that Reinhard acted as if it was all news to him. Goodman had requested Reinhard's presence, Hutner told him, and Reinhard said he would make himself available.

Some time later, Goodman arrived for his meeting with Hutner and Reinhard. Goodman wanted to discuss a serious matter, he said, but he first needed a clearer understanding of the attorney-client privilege, and he asked a series of hypothetical questions, such as, "If I told you something, who else would you have to tell?" "It would depend upon what you told me," Hutner responded. Goodman asked, "Why don't you ask me some questions and maybe I can give you enough information for you to give me an answer." The cat-and-mouse game continued.

"Well, does this something you are going to tell me about relate to OPM?" Hutner asked.

"Yes it does," Myron said.[9]

More questions led Hutner to believe the problem involved wrongdoing, although Goodman never said so explicitly. Hutner asked, "Is it criminal?" "I'm not sure," Goodman responded, but whether it was or wasn't, Goodman said he did what he did for OPM *and* for Singer Hutner.

Goodman was agitated, much more so than he had been the night before, Hutner remembered. It was clear that he wanted to tell Hutner, that he wanted to get the load off his chest, but he would not communicate anything until he was certain Hutner wouldn't tell anyone else.

> "Does it involve financial matters?" Hutner continued.
> "Yes."
> "Is it substantial?" to which he didn't get a direct response, so he asked, "Well, if it is substantial, is it something that can be rectified?"
> "Yes, it could," Goodman said.
> "If this could be cured with money and is a financial matter only, why don't you sell the bank stock?" an asset Hutner believed was worth about $10 million to OPM.
> "It wouldn't be enough," Goodman responded.[10]

Goodman was worried about Hutner telling Mordecai Weissman and possibly others. He asked Hutner question after question. Hutner had a difficult time answering, claiming that Goodman was making him "deal with hypothetical upon hypothetical," but nonetheless the attorney gave him a quick lesson on the attorney-client privilege and on legal ethics. Hutner said he hadn't focused on the privilege rules for some time, but he believed Goodman or the law firm would have to tell Weissman since Weissman was a director of the company. "That gives me a lot of trouble," Goodman told him, appearing upset about the prospect of Weissman's being told. Goodman was just staring at the floor, and Hutner began asking him more questions.

> "Does it involve double-hocking?"
> "No."
> "Is the activity, whatever it was, completed?"
> "Absolutely," Goodman said.[11]

Goodman wanted to know whether Singer Hutner would have to resign. Hutner responded, "I can't answer that before I know the facts, but I can't think of any reason off the top of my head why we would have to if this thing was completed." On the other hand, if the crimes were ongoing, Hutner went on, a lawyer has "got to try to convince the client not to commit the fraud and if he's unsuccessful, he has certain options, and my recollection is that these options are to resign, and if he chooses to, even to warn the party about to be defrauded."

Goodman replied, "Well, I'm very troubled about this Mordy thing. Are you sure about it?" Hutner told him he was pretty sure. "Well, I really got to think on this," Goodman stated, now that the lesson on legal ethics and the attorney-client privilege was over. Hutner asked, "Does that mean you are not going to tell me now?" "Yes," Goodman replied.

Goodman further revealed that John Clifton was resigning at the end of the week and that Clifton was writing a letter to the firm, specifically to Andrew Reinhard, "which made some reference to the facts, and that the facts as set forth in the letter . . . were fragmentary and misleading," Hutner recalled Goodman saying.

At one point during the meeting, Hutner testified, "A time came when Goodman, who had left the room, my room, either to go to the bathroom or for some other purpose,[12] returned standing at the threshold to my room and identified a document . . . in his hand as the Clifton letter." Hutner couldn't recall whether Goodman said he took it off the corner of Reinhard's desk or whether he took it out of Reinhard's hands.[13] Hutner claimed he asked Goodman for the letter and Goodman refused to give it to him since he hadn't yet decided whether to tell Hutner the underlying facts. Before they parted, Hutner told Goodman he should reconsider telling his attorneys so that they could assist in resolving the matter.

The next morning, Friday, June 13, OPM closed a bridge loan with the First National Bank of St. Paul for nearly $2 million, and a permanent loan from Lincoln Leaseway for nearly $6 million. Singer Hutner represented OPM at the closing. Both loans were fraudulent.[14]

Myron Goodman had placed Joseph Hutner in a difficult position. Since Andrew Reinhard brought the company to the law firm in 1971, OPM had become the firm's largest client by far. From 1976 through 1980, OPM had paid Singer Hutner almost $10 million in legal fees and expenses, accounting for 60 to 70 percent of the law firm's total billings. Since the relationship began, the firm had more than doubled in size. In 1971, the firm employed twelve attorneys; by 1981, it employed twenty-seven, many of whom were graduates of the best law schools in the Northeast. Moreover, the firm opened branch offices in New Orleans and in Los Angeles at the insistence of Myron Goodman. As OPM grew, so did Singer Hutner, and no one knew that better than Hutner.

Joseph L. Hutner, then forty-seven years old, was a tough, aggressive lawyer—and smart. Some thought him obnoxious and arrogant, but he could just as easily turn on the charm. He had once turned his skills to the political arena, but when he lost an election for the congressional seat for New York's 26th District to Ogden Reid in 1966 by an almost three-to-one margin despite the support of Robert F. Kennedy, Hutner abandoned his political aspirations. Since that time, Hutner, a Harvard Law School graduate, concentrated on building a successful—and lucrative—law practice, one that provided its partners with equal shares of the firm's profits in the amount of $130,000 for 1980 alone. For the most part, the firm's success was due to OPM. And Hutner knew it. The prospect of losing his most important client was unsettling, to say the least.

OPM had presented its share of problems over the years, however, and the Singer Hutner lawyers "knew" or had "substantial reason to suspect," according to Trustee James P. Hassett, that Goodman and Weissman had been committing crimes, including lease fraud, commercial bribery, and altering financial statements. Several witnesses testified that they had had conversations with Singer Hutner lawyers concerning OPM's early crimes. Mordecai Weissman, for instance, claimed that Henry Singer, another Singer Hutner partner, was a party to the decision to terminate the hostile takeover of Century Factors in mid-1977, and that the primary reason for ending the takeover bid was a fear that ensuing litigation would lead to a discovery of the early frauds.[15] Singer, according to Weissman, was told about the crimes and was privy to the discussions that led to the decision to withdraw the tender offer. Other Singer Hutner attorneys also learned about the frauds. Marvin Weissman, for instance, testified about conversations he had had with Hutner in 1979 about the early frauds.

Singer Hutner lawyers Jay W. Seeman and Eli Mattioli, on two separate occasions, each had good reason to believe Goodman and Weissman had engaged in lease fraud. In 1972, OPM fraudulently leased a minicomputer to Blau Sportsmates Corporation.[16] By 1974, Blau was delinquent in its payments on the lease and, apparently forgetting about the fraudulent financing, Goodman ordered Singer Hutner to file a lawsuit against it. While in the middle of a deposition connected to the suit, Goodman or Weissman suddenly recalled that the lease was fraudulent. Halting the proceedings, Myron claimed Seeman had been informed about the altered lease. Seeman asked Goodman whether OPM had similar leases on the books, and Goodman said there were several double-discounted leases that they were in the process of buying out. OPM subsequently settled the Blau case at a great loss. Seeman denied ever being told by Weissman or Goodman about OPM's double-discounted leases.

In 1977, Vincennes Manor, a nursing home, wanted to lease an elevator from OPM, but the leasing company's financing sources balked at financing an elevator. A computer, yes; an elevator, no. Unwilling to lose the lease, Weissman decided to prepare a lease for Vincennes Manor but to substitute a minicomputer for the elevator. In that way, he could provide the elevator for Vincennes Manor with the financing obtained with the fictitious minicomputer lease, and nobody would be the wiser. To make matters worse, Goodman and Weissman then double-financed the minicomputer lease. In the fall of 1977, the forgetful Goodman directed Singer Hutner to bring a suit against the nursing home for its failure to keep up with its payments.

Eli Mattioli, who handled the case for OPM, not surprisingly uncovered some serious problems with the lease. Mattioli wrote OPM and said he could find no record of the title documents for the Vincennes Manor minicomputer. "What equipment can we prove was purchased by OPM for use by Vincennes," Mattioli asked, "a computer system and elevator system, or two elevator systems, or possibly one elevator system?" Later, Goodman told Mattioli to end the legal action against Vincennes Manor.[17]

Several Singer Hutner attorneys also knew about payoffs to employees in various corporations. Several others knew that Goodman had furnished Kent Klineman with false financial statements in 1978. And, of course, most of the attorneys were aware of OPM's check-kiting conviction in March 1980. Many of the Singer Hutner lawyers realized

Goodman and Weissman were far from angels, but none knew it more than Reinhard.

The Reinhard Question

Andrew B. Reinhard had been Myron Goodman's friend for a long time.[18] Goodman was four years younger than Reinhard and was good friends with Michael Reinhard, Andy's younger brother. Goodman claimed he "almost lived in" the Reinhard household while growing up in the Flatbush section of Brooklyn. He had idolized the older Reinhard and looked forward to the times when Andy Reinhard and his twin brother, David, would take the younger Reinhard and Goodman to basketball games at Madison Square Garden.

When Reinhard began attending Columbia University in 1960, Goodman saw less of him and less still when he went on to Harvard Law School, where he graduated with honors in 1967. Two years later, Reinhard joined the Singer Hutner law firm, and within five years he was made partner.

On the evening of June 3, 1969, Myron Goodman's wedding night, he and his wife Lydia were issued a summons for making too much noise moving furniture in their apartment on Ocean Parkway in Brooklyn. Needing an attorney, Goodman called Reinhard, who took the case as a favor to his friend from the old neighborhood. The charges were eventually dismissed. Now Goodman owed Reinhard a favor. It was a favor Reinhard probably *now* wishes he had never done.

Several weeks after joining OPM in January 1971, Goodman again called Reinhard to see whether he'd be interested in preparing lease documents and providing other legal services to OPM. Singer Hutner became OPM's outside general counsel shortly afterward and continued in that capacity until late 1980. For the first three to four years, there was only a limited amount of work for the law firm to do, but when OPM began leasing mainframes in 1975, the leasing company gradually became Singer Hutner's most important client; it was well on its way to becoming a "captured" law firm.

The Singer Hutner-OPM relationship was an intimate one; indeed, the boundary line dividing the two organizations at times was so thin it appeared imperceptible. Reinhard was made a director of the company in 1972 because Goodman and Weissman believed having a lawyer on the board would be influential with outsiders. Other Singer Hutner attorneys were officers of OPM subsidiaries. Hutner was a director of the First National Bank of Jefferson Parish. Goodman advised Singer Hutner on the law firm's organization and staffing; the law firm even opened branch offices in New Orleans and in Los Angeles at Goodman's request. Goodman's influence on the law firm was enhanced by the friendships he struck with Singer Hutner partners, including, of course, Andrew Reinhard, Alan Jacobs, Henry Singer, Jr., Joseph Hutner, and Carl J. Rubino. In 1976, Goodman, Reinhard, Singer, and their wives traveled together to Europe. In late October 1978, Hutner rented the Stadium Club at Yankee Stadium for Goodman, an avid Yankee fan, to celebrate Goodman's thirty-second birthday. A year later, Hutner, stroking the enormous egos of Goodman and Weissman, wrote to *Who's Who* nominating the two entrepreneurs for inclusion in the next volume. Goodman and Weissman "experienced a meteoric rise in American business circles," Hutner wrote, and claimed their climb in the computer leasing business "has been extraordinary."[19]

Gifts exceeding $100 from Goodman to Singer Hutner attorneys were not uncommon. Reinhard did quite well. Goodman sent him on a trip to Israel, and gave him tickets to Florida, a car, and $5,000 to invest in his wife's business. Goodman also gave a car to David Reinhard, Reinhard's twin.

Some time around mid-1974, Goodman decided to clean up OPM's books and buy out the early fraudulent loans. He turned to Reinhard to help "discipline" him, he said, to "help me to watch over, to make sure the deals were bought out, to make sure the cash . . . coming into the company was not diverted."[20] Reinhard was furious when Goodman first told him about the bad loans. "How the f . . k can you do something like this?" Reinhard questioned. Goodman played the "little boy," emphasizing he "wouldn't do it again" and that he had been wrong. The kind and generous Reinhard agreed to help Goodman, at least according to Myron.[21]

From that point on, Goodman said he had "many, many, many conversations" with Reinhard about the early frauds. He reviewed a schedule of the fraudulent loans with Reinhard and reported on his meetings with Marvin Weissman, who was also enlisted to bring Goodman under control. But Reinhard never met with Weissman about them, at that time. And although Goodman testified he promised Reinhard he would never commit fraud again, he said he confessed to more swindles in 1976 or 1977.

Goodman claimed Reinhard also knew about payoffs made to vendor salesmen. But his most serious charge against Reinhard was that the attorney knew about and facilitated the Rockwell fraud during 1979 and 1980. On a flight from the West Coast on February 1, 1979, Goodman testified that he told Reinhard about his plan to commit the Rockwell frauds.[22] "You can't do it," Reinhard argued. "[If] we don't do it, I'll have to close the doors," Goodman responded. Goodman went on to say that OPM's cash shortage was only temporary and that he'd be able to buy out the fraudulent deals within weeks. "You have got to go along with me," Goodman pleaded, "you have got to do me a personal favor."[23] Once again—according to Goodman—Reinhard couldn't say no.

For the next year and a half, according to Goodman, Reinhard learned more and more about the frauds at OPM. Goodman testified that on occasion Reinhard reviewed fraudulent documents to determine whether they appeared authentic, and that he approved the change in Singer Hutner's procedures that led the company to forward Rockwell documents to OPM instead of sending them directly to Rockwell, which made it easy to switch the materials. Other witnesses testified about conversations they had had with Reinhard regarding the crimes, but the ever-careful attorney avoided terms like "crime" or "fraud." Unsure about exactly how much Reinhard knew and unwilling to reveal the extent of their own knowledge, Reinhard's interlocutors also spoke ambiguously. Stephen Lichtman had several discussions with Reinhard and complained that Goodman was doing "a lot of crazy things, making bad decisions" and so forth. Reinhard never inquired about the details.

In April 1980, Lichtman was so upset about the frauds that he refused to work for about a week. To bring Lichtman back into the fold, Allen Ganz arranged a telephone call between Reinhard and Lichtman from OPM's offices, and Ganz listened to the conversations. Avoiding the word "fraud," Lichtman told Reinhard he no longer wanted to work on the Rockwell account because of the "problem" or the "bad" deals. Reinhard told him to calm down and said he would speak to Goodman. Reinhard never asked Lichtman why he was so upset about these leases.

The same month, Reinhard reluctantly met with Marvin Weissman to discuss the "hypothetical" Rashba & Pokart client who was engaged in fraud. Through his attorneys, Reinhard admitted he knew that Weissman was talking about Goodman and OPM.

Whatever Reinhard knew, it was never revealed to the other Singer Hutner attorneys—at least, according to them.

Hutner's Version of His Meeting with Davis

On the morning of Friday, June 13, 1980, Goodman called Hutner and told him he had met with John Clifton and had informed him of the purloined letter. Clifton had since spoken to his attorney William Davis, Goodman said, and Davis tentatively concluded that since the letter was intercepted, Clifton might now have to go to the authorities with information concerning the fraud—otherwise, he might be guilty of a felony under the misprision statute. Hutner wasn't absolutely certain but, based on his meager understanding of the criminal law, he didn't think that Davis's conclusion was right. Hutner and Goodman decided it would be a good idea for Hutner to speak with Davis. Hutner claimed he didn't want Davis to be advising Clifton to take certain action based on Davis's misunderstanding of the law. Hutner's notes of his conversation with Goodman read: "Stop Davis."[24]

Hutner's version of his meeting with Davis is different from the one offered by Davis in at least two respects. First, Hutner claimed—and Mattioli's testimony supported him—that he never proposed that Clifton take back the letter. Second, Hutner claimed it was Davis, not he, who seemed reluctant to reveal the letter or its contents. Although they knew of no legal or ethical prescriptions preventing them from asking, however, Mattioli and Hutner acknowledged that they never asked for a copy of the letter nor asked about its substance. Hutner testified that it was clear to me from the very circumspect, guarded way in which he [Davis] was dancing around the letter that it would have been pointless [to ask]. You know, after all, I was sitting there. He didn't offer me a copy.... It would have been the most natural thing in the world. Here's a lawyer who recommends to his client send a letter to the offices of Andy Reinhard. He learns the letter is intercepted. Lo and behold, the attorney arrives at his doorstep. He didn't offer me a copy.[25]

Hutner remembered Davis saying, however, that the Clifton letter contained information disclosing what OPM had done. "I don't remember the word he used," Hutner testified, "but it was something like 'wrongdoing' in substantial amounts, and he used the term 'it dwarfs or would dwarf New Orleans,'" a reference to OPM's check-kiting conviction, which Hutner knew amounted to about $4 million. Davis also said the information contained in the Clifton letter was supplied by one or more OPM employees. He also revealed that Singer Hutner had been provided false documents rendering some of its opinion letters inaccurate. The letter also expressed Clifton's view that the wrongdoing would have to continue for OPM to survive, Davis told him.

From June 16 on, no Singer Hutner attorney tried to obtain the Clifton letter from any source other than from Goodman. No attorney ever spoke to Davis again, nor to Clifton. Nor did they try to discover the information on which his letter was based. They didn't try to interview the two OPM employees who provided Clifton with the information in his letter. They didn't even try to learn their identities.

The Lawyer's Lawyers

On Tuesday morning, June 17, Mattioli, Rubino, and Reinhard met in Reinhard's office, and Mattioli briefed his colleagues on the most recent events. Hutner was in New Orleans attending to business involving the First National Bank of Jefferson Parish. Rubino, the most experienced of the three, said the problem raised hard ethical questions and recommended that the firm engage its own legal counsel to advise them. Rubino also suggested that they consult with Joseph S. McLaughlin, dean of the Fordham Law School and now a federal district court judge in the Eastern District of New York.[26] After receiving Hutner's consent to approach McLaughlin, Mattioli called the dean and told him he had an evidence problem that his firm needed advice on and asked if they could meet with him as soon as possible. The dean said he could make some time around 4:30 P.M. Thursday if they would like to come by his office then.

In the late afternoon on June 19, Hutner, Mattioli, and Rubino walked into Dean McLaughlin's law school office in upper Manhattan. The dean remembered all three appeared "distressed" and "over-wrought." After the usual amenities, Hutner led the discussion, providing the dean with a brief history of the client—not yet mentioning OPM by name—the nature of its business, the bank acquisition, and the subsequent check-kiting conviction. He told the dean about the events since June 11—Goodman's phone call and, as the dean later called it, "the bizarre incident" where the principal of the client seized a letter to Reinhard. Hutner also told McLaughlin he was fairly certain that the crimes were over.

Hutner remembers telling McLaughlin about an earlier incident involving the client in which the principal admitted to several partners in the law firm that he had double-financed loans. Hutner told McLaughlin:

> There was a time when Henry Singer and I were in a cab . . . sometime before that there was a meeting with representatives of Fox attended by Reinhard, Singer, Goodman and that the subject was the double-pledging of a single minicomputer lease in the neighborhood of, I don't remember the figure, $300,000 or $400,000, and that had been picked up by the auditors, the accountants, rather. . . . And that amount had been repaid, and that Fox, notwithstanding this revelation, agreed to issue its certificate, and that Myron had agreed at the insistence of one or more Fox partners that he would never do it again, and that Goodman had extracted from Singer and Reinhard a promise not to reveal these facts to anybody, including other partners at Singer Hutner.[27]

Hutner was impressed by the dean and asked him if he were interested in taking on the case. McLaughlin told him he was, but he thought it would be appropriate to engage cocounsel to assist him on the problem because he was jockeying for a Court of Appeals appointment; should he be selected, he wouldn't be able to continue the Singer Hutner engagement. He also said the Singer Hutner problem raised legal ethics questions that demanded the support of an expert on such matters. The dean suggested Henry Peter Putzel III, a graduate of Yale Law School, former assistant U.S. attorney in the Southern District of New York, and now in private practice. Putzel also taught a course on professional responsibility at Fordham. The dean said he would contact Putzel if they agreed with his choice.

Hutner and the others did not have a problem with a co-counsel, but since Hutner was so impressed with the dean, he wanted the dean's assurance that it would be his advice and judgment that the firm would be relying on. Hutner later testified, "I told him we were going to count on him being fully involved and he was going to be the man we were going to be looking to." Hutner further stated, "We had the impression that Peter Putzel was going to take the laboring oar," but, he continued, "it was our clear understanding explicitly that on all important decisions, meaning all important substantive advice given to us by Putzel, that he would consult with Dean McLaughlin." Asked whether he thought the dean understood that, Hutner replied, "Absolutely . . . that was expressly set forth as a condition of his employment. We wanted his mind as well as his name."[28]

McLaughlin had a different view of the conditions for his engagement. He recalled telling the Singer Hutner attorneys that he wouldn't become involved unless Putzel did most of the work. After all, he had a school to run, and he didn't have time to get involved in the day-to-day activities of that particular case. He first wanted to turn the whole thing over to Putzel, but Hutner objected, so McLaughlin agreed to "look over" Putzel's work. He said his role was "avuncular." He also testified that the principal reason Putzel was brought in was because of his expertise on legal ethics, an area in which McLaughlin didn't feel competent. He claimed it was clear that Putzel would handle matters on ethics—the dean would serve as a "sounding board"—and he would provide advice only on attorney-client privilege questions.[29] But in an affadavit filed by the dean on March 23, 1981—eleven months after he was engaged by the Singer Hutner law firm—the dean contradicted the testimony he gave in the bankruptcy proceeding. In the affadavit, the dean specifically stated he was retained to advise on ethical matters —he did not distinguish legal ethics from attorney-client privilege questions. The affadavit reads, "On June 19, 1980, I was retained by the law firm [Singer Hutner] to counsel it as to its ethical obligations with respect to its representations of OPM Leasing Services, Inc." In paragraph three of the affadavit, the dean further stated, "The full extent of my representation and the advice rendered in connection therewith are confidential. I am authorized to state, however, that my engagement related to the ethical responsibilities of the firm concerning the clients identified above, with particular respect to the continued representation of such clients by the firm." The affadavit continued, "Mr. Putzel and I have counseled the law firm with respect to such matters on virtually a daily basis from June 1980 to the present." The judge later testified that this last statement was misleading and that it was Putzel, not he, who consulted with the client on a daily basis.

At the close of the meeting on Thursday, Joseph Hutner provided the dean with a retainer of $5,000 and agreed to pay him $400 an hour for his services. There was no engagement letter that described his responsibilities. Hutner and the dean merely shook hands.

8

The Summer of Nondisclosure

FOLLOWING his meeting with the Singer Hutner Levine & Seeman attorneys, Dean Joseph S. McLaughlin called Henry Peter Putzel and told him about the case. Putzel agreed to meet McLaughlin and the Singer Hutner attorneys the following day.

Around 2:00 P.M. on Friday, June 20, Joseph Hutner, Carl J. Rubino, and Eli Mattioli met with McLaughlin and Putzel in Hutner's office. At the outset, Hutner, who led the discussion in this meeting and in those that followed, made it clear that McLaughlin and Putzel were being retained to furnish advice on the ethical obligations of the Singer Hutner attorneys. The client represented 60 to 65 percent of Singer Hutner's business, he began, and the law firm was heavily dependent on them for its success. "If it was ethically permissible," Putzel recalled Hutner saying, "they would like to continue representing the client."[1] But, according to McLaughlin, Hutner made it equally clear that the firm was prepared to walk away if legally required to do so. Putzel and McLaughlin, however, weren't told that walking away would not be so easy. At the end of May, just three weeks before the June 20 meeting, OPM owed the Singer Hutner law firm $700,000.

Hutner went on to describe the company's history and the backgrounds of the principals in much greater detail than McLaughlin or Putzel had heard before. He continued to use pseudonyms, and so Goodman was referred to as "Sam," Weissman as "Harry," and OPM was called the "XYZ" company. The XYZ Company was a privately held firm, owned entirely by Sam and Harry, Hutner told Putzel and McLaughlin. Andrew Reinhard, a partner at Singer Hutner and a boyhood friend of Sam's, served as the third director of the company. Sam was only thirty-three years old but in very fragile health, they were told. He went on to describe Sam's extravagant living—his fifty pairs of shoes, his taste for fine, expensive wines, the purchase of the former Wardwell estate—which amused Putzel because he had once worked at Davis, Polk, and Wardwell—and about Sam's predilection for helicopters. Hutner also made known the purchase of the bank stock and that Hutner sat on the bank's board.

Hutner told them about the check-kiting conviction and how Carl Rubino was able to get the indictment switched from Sam to the company. Based on this experience, Hutner believed Sam had a morbid fear of criminal prosecution; Sam believed Rubino had saved his life.

Hutner repeated his story about the past double-hocking, and there was some discussion about whether the present problem was double-hocking. Mattioli then revealed an oddity that has yet to be explained.[2] In April 1980, Mattioli told the group, Andrew Reinhard and Alan Jacobs received anonymous postcards that stated the following:

MEMORANDUM

TO: ALAN S. JACOBS & ANDREW REINHARD
GENTLEMEN:
          YOUR CUNNING MACHINATIONS AND SUBTERFUGES ARE DESPIC-
     ABLE, A DISGRACE TO THE FIRM PER SE, AND TO THE LEGAL PROFES-
     SION AT LARGE.
          YOUR CUNNING IS NOT FOOLING ANYONE.
CC: LEVINE, HUTNER, SINGER, SEEMAN

No one offered any speculation about the meaning of the anonymous postcards or about who might have sent them.

Hutner then recounted the recent events, beginning with the resignation some five weeks earlier of an outside accountant (Marvin Weissman), who had worked on XYZ's books for a number of years. The accountant had apparently resigned because of the huge cash flow problems facing the company.[3] According to Sam, the accountant knew very little about the underlying facts. Putzel remembered being told about the accountant's call to Hutner a week earlier and about Sam's partial confession to Hutner. Putzel was also told that Reinhard and Harry didn't know the underlying facts, according to Sam.

The Clifton resignation—John Clifton was referred to as "Paul" —and the "snatched letter" were described by Hutner, and Mattioli briefly reported on the misprision research and some of the discussion he had had with "Paul's attorney." Putzel didn't recall any conversation about asking Paul to withdraw the letter. Hutner recounted his talks with Paul's attorney, whom he said he didn't trust and found "sleazy." Nevertheless, the attorney told them the firm had been given fraudulent documents, including false financial statements, and Hutner himself believed that the firm was also provided phony bills of sale. Hutner further speculated the fraud may have commenced around March 1979, which, in fact, it did, but he offered no elaboration in his testimony. Hutner also guessed the amount of fraud was around $10 million because Sam told him the problem couldn't be rectified by the sale of the bank stock, which Hutner knew was worth around $9.5 million.

Toward the end of the meeting, Putzel and McLaughlin told the Singer Hutner lawyers they would like more information before they offered a formal opinion. They suggested that one of the Singer Hutner attorneys prepare a memorandum outlining the facts and specifying the issues on which the firm was seeking advice. Mattioli said he would draft the memorandum over the weekend.

But Putzel and McLaughlin tentatively advised that it wasn't necessary for the law firm to resign and, indeed, they implied that it would be unethical to do so[4] since Sam had told Hutner the fraud had ended. "Everyone at the meeting believed Goodman's representation to them that the fraud, whatever it was, had taken place in the past,"

Putzel later testified, "and this was why he was in a confessional mood about it. He wanted to get something off his chest about something he had done. It was clear, at least to me, and I believe to Dean McLaughlin, that this was perceived as a past act." Putzel went on to say, "Certainly, however, the possibility of future recurrence was something that had to be considered."[5] No one recalled discussing whether the firm could really know if the fraud had ended until Goodman disclosed the underlying facts. No one remembered a discussion about the steps the law firm would take to prevent future frauds. And no one recalled discussion about whether the firm should cease closing OPM transactions until disclosure was made by Goodman.

To continue representing OPM, the group of Singer Hutner attorneys had to believe the fraud was over. If they believed otherwise, legal and moral precepts required additional measures be taken, which included termination. They had strong reasons for wanting and for wishing that the fraud had ended; after all, OPM owed them a substantial amount of money, and the leasing company was, by far, their largest client; indeed, they were dependent on OPM's continued business. Singer Hutner had little choice; without OPM, there would be no law firm.

Putzel and McLaughlin may have believed the crimes were over, but Hutner and others had every reason to believe the frauds might continue. At least since the check-kiting investigation, the lawyers had known about OPM's cash flow difficulties. Indeed, Reinhard had been attending the Coopers & Lybrand progress meetings throughout the late winter and spring. Moreover, Clifton—through William Davis—suggested OPM couldn't survive without continuing the frauds. These facts, combined with OPM's past record—much of which was not told to McLaughlin and Putzel—should have made the lawyers more skeptical and circumspect than they were.

Some time that day, OPM closed a bridge loan with the First National Bank of St. Paul for nearly $2.4 million. Singer Hutner represented OPM at the closing. The deal was fraudulent.[6]

Over the next few months, this group of attorneys interpreted the American Bar Association's (ABA) code of professional responsibility in a way that allowed their continued representation of OPM. They were not technically wrong. But there were other courses of action open to them. For instance, they could have immediately resigned from the OPM engagement. Second, they could have refused to close OPM transactions unless Goodman turned over the Clifton letter or made full disclosure. Third, they could have implemented a system of third-party verification of OPM transactions. Fourth, they could have turned to other OPM officers to help prevent further fraud. Fifth, they should have informed Weissman since he was a director of the company. Whether or not this would have brought the matter to a head is open to question; nonetheless, informing members of the board about corporate wrongdoing is one area where the ABA's Code of Professional Responsibility is clear. Sixth, they could have sought independent verification of Davis's assertions, particularly those concerning OPM's financial condition. For example, they might have examined the leasing company's financial statements or tried to speak to Clifton. They never even explored OPM's finances with Marvin Weissman, with whom they had contact during the summer of 1980. Seventh, they could have gone back to Davis to elicit specific information or to obtain the Clifton letter. Eighth, they could have: (a) audited their own procedures to determine where they might have been the recipients of false documents, which rendered their opinions false (as Davis had told them) and (b) redesigned those procedures to prevent future frauds. For instance, one of the ways Goodman was able to carry out the frauds was by keeping separate the Rockwell International and lender versions of the financing documents. Singer Hutner facilitated this practice by forwarding Rockwell's documents to OPM—where the switch was made—instead of sending them to Rockwell as they previously had done. Had Singer Hutner carefully examined its own practices and uncovered situations where it might have been swindled, the firm could have taken steps to prevent fraud or, at least, make it more difficult for them to be duped.

Few of these options were raised in the group's deliberations, and those that were discussed (resignation, informing Weissman, and third-party verification) were not considered for very long. Moreover, they failed to ask penetrating questions of each other and of Goodman. Why didn't they canvass the full range of alternatives open to them? Why were they taken in by incomplete and inconsistent answers?

The group of lawyers shared an illusion of invulnerability, an illusion derived primarily from a belief and trust in Myron Goodman's

representations. Goodman had told Hutner the wrongdoing was over
—it was a past crime. Putzel insisted it was much more than that.
Goodman was devoted to the Singer Hutner law firm, particularly to
Hutner. He was terribly upset about what he had done; he was embarrassed and swore it wouldn't happen again. It was illogical for him to
commit more crimes, the lawyers believed. In part, he had already
confessed. Why would he commit more fraud? Better yet, *how* would
he commit more fraud once they were on to him? Which leads to
another factor that strengthened the group's illusions. The attorneys in
the group were all extremely bright and experienced. Goodman had
also retained Andrew Lawler, a lawyer everyone respected. The group
undoubtedly believed Goodman not only *wouldn't* commit more fraud,
but *couldn't* deceive such an experienced and prestigious group. Indeed, one lawyer said the only way the group could have anticipated
what actually happened was to realize just how crazy Myron Goodman
really was.

To arrive at their choice of action—or rather inaction—and stick
with it, the group ignored numerous signals indicating their decision
was in error. First, the lawyers should have been aware of the extent
of OPM's financial problems, which led to the crimes in the first place.
Over the course of the previous two years, they had received ample
warning. They knew about the check-kiting, potential problems stemming from early terminations, Marvin Weissman's concerns about the
enormous cash flow problems, and the ominous signals coming from
Coopers. But the group chose to ignore these signals—signals suggesting Goodman had to continue his crimes if OPM was to survive, as
Davis had told them. Instead, group members cited evidence of OPM's
"brisk and profitable" business. The company was considering the
purchase of a forklift company in New Jersey, and it was forming OPM
Data Services in California, Hutner remembered—hardly moves made
by a company in financial trouble. Moreover, Singer Hutner was closing
numerous deals; Jacobs had been working night and day. How could
the company be in serious financial difficulty?

The warnings provided by Davis were the most clear. Davis told
Hutner and Mattioli that (1) OPM could not survive without committing more crimes; (2) Goodman had submitted false documents to the
lawyers rendering certain opinion letters false; and (3) the wrongdoing
was in excess of $4 million. Instead of trying to determine the veracity

of Davis's claims, the lawyers chose to ignore them. Hutner discredited Davis, claiming he was "sleazy," "untrustworthy," and couldn't possibly know what he claimed he knew. When Putzel asked whether he should try to contact Davis, Hutner told him to "forget it"—that he wouldn't get anywhere with him.[7]

Signals that the frauds were continuing were explained away by the group, and Goodman's stalling was collectively rationalized as symptoms of his embarrassment. At no time during the summer of 1980 did the group seriously consider the possibility of ongoing fraud. Instead, they concentrated on a narrowly defined problem—a client's partial confession of a past crime—and virtually ignored any warning challenging that view. They failed to probe, to examine carefully the evidence before them, or to consider alternative scenarios.

Students of group dynamics will recognize the lawyers' behavior as characteristic of a phenomenon called "groupthink." Irving Janis, who developed the theory, describes groupthink as "a mode of thinking that people engage in when they are deeply involved in a cohesive ingroup, when members' strivings for unanimity override their motivation to realistically appraise courses of action."[8] "When a group of people who respect each other's opinions arrive at a unanimous view, each member is likely to feel the belief is true. This reliance on consensual validation," Janis says, "tends to replace individual critical thinking and reality-testing. . . . The group leader and the members support each other, playing up the areas of convergence in their thinking, at the expense of fully exploring divergences that might disrupt the apparent unity of the group."[9] No strong voice of opposition was ever raised during the group deliberations studied by Janis and, as usually happens in small, cohesive groups, members assumed "silence gives consent."[10]

During the five months of meetings held by the Singer Hutner attorneys, there were few disagreements about how to proceed. On the few occasions where other courses of action were discussed, the group immediately dismissed them as "cumbersome" and "harmful to the client." Other events also indicate the appearance of a concurrence-seeking tendency—striving for agreement and group cohesion—rather than a realistic appraisal of alternative courses of action.

Whenever unfavorable events emerged that countered the group's preconceived conceptions of reality, they shielded themselves from becoming aware; they ignored stark warnings; they failed to seek fuller information and to ask incisive questions that would have made clear their erroneous strategy.

On Monday afternoon, June 23, Putzel, Hutner, Mattioli, Rubino, Jacobs, and Reinhard met to discuss the procedures used by Singer Hutner in handling the OPM transactions. Since Jacobs and Reinhard were most familiar with the lease-financing documentation, they described the procedures and materials to Putzel and Mattioli, who also were inexperienced in these matters. The conversation also focused on several prophylactic measures that could be taken to prevent future fraud. Although he believed taking steps to prevent future fraud was a prudent thing to do, Putzel didn't believe the fraud was continuing. "The fact that Goodman had acknowledged some sort of wrongdoing, and that he was assuring the firm that this was all in the past," Putzel asserted, "was considered by me as some evidence that there was no reason why the man would have acknowledged wrongdoing and concealed the ongoing nature of it. It struck me as 'illogical.' "[11]

One attorney suggested contacting the lessees directly to verify the terms of each deal, but Jacobs rejected the idea as being cumbersome and showing mistrust of OPM. According to Mattioli, verification of that kind would have had a "detrimental effect on the client in the sense that possibly being interpreted by third parties as a sign of mistrust on the part of our law firm with respect to our client."[12]

Putzel offered an alternative that, he believed, satisfied the attorney's responsibilities to serve as an advocate for OPM while, at the same time, encouraging them to remain within the bounds of the law. He suggested the law firm obtain officers' certificates from Goodman verifying the terms of each deal. "The prophylactic purposes that would be served by the certificate," Hutner later claimed, "is it would be making Myron focus afresh each time he was presented with a certificate that not only was he called upon to tell the truth, but that he was asking us to rely on his word."[13]

Carl Rubino objected to the idea of using officers' certificates. He argued that the firm could not rely on Goodman to certify the authenticity of documents since he had already deceived the lawyers by providing false documents. Before they learned the details of the fraud, Rubino reasoned, the firm should take "every step to prevent further fraud." By doing so, the lawyers would be in a better position should it turn out the crimes were ongoing.[14]

Asked whether it made sense to get a certificate from the alleged malefactor, Hutner remembered being advised "that a lawyer should not assume that his client is lying to him even when he admits to him that he has been guilty of prior wrongdoing."

Putzel testified:

The fundamental questions that I know that Dean McLaughlin and I discussed was whether a lawyer has an obligation to disbelieve his client and . . . I know he and I reached the same conclusion that the lawyer is entitled to believe the representations made to him by his client, absent evidence to the contrary. We knew of no such evidence in this case.[15]

He further stated:

the attorney is not the policeman of his client. He is a—or she is—an agent of the client and a representative of the client. Now that doesn't mean that the attorney can put blinders on and blindly do whatever the client says. But it does, in my judgment . . . absent evidence to the contrary, the attorney is entitled to believe the representations made to him by his client.

Asked what legal principles or cases he reviewed where officers' certificates were relied on, Putzel responded, "I don't think I found any."[16]

By the close of this meeting, Hutner had "dismissed double-hocking as the possible underlying problem." He remembered Jacobs offering "what seemed to be sound reasons" for concluding it was not double-hocking, "that it [double-hocking] would have shown up in a UCC [Uniform Commercial Code] search to someone who was sensitive to the issue."[17]

On the following day, June 24, OPM obtained a loan from the Rhode Island Hospital Trust National Bank for a little over $3.2 million. Singer Hutner represented OPM at the closing. The deal was fraudulent.[18]

That same morning, Hutner, Rubino, and Mattioli were in Hutner's office when Alan Jacobs entered and said he had some questions concerning recent OPM equipment purchases in the amount of about $5 million, equipment that was about to be financed and leased. The bills of sale and invoices indicated the equipment was purchased some weeks before, Jacobs told the group, yet he wasn't aware of any financing obtained by OPM to acquire the machines. Where did they get $5 million? Jacobs showed the documents to his colleagues, and Mattioli observed something odd. "I recognize, I think I recognize the handwriting," he told the others. "That looks like Myron Goodman's handwriting," he said, pointing to the signature of a vendor representative on a bill of sale. Rubino suggested they consult a handwriting expert and notify Putzel and McLaughlin immediately.

Hutner called Putzel and reported what Jacobs had found and said Rubino recommended they consult a handwriting expert to determine whether Mattioli's observation was valid. Putzel asked Hutner to send copies of the documents to his office so that he and McLaughlin could review them.

The following day, Mattioli delivered copies of the suspect documents to Putzel and McLaughlin. Within the next day or so, Putzel called Hutner, Mattioli remembered being told. Hutner told him that Putzel thought that perhaps Mattioli was "overreacting," "seeing ghosts," and "seeing things that weren't there."[19] He also told Hutner that engaging a handwriting expert to examine copies of signature pages would be fruitless since no handwriting expert would render an opinion based on a Xerox copy. No one had informed Putzel that closing requirements on OPM lease transactions required original title documentation. Originals should have been in Singer Hutner's files, but no one ever looked.

The suspect documents sent to Putzel and McLaughlin were part of the closing documentation on OPM/Rockwell Equipment Schedules 0–39–80, 0–42–80, and 0–31–80. The First National Bank of St. Paul and Bankers Life Company of Des Moines provided OPM with nearly $10 million worth of loans related to this equipment. On June 27, the deals were closed. Singer Hutner represented OPM at closings. Both deals were fraudulent.[20] Myron Goodman had forged the vendor's signature on the bill of sale.

On June 24, Eli Mattioli sent copies of the fourteen-page "Sam and Harry" memo to McLaughlin and Putzel, outlining the facts that had already been conveyed orally and asking a series of questions on which they were seeking advice. The memo stated that Sam told Hutner, "that the matter related to past wrongful transactions conducted through the Company."[21] At another point in the memo, Hutner and Mattioli—the two principal authors of the document—wrote that Paul's (Clifton's) attorney (Davis) told Hutner and Mattioli that his client's letter revealed a matter "*possibly* involving a felony" (emphasis mine). Lawyers frequently draw a distinction between "knowing" in a legal sense and strongly suspecting or believing something is true or not. Did the Singer Hutner attorneys really "know" that Goodman had committed crimes? Certainly. Did they "know" in a legal sense? That is another matter entirely. The following paragraph appeared at the close of the memo. "The Firm has no actual knowledge or information of wrongdoing, if any, by the Company. Nor does the Firm have any knowledge or information as to whether the statements of Paul's lawyer mentioned above are accurate or inaccurate."

On Wednesday, Putzel arrived at Dean McLaughlin's office with written answers to the questions asked by the Singer Hutner firm in the "Sam and Harry Memo." Putzel and McLaughlin discussed the memo and the advice they were about to offer the law firm before calling Mattioli. They did not provide advice in written form because, in McLaughlin's view, Singer Hutner was "in a hurry"; they were closing deals and wanted advice before they went much further. They first told Mattioli that Reinhard must resign as a director of OPM. It was inappropriate, in their view, for Reinhard to continue to serve both as a director of the company and as counsel to the company. Should Reinhard receive information while serving as a director, the information would not be privileged. Hutner replied that Reinhard had attempted to resign but was begged by Sam not to do so.

Second, the lawyers' lawyers believed that Singer Hutner had to straighten out what appeared to be a clear conflict of interest in continuing to represent both Goodman and OPM. McLaughlin later testified, "[Singer] Hutner represents OPM, and that is the corporate client. Unhappily, [it] . . . also represented Goodman in an individual capacity. . . . If there was any fraud here," the judge said, "the principle perpetrator would have been Sam, or Goodman . . . and for that reason [Singer] Hutner could not represent both of them . . . because OPM would have been the victim of the crime."[22] Putzel and McLaughlin suggested that Goodman retain his own attorney, and they recommended Andrew Lawler, another Fordham Law graduate—indeed, a former classmate of the dean's—and a close personal friend of both Putzel and McLaughlin.

Third, McLaughlin and Putzel concluded that it was a "nature of law" that all the members of the board of directors—and that, of course, meant only Weissman, since Reinhard already knew—had to be told about the foregoing events.

Fourth, predicating their advice on the belief that the crimes were over, the two reiterated their position that the firm had no obligation to resign, since resigning would be detrimental to the client. Putzel remembered being told that if Singer Hutner resigned, OPM would have great difficulty continuing and, Putzel later testified "that made it a matter of great seriousness to determine what its [the law firm's] obligation was to the client." Hutner had made it clear that if the law firm were to resign, Lehman Brothers Kuhn Loeb would also resign, and if Lehman resigned, Hutner said, "It wouldn't be likely that any substantial, responsible investment banking house . . . would become involved with OPM." Hutner further stated, "It would be very difficult for OPM to function without an investment banker."[23]

The final piece of advice offered by Putzel and McLaughlin concerned the lawyer's duty to keep the "secrets" and "confidences" of their client in regard to past crimes. In New York State, Disciplinary Rule 7–102(B)(1) reads:

> A lawyer who received information clearly establishing that:
> (1)   His client has, in the course of the representation, perpetrated a fraud upon a person or tribunal shall promptly call upon his client to rectify the same, and if his client refuses or is unable to do so, he shall reveal the fraud to the affected person or tribunal, except when the information is protected as a confidence as secret.

Continuing to play this academic game, Putzel and McLaughlin claimed the firm had not received any information which *clearly established* fraud, although the information Davis provided raised some question as to whether they received such information or not.[24] But in either case—whether they had received information of wrongdoing or not—such information was privileged.[25]

Armed with the advice they wanted to hear, the Singer Hutner lawyers set out to do business with OPM as it had always been done. There was only one change. That week the Singer Hutner partners voted in favor of using the officer's certificates on OPM transactions. According to Mattioli, no one spoke against the procedure—other than the objections made earlier by Rubino. Despite Goodman's confession, Singer Hutner didn't even have to alter its opinion letters, according to Putzel.[26] He did tell the lawyers, however, that they had to "keep their eyes peeled" and they could not "stick their heads in the sand."

Goodman and Andrew Lawler met at the Singer Hutner offices on Thursday, June 26, for the first time. Emerging from behind closed doors at around 9:00 P.M., after discussing the problem for about five hours, Goodman announced he was retaining Lawler as his personal attorney. However strong the Singer Hutner attorneys' beliefs were that the fraud had ended, those beliefs were made stronger by Lawler's involvement in the case. Lawler was a man of the highest integrity with wide respect in the New York Bar. His friends, Putzel and McLaughlin, had the utmost admiration for him, and they seemed to relax knowing he was advising Goodman. Putzel later testified, "I knew darned well that Andrew Lawler would never permit his client to perpetrate a fraud while he was representing that client."[27] McLaughlin said, "I have known Andy since law school. Andy is an absolutely unimpeachable lawyer . . . his character is above reproach. I knew that if anybody could get into a sticky situation like this and handle it with professionalism, it was Andy Lawler."[28]

Hutner, who hadn't known Lawler prior to this time, said, "We were relying on our understanding of Lawler's competency and probity that there was not a fraud." He continued:

> I cannot conceive of a man, like the man I believe Andy is, continuing to represent Myron Goodman if the frauds were ongoing and [unless] he too was defrauded. . . . Also the relationship between Lawler and McLaughlin, between Lawler and Putzel, Lawler was also a friend of my law school roommate. It was inconceivable that Lawler would remain in the picture one moment after learning that he had been defrauded and we had been defrauded.[29]

What didn't occur to this group of attorneys, however, was that Lawler was bound by the same ethical code that prevented Singer

Hutner from divulging what it knew. Lawler wouldn't be permitted to reveal what he knew in regard to past frauds; and since Goodman wouldn't confess to Hutner, what made them think he would disclose the crimes to Lawler?

Asked whether Lawler made assurances that the fraud had ended, Putzel said that "in sum and substance" he had. But asked about the steps Lawler was taking to ensure the fraud had ended, Putzel replied, "Well, I don't know what else he was doing, but I do know that he was sitting down and spending a lot of time with Goodman getting the facts from him."[30]

Throughout the next several weeks, meetings were held regularly between the Singer Hutner attorneys, Putzel, and, on occasion, with Lawler, to discuss what to do next. They continued to await Goodman's disclosure, and they relied on Lawler to arrange a meeting so that Goodman's confession could be heard; they assumed this would soon occur.

On July 15, while reviewing some OPM documentation in preparation for a meeting with Lawler, Alan Jacobs brought another bill of sale problem to the attention of Eli Mattioli. Jacobs told Mattioli he was processing an OPM-related deal and had become aware of two bills of sale supposedly for two different leases and financings, yet each contained identical equipment descriptions, including identical serial numbers. (Alan Jacobs testified that he didn't recall this incident.) Mattioli immediately called Putzel and told him what Jacobs had discovered. He also brought the problem to the attention of Hutner and Rubino. Putzel told Mattioli he would meet with Jacobs following the scheduled meeting with Lawler the next day at the Singer Hutner offices.

Mattioli remembered Putzel and Jacobs meeting the next day, and he was subsequently told they had talked about the problem several times. Jacobs told Mattioli that Putzel recommended contacting the OPM officer responsible for that particular transaction to ask for an explanation.[31] Jacobs contacted the OPM officer—a member of Goodman's team—and the officer explained it was apparently a "typographical error" and said that he would provide Jacobs with a correct copy of the bill of sale.

Putzel's recollection is a bit different. First of all, Putzel said he never saw the documents in question and he doesn't believe he told

Jacobs how to resolve the matter; he just insisted, "Get to the bottom of it. Find out what the problem is." He didn't recall telling Jacobs to check with an OPM officer. Putzel said Jacobs later claimed it was a false alarm, "that there had been a typographical error which made it appear that the equipment was identical, whereas in fact a number had been miscopied."[32]

The "typographical error" or "miscopied number" on the bill of sale was quite an error. It included a machine number, a model number, and the following description:

> Mass Storage Facility
> S/N 65415
> Twin Port
> Two Channel Switch

The serial number for this unit—65415—matched the serial number on equipment that was a part of OPM/Rockwell Equipment Schedule 0–13–80, which had closed some three months earlier, on April 16, 1980. That transaction was fraudulent.

The "corrected" bill of sale Jacobs received from OPM was part of the documentation on OPM/Rockwell Equipment Schedule 0–43–80, which closed on July 11. Needless to say, it too was fraudulent.

Five weeks after first learning of the wrongdoing, the Singer Hutner attorneys had not heard Goodman's disclosure of the underlying facts. Nor had they informed Weissman about what they knew; Goodman insisted that he be the one to tell Weissman. But Goodman hadn't told him as far as any Singer Hutner attorney knew. Reinhard hadn't resigned as a director of OPM, either. Goodman was orchestrating everything exactly the way he wanted, and Singer Hutner played along. Certainly, Hutner pressed Goodman to confess. In fact, Hutner claimed he often spent full days with Goodman pleading with him to disclose. Beyond his pleading with Goodman, Hutner recalls little about these private meetings. And, of course, Putzel kept after Lawler, but time continued to pass, fraudulent deals were closed, and Goodman's excuses kept coming. But on July 21, the Singer Hutner firm received some indication from Lawler that Goodman was planning to confess in some general way but not make a full confession. Hutner was furious. During a lengthy meeting with Putzel, Rubino, and Mattioli on June 22, Hutner, quite agitated, called Goodman. He told Goodman that if he didn't inform Weissman by Monday, that he, Hutner, would tell him. Goodman, in substance, responded, "You are pushing me too far. If you don't back off, I'm going to kill myself." Hutner remembered Goodman threatening to jump from his ninth-floor window. Hutner pleaded with him not to.

Putzel remembered the incident vividly—it was right out of a grade C movie. At the time of the phone call, there was the worst lightning and thunderstorm he had ever seen taking place, and he recalls "wild lightning, claps of thunder, Hutner pleading with Goodman to be rational, and more than once, some indication that Goodman was threatening to go out a window or otherwise harm himself."[33] Mattioli recalled Hutner saying, "No, Myron, don't say that," and then Hutner becoming visibly upset—in tears at one point—as he indicated to those in the room that Goodman was on the windowsill of his ninth-floor office threatening to jump. They all believed Goodman must have been in a state of extreme emotional strain and stress.[34] Hutner continued to plead with Goodman, to speak rationally with him, and finally, after several lengthy conversations, he agreed to tell Weissman on July 29, when the two of them would be together on a trip to the West Coast, and he agreed to tell Singer Hutner on August 6—still two weeks away. Hutner agreed.[35]

On August 6, the Singer Hutner attorneys anxiously awaited Goodman's arrival. After six weeks of waiting for his confession, they were finally going to hear what had happened. In the late afternoon, Goodman and Weissman arrived at the Singer Hutner offices, and they met with Lawler, Hutner, Reinhard, Rubino, and Mattioli. Putzel was on vacation. Before anything was discussed, Andrew Reinhard submitted his letter of resignation from OPM's board of directors to Goodman and Weissman without comment. Hutner opened the meeting by explaining why they were all drawn together—to hear Goodman's confession. But before Hutner went any further, Weissman, appearing very impatient, interrupted him saying, "Why are you boring me with all of this, Joe?"[36] Weissman told the group that before the meeting commenced, he had something to say. He said that he decided to sell his half interest in the company to Goodman but that he would stay on as a consultant. He claimed that his decision was not based on any negative development in his relationship with Goodman—there was no falling out, he said—but after long deliberations with his partner, he decided he would retire. It had always been his objective to retire before the age of thirty-five. It wasn't his goal to run a large company—that was Goodman's aim; he thought there were more important things in life. At that moment, Weissman was interrupted by a phone call for him and left the room. There was complete silence when he exited.

When Weissman returned, Hutner said he believed the proposed buyout was nothing but a charade, and whether or not Weissman was to sell out in the future, he was presently an owner and member of the board of directors of OPM and that Singer Hutner "had waited as long as they wanted to"—they were there to listen to Goodman's confession. Weissman then protested that he didn't want to hear any disclosure about a company he was about to sell, as though hearing something bad about the company would somehow devalue his interest in OPM. He told Hutner, "Hey, you know, I'm in the midst of negotiating the sell-out to Myron, and you are trying to tell me that I'm going to sit here and hear something that's going to make my stock worthless. I don't understand this situation." Neither did anyone else.

Hutner said, be that as it may, they were there to hear Goodman's disclosure. Hutner asked Weissman if Goodman had disclosed anything to him. Weissman said that he had. Hutner then turned to Goodman and asked him to proceed. "I'm not going to make disclosure at this time," said Goodman, rather indifferently. Hutner looked beseechingly at Lawler, who responded only with a stony silence. Surprised by what had taken place, Hutner said, "We're having this meeting with the understanding you were going to come here and make a disclosure. We've waited for this meeting for you to make a disclosure. Will you please make it?" Goodman declined. Hutner pleaded with Lawler, who looked as though he wasn't shocked by what had taken place, to urge Goodman to keep his commitment to the law firm. All to no avail.

Following the meeting, Hutner called Putzel at his vacation home to inform him of the "nondisclosure meeting." Putzel later testified that he was concerned about what had taken place, but he said it did not raise any new worries about Goodman concealing an ongoing fraud. "It simply caused me to believe that what he had done was something of gravity," Putzel said, and "he was therefore very embarrassed about disclosing."[37]

9

The View from the Outside

I N ADDITION to Singer Hutner, a number of organizations doing business with OPM in 1980 began to get concerned about OPM's viability. Coopers & Lybrand, Lehman Brothers Kuhn Loeb, the First National Bank of St. Paul (FNBSP), and Rockwell International were among them. Correctly sensing something wrong, representatives of these organizations initially acted responsibly. Lehman, for instance, caused OPM to hire Coopers. Rockwell attempted to learn more about OPM's financial condition and to limit its future business with the leasing company. But in each instance, with the exception of Coopers, representatives of these institutions reacted slowly in response to further warnings coming from OPM, and they frequently interpreted such signals in a favorable or, at least, neutral way. Goodman's explanations were accepted without verification. Inconsistencies were not carefully examined. In several cases, people seemed satisfied merely that they had checked, that they had asked or made halfhearted attempts to probe. Although the answers seemed suspect, that did not appear to matter. And when OPM's performance became so poor and they finally did exit, they still failed to warn others who went to work for OPM. And the frauds continued.

Coopers & Lybrand Resigns

Throughout the month of June 1980, several events began to concern Robert Lage at Coopers and, eventually, even Louis Moscarello became alarmed. The accounting firm was having trouble collecting its fees from OPM and was forced to demand payment within ten days of billing. In addition, Coopers became more disturbed over OPM's financial condition. In a memo to the file written on June 30, Lage wrote:

> It appears that OPM is able to generate an overall profit only if it continues to generate sufficient new leases to compensate for the recurring annual loss sustained with on-going leases. This will become increasingly difficult each year.[1]

About the same time, a Coopers' employee discovered two OPM ledger cards revealing cash advances to Goodman and Weissman in the amount of $9.8 million, approximately $5 million more than the amount recorded in 1978, the last time OPM was audited. Several shareholder loans were made when the owners purchased the First National Bank of Jefferson Parish (FNJ) stock, but that didn't satisfy Coopers. Lage and Moscarello were uneasy about Goodman and Weissman taking large sums of money from an apparently insolvent company; they were borrowing money that wasn't theirs to borrow— the money belonged to OPM's creditors. Moscarello later testified:

> This [officers' loans] immediately raised a number of specters in my mind: Preferential payments, possible illegalities, all kinds of problems where I knew I had to consult with my attorney . . . [I] made the judgment I no longer wanted to be associated with this kind of a situation.[2]

Moscarello discussed the situation with Coopers' general counsel and decided to suspend the engagement until the firm received an adequate explanation for the loans. Coopers also decided to inform Lehman of their findings.[3]

Lage tried calling Goodman in California to inform him of the firm's decision, but Goodman, worried that Coopers had uncovered the

Rockwell fraud, wouldn't accept the call. He had Michael Weinberg phone Lage, but Lage refused to speak to anyone but Goodman. Finally, Goodman returned the call, and when he learned that Coopers was upset about the officers' loans, he couldn't have felt more relieved. Compared to what was hanging over his head, being called to task on the officers' loans was like issuing a traffic ticket to a bank robber. He agreed to meet with Lage and Moscarello at the next progress meeting when he returned to New York later that week.

On Thursday, August 7, around 9 A.M., Thomas Walther, Robert Lage, and Louis Moscarello entered OPM's ninth-floor conference room to conduct the previously scheduled progress meeting. Goodman, David Lesnick, and Michael Weinberg from OPM were present. Stephen Kutz from Fox & Company and Joel Peck from Lehman were also in attendance. At the start of the meeting, Weinberg suggested Moscarello first discuss the issue in private with Goodman. Moscarello acknowledged Weinberg's request but added that Coopers was "duty bound" to disclose what it knew to Lewis Glucksman of Lehman. Kutz, Lesnick, and Peck were then asked to leave the room. Goodman began by saying that he would decide whether anyone else would be told about the loans. He had given Coopers access to OPM's records "in confidence," he reasoned, and Coopers should not reveal the contents of these materials to anyone without his prior approval. He said he was going to inform Lehman about his position on disclosure "right now." Prone to dramatize the points he made, Goodman then left the room to call Alan Batkin.

About twenty minutes later, Goodman returned and restated his position. "No one," he said, would discuss the issue with Lehman unless he decided it was okay. Moscarello reiterated his intention to disclose to Glucksman despite Goodman's insistence that he not.

Moscarello then began by saying he was "making no allegations, [that Coopers] has not conducted an audit and does not intend to perform an audit."[4] However, in the course of its work, it had discovered $9.8 million in officers' loans, many of which had been made while the company was insolvent. Moscarello further said his firm was uncomfortable with the situation, and until it received a satisfactory explanation, it was suspending the engagement. Moscarello also told Weinberg and Goodman they could respond to Coopers or not, as they wished.

Weinberg explained that $6.4 million of the $9.8 million in loans to Goodman and Weissman was related to the acquisition of the First National Bank of Jefferson Parish. Moscarello was aware of that, but he was still not satisfied. "I indicated that Coopers and Lybrand chose not to be associated with such a situation," Moscarello later wrote in a memo to the files, "and restated our position that OPM executives were free to respond or not to respond to us as they saw fit but that we would perform no further work until we had received what we considered a satisfactory explanation."

Moscarello Calls Batkin

On August 15, Moscarello called Batkin and told him Coopers had suspended its engagement with OPM because he "questioned the integrity of Myron Goodman, and that [he] chose not to be associated further with Myron Goodman." Furthermore, Moscarello told Batkin, "Basically we have a situation where [there is] a negative net worth which means that it's not the shareholders' money anymore. It's somebody else's money, and under those circumstances, when you're taking money out of the business, you're not taking your money out of the business." Batkin's notes of the conversation read: "he didn't want to be associated with this crap"; "he was suspicious about what was going on"; "withdrawals in anticipation of bankruptcy"; and "maybe another Continental Vending,"[5] a reference to a case where false financial statements were prepared by the predecessor firm of Coopers for Continental Vending Machines Corporation, a company that was being looted by its president.[6]

Batkin countered by telling Moscarello that most of the withdrawals were made during a period when OPM was solvent. Batkin also said that a substantial portion of the officers' loans were collateralized by the bank stock. Moscarello was unpersuaded. He didn't argue with Batkin; he just repeated that Coopers was uncomfortable with the situation and preferred to suspend the engagement.

Although Weinberg and Kutz analyzed the officers' loan account and attempted to justify the figures, Coopers was never satisfied with Goodman's explanation. Coopers never returned to OPM.

Believing things were crumbling around him, Goodman viewed the accounting firm's discovery as a blessing in disguise, since it withdrew before it had uncovered any evidence of fraud. Goodman found another blessing in Coopers' decision not to inform third parties of its discovery. Following the code of professional ethics of the American Institute of Certified Public Accountants (AICPA)[7] and the advice of its legal counsel, Coopers kept silent about OPM's looting.

When Lehman induced another accounting firm, Oppenheim, Appel & Dixon (OA&D) to pick up where Coopers left off in the fall of 1980, Lage failed to mention Coopers' concerns about shareholder loans to OA&D's Paul Spindel when he called Lage about OPM. Coopers forwarded documents to OA&D as required by the AICPA, but none of the material related to the officers' loans, although Lage had told Spindel the documents were complete. Lage did, however, tell Spindel that OPM was a difficult engagement and that he was glad it was over. He also told him to check with Michael Weinberg about why Coopers withdrew. He never mentioned the looting. And he never suggested that OA&D ask Goodman's permission to allow Coopers to freely discuss the situation with the firm. The OPM trustee wrote that such a course of action was required by the professional ethics division of the AICPA in a similar situation.[8]

Over the course of its engagement, Coopers had received more than $178,000 in fees; OA&D had received $27,000.

Lehman's Response

Following his conversation with Moscarello, Batkin met with Lehman's operating committee—David Sacks, Lewis Glucksman, and Harvey Krueger—and told them about the foregoing events. The Committee was distressed, and initial reaction was to withdraw from the OPM engagement, but it was subsequently decided to first get the facts.

Batkin later spoke with Weinberg about the officers' loans. Weinberg, Kutz, and Joseph Datuin had conducted an analysis of the officers' loans, which Weinberg presented to Batkin. Of the nearly $10 million in officers' loans, approximately $7.7 million was attributable to the bank purchase, Batkin was told. Of the $2.3 million in loans that were not related to the bank purchase, only $1 million was taken during the period December 31, 1978, to July 30, 1980, the period the company was allegedly insolvent. The major problem for Batkin was that the OPM loans to Goodman and Weissman for the purchase of the bank stock were unsecured; the loans were not collateralized by the stock, as he had originally thought.

Weinberg's apparent lack of concern about the officers' loans is perplexing, particularly in light of his own experiences with Goodman taking money from the company. In January 1979, Goodman and Weissman established the Michael B. Weinberg Fiduciary Account, which allowed them to make anonymous charitable contributions. Every so often, Goodman would tell Weinberg to issue a check to a charity; Weinberg said he didn't know how funds got into the account or the source of such funds—he just concerned himself with how much went out and to whom it went. But there came a time when he didn't even get that much information.

On July 18, 1980, a month after Goodman had made his partial confession to the Singer Hutner attorneys, Goodman asked for and received from Weinberg a blank check in the amount of $600,000. Shortly afterward, the check was returned to Weinberg, and Goodman told him to make the check out to Chemical Bank account number 327. Weinberg asked Goodman the identity of the charitable organization. Goodman said he was very rushed and would tell him who the recipient was in a couple of days. He assured Weinberg that it was a charitable organization, and he could verify that by talking to Andrew Reinhard. Weinberg called Reinhard, who said that he would prefer that Goodman provided the information on the charity. Weinberg asked whether the check was going to a legitimate charitable organization. Reinhard said that it was. According to Weinberg, "Reinhard gave me comfort that this was an appropriate check to an appropriate charitable organization and that it was appropriate to issue such a check."9 Weinberg issued the check.

Despite attending several Coopers meetings covering OPM's financial problems and the size of the officers' loan accounts and even writing memos on the subject himself during this same period, Weinberg never asked about the source of the $600,000. He claimed he never made the connection between the size of the officers' loan accounts and the $600,000 check. On March 13, 1981, two days after OPM filed for bankruptcy, Weinberg learned that Chemical Bank account number 327 was a Myron Goodman personal account. (It is believed these funds eventually found their way to Yeshiva University.)

The day after Batkin spoke to Weinberg, he met with Goodman, who walked him through the ledger cards that itemized each loan made to the two principals. Myron showed Batkin that a number of the loans were related to the purchase of the bank stock. A large portion of the remainder was used to purchase securities through several brokerage houses. Goodman also told Batkin that he had $5.5 million in cash in his account at Chase Manhattan Bank and $3 million in cash at the FNBSP.

Batkin didn't see any inconsistency in Goodman's borrowing from the company during a period in which it had millions in cash reserves at two banks. Nor did he find it unusual that there were complaints about OPM bouncing checks during the same period they had this much cash, particularly since Goodman told him the bounced checks were due to a computer foul-up. Batkin registered no surprise at the size of the cash reserves. Nor did he conduct any independent check to see whether or not Goodman was being truthful.

Batkin reported his findings to the operating committee at Lehman. They decided it was important to get the officers' loans collateralized and have Goodman replace Coopers with another Big Eight accounting firm. Until Goodman complied with Lehman's conditions, Batkin said, they wouldn't place any OPM debt. The Lehman freeze lasted two weeks, ending in early September.

The FNBSP Learns about the Coopers Suspension

Although it took several conversations with Alan Batkin to get the full story—or what he thought was the full story—Jeffrey Werner learned that Coopers had terminated its engagement with OPM. Werner was concerned and surprised since Batkin's memos about

OPM the previous several weeks "had less of crisis tone" than did earlier reports. Werner was so concerned, in fact, that he flew to New York to meet with Batkin and Goodman. Batkin told him Coopers had resigned because it was upset about the size of the officers' loans. But, he added, no one should have been surprised about the increase in those loans since much of the money went toward the purchase of the bank stock. Werner remembered Batkin saying that he believed Coopers actually resigned because of the personality clashes between OPM and Coopers' personnel, not over the size of the officers' loans.

On September 8, Werner and another officer from the FNBSP met Goodman, Weinberg, and Batkin at the OPM offices in lower Manhattan. Goodman told Werner that OPM was not going to have audited financial statements for the 1979 fiscal year, but they were just about to retain Ernst & Whinney as their auditors. He went on to say that he was selling the FNJ bank stock, and that the sale combined with the $8 million cash he claimed he had in the bank would put the company in a pretty good position. In addition, he said the market for the IBM 370 series was good, which meant OPM's residual values would hold up. Goodman also told Werner that he and Weissman would provide personal guarantees on the loans made by the FNBSP to OPM.

Werner felt better after his visits to Lehman and to OPM. He discussed his trip with Andrew Sall, the senior vice-president and head of the commercial banking group at the FNBSP; neither one considered terminating business with OPM. But what Werner hadn't been told by Batkin or by anyone else was that those officers' loans were made during a time when Coopers felt OPM was insolvent. No one told Werner about the predictions made by John Clifton, Martin Zelbow, and Stephen Kutz that OPM would show a negative net worth—if the financial statements were ever completed. Nor did Batkin, when he subsequently learned the facts, tell Werner that Ernst & Whinney had declined the OPM engagement. Nor did any of these men check to see whether Goodman had the $8 million in bank accounts or whether business on the IBM 370 series was as good as Goodman had alleged. Had these men bothered to investigate the market value of the IBM 370 series, they would have known OPM was losing a great deal of money on mainframe computers. Goodman knew this all too well; he was losing his shirt on equipment he subleased for Rockwell. But Goodman also knew the men in that room wouldn't know that.

Rockwell

Most Rockwell representatives were unaware of the growing problems at OPM throughout 1979 and 1980; they faced a set of problems of their own with Myron Goodman and with Sidney Hasin during the same period—problems that, if left unresolved, could cost Rockwell millions of dollars.

For several years, OPM not only leased computer equipment *to* Rockwell, they also leased equipment *from* them. As a favor to Rockwell, or more specifically to Hasin, OPM subleased unwanted Rockwell equipment under a sublease agreement. For example, Hasin sometimes produced forecasts that indicated a need to expand Rockwell's computer capacity, often causing the aerospace company to acquire more equipment than it needed. Or, on other occasions, Hasin wanted to rid himself of obsolete equipment Rockwell held on long-term leases— leases he had negotiated. In either case, Hasin sought to unburden Rockwell of the obligation, and Goodman, seeking favored treatment from the canny Rockwell engineer, assumed responsibility for the outdated machines. Time and time again, Goodman provided Hasin and Rockwell with short-term fixes for their predicament, but it was like being rescued by a ship riddled with holes, for Rockwell was still responsible to the financial institutions for loans on the subleased equipment.

Some Rockwell officials were beginning to sense the danger. Thus, when Hasin pushed for a formal sublease agreement with OPM in 1979, whereby OPM would assume responsibility for subleasing a significant portion of the Rockwell portfolio, his superiors were hesitant. Worried about Rockwell's exposure on the equipment and their growing dependence on OPM, Robert DePalma, Rockwell's vice-president of finance, wanted OPM checked out thoroughly. He ordered William Neely, the company's treasurer, to pay OPM a visit and analyze its financial statements.

When William Neely, Sidney Hasin, and Maury Dahn, vice-president of Rockwell's ISC, arrived at OPM on August 1, 1979, Goodman was well prepared. He had planned a "dog and pony show," complete with a guided tour of the three floors OPM occupied in the former U.S. Steel building on lower Broadway. He left less than an hour for the on-site review of the company's financial statements; the reports were not to leave the premises, Goodman told the group. But even this carefully staged performance wasn't enough for Goodman. Knowing that the Kutz method—reporting equity as income immediately rather than amortizing it over the life of the lease—might not get him through this one, Goodman had created his own financials.

So that he would know exactly which figures were suspect and, therefore, required changing, the week before the Rockwell visitors arrived, Goodman sat down with John Clifton to review OPM's financials for fiscal 1978. Unaware of Goodman's fraudulent plans, Clifton pointed to the figures that would draw questions from an astute observer. After his session with Clifton, Goodman improved OPM's financial picture overnight by inflating the company's total assets by $200 million while raising liabilities only $159 million. He increased income by $8.4 million, retained earnings by a whopping $34.4 million, and he changed OPM's net worth from $4.2 million to a staggering $44.9 million. He even modified the footnotes and removed the controversial footnotes 2 and 4. But even Goodman's Promethean efforts couldn't hide the company's difficulties; the altered financials revealed a $203.6 million gap between equipment-related debt and minimum lease receivables—almost as egregious as the $283.6 million gap in the "real" financials.

Still concerned that he hadn't done enough to cover OPM's fiscal distress, Goodman asked Hasin how to handle Neely. "He doesn't understand financial statements," he remembered Hasin saying, "so you can doubletalk your way around it. And you should have no problem."[10] Indeed, Goodman had little trouble convincing Neely of OPM's viability. Neely walked away satisfied with OPM, and although he noticed the gap between equipment-related debt and minimum lease receivables, he didn't become alarmed—he was probably too impressed by OPM's $44.9 million net worth. And since it was to their advantage to have Neely approve of OPM and the proposed sublease agreement, Dahn and Hasin didn't raise any questions during the meetings. According to Hasin, Dahn even instructed him not to raise questions about the financials, and although he noticed several problems with the documents, Hasin kept quiet. "Mr. Neely was in charge of that part of the meeting," Hasin said, "and I was told not to say anything."[11]

Back at Rockwell's corporate headquarters in Pittsburgh, Neely wrote DePalma and recommended the sublease extension agreement (SEA)[12] with OPM. Once he received the green light from Pittsburgh, Hasin, in keeping with Rockwell's competitive bid procedures, requested proposals from other lessors on the SEA. But he only gave them eight days to respond to the complicated deal, and since OPM had more than a year to prepare for the agreement, it was the only responsive bidder. On September 30, 1979, Rockwell and OPM signed the SEA, tying the noose around Rockwell's throat even tighter. Under the SEA, OPM subleased outdated equipment from Rockwell for a total rent of approximately $12 million. Goodman saved Rockwell millions of dollars on the transaction, and once again, saved Hasin's neck. But Hasin wasn't out of hot water for long.

One month before the SEA was signed, Robert Scheussler, who headed Rockwell's EDP audit staff, completed a review of procurement practices at the Information Systems Center (ISC). Although he was generally complimentary of Hasin's cost-saving policies, Scheussler was critical of Hasin's sloppy recordkeeping and violations of Rockwell bidding procedures. The problems were accentuated, Scheussler claimed, by concentrating the entire procurement process—from preparing acquisition requests to the review of bids and negotiating the leases—in the hands of one person—Sidney L. Hasin.

Following Scheussler's audit, procurement procedures were changed at the ISC, and Hasin was relieved of responsibility for bids. But because Hasin's replacement, who assumed that task, was less experienced, Hasin remained in effective control of the bidding process. Needless to say, OPM's favored treatment continued. From 1976 until February 1981, Rockwell awarded over 190 leases to OPM without competition from other lessors; most were granted after the 1979 audit. Even with competitive bidding, the process was often rigged in OPM's favor. At times, Hasin asked his cronies in the leasing business to submit bids higher than OPM's. On other occasions, on receiving all the bids from other lessors, Hasin would call Goodman and provide him with a ballpark figure for him to submit to guarantee a lock on the deal. "I was always careful," Hasin said, "I would never quote a precise number." The logistics of the "wire-type" system, however, made it difficult for OPM to submit its bids on time, so Goodman gave Hasin a stack of OPM stationery with his signature affixed to the bottom of the page. In the event the two connivers were pressed for time, Hasin entered bids on OPM's behalf. On several occasions, Hasin called Goodman and told him what OPM's bid was.

But the new rules and changes in procedure made it more difficult for Hasin, and he became more and more careful and more conscious of audits. Once a one-man show, Hasin's power base was gradually being eroded. He thought he wasn't being recognized for his efforts, and he gradually began to think about new opportunities. In the winter of 1979, Hasin proposed a new business venture to Goodman.[13] Hasin convinced the enterprising Goodman that OPM needed to diversify and suggested he acquire a data services business owned by two of Hasin's friends, William Graham and Robert Madariaga. Once established, OPM Data Services, as the new company was to be called, would be managed by Hasin—at well over twice the salary he received at Rockwell. Goodman, Hasin, Graham, and Madariaga made plans and negotiated well into the summer of 1980, and despite the series of OPM problems that surfaced over that period, Hasin never wavered. He was determined to leave Rockwell and go to work for OPM and collect that six-figure salary.

If Hasin wasn't worried about OPM, his superiors were. They had reason to worry. In March 1980, several events occurred that had Rockwell representatives concerned about OPM's financial viability. OPM's exposure alone on Rockwell's early terminations was more than $40 million, and that didn't include the contingent liability on equipment covered by the SEA. At about this time, Rockwell officials learned that approximately half a million worth of OPM checks had bounced. Hasin was furious, and he called Goodman to tell him so. Goodman said it was a mix-up, but Hasin couldn't understand how they could do anything "so stupid"—not realizing such mix-ups were inescapable and likely to reoccur, given OPM's dire financial straits.

That same month, Robert DePalma became enraged when he read about OPM's check-kiting conviction in the *American Banker*.[14] DePalma went "berserk," according to Goodman. DePalma immediately called Dahn, who called Hasin. After reading the article himself, Hasin called Goodman, who mollified him by claiming that the article was unfair—that he had pleaded guilty only to avoid a long, involved trial. Moreover, all they did was borrow money from themselves, Goodman argued, "which was considered normal practice in New York City."[15] DePalma was unpersuaded and demanded a review of OPM's financial condition and a report on Rockwell's potential exposure should OPM go under.

The possible damage to Rockwell following an OPM collapse would be considerable, and DePalma had only begun to see it. Despite Hasin's attempts to minimize the severity of OPM's conduct and ignore the risk to his own company, DePalma imposed a freeze on all future OPM transactions and ordered Neely again to review OPM's financial statements. But the steadfast Hasin remained loyal to Goodman. He knew that without OPM, his power at Rockwell would diminish further. Goodman claimed Hasin couldn't operate his "throne" without OPM since no other leasing company would provide the deals his firm did. On July 7, Hasin wrote Neely asking for exemptions from the freeze on OPM transactions that were "in the pipeline." At the close of his letter to Neely, Hasin added that it was "unfortunate that a one-man scandal sheet . . . should have such an influence on the OPM-Rockwell relationship."[16] Hasin even went outside Rockwell to get the freeze lifted. Three days after his note to Neely, he wrote a confidential letter to the senior U.S. Defense Department official who supervised defense contracts at Rockwell, asking him to intercede on OPM's behalf since the leasing company saved Rockwell, and indirectly, the Defense Department, so much money.

Even though he tried to get the freeze officially lifted, as far as Hasin was concerned, there was never much of a freeze. He said the freeze was a "little ambiguous," that management "blew hot and cold" on it, and there was never any hard-and-fast rule that "thou shalt not . . . take OPM bids." Hasin claimed Neely gave him the "green light" on a "discrete basis,"[17] which was quite often. Indeed, the freeze had so little effect on the OPM-Rockwell relationship that Stephen Lichtman was hardly aware of its existence. But miles away in Neely's office, the freeze never thawed. The Rockwell treasurer categorically denied lifting the freeze later that summer, as Hasin claimed. The freeze was to remain in place until he received OPM's 1979 audited financials, according to Neely—which, of course, he never saw. Nor did anyone else.

Signals of OPM's impending financial doom repeatedly reached Rockwell during much of 1980. Earlier that year, Hasin learned that IBM had placed OPM on COD. Lenders were calling Rockwell complaining about bounced checks, delinquent payments, and installments made by OPM rather than by Rockwell. In that disastrous month of March, LeRoy McClellan of the Philadelphia Savings Fund Society (PSFS) began to get concerned about late payments on fifteen OPM-Rockwell leases, including Equipment Schedule 81 and five phantoms. Already angry over the check-kiting conviction and unable to get OPM to resolve the matter, McClellan decided to call Rockwell. Turning to *Moody's Manual*, McClellan found Neely's name and called him. McClellan told Neely that Rockwell was in arrears on several payments. Somewhat indignant, Neely claimed Rockwell was never late with its payments. To support his claim, McClellan read Neely the list of delinquent OPM-Rockwell transactions. Jotting down the list of equipment schedule numbers, the embarrassed Neely told McClellan he'd look into it.

Neely called Hasin and read him the list of equipment schedule numbers and told him to get to the bottom of it. Goodman and his entourage happened to be in California when Hasin got the call, and later, after showing Goodman the list but apparently failing to notice the five fictitious leases and the "forgotten" Equipment Schedule 81, Hasin questioned Goodman about the late payments. Predictably, Goodman said it was a mistake, an "error" by the PSFS, but he'd look into it anyway. When Goodman reached New York, he sent his father-in-law, Sam Ganz, to Philadelphia to pay the PSFS in person, hoping that this would resolve the problem, and it did, so far as McClellan was concerned.[18] But when Neely learned from Hasin that the problem was resolved and that the whole thing was the result of an error made by the bank and not due to Rockwell's tardiness, he became enraged and demanded an apology from McClellan. Hasin called Allen Ganz and told him about Neely's anger. Determined not to be exposed by such a slip-up, the fraud team decided to impersonate McClellan and call Neely apologizing for the error. Unable to play McClellan himself because it was the Sabbath eve, Goodman assigned the role to the willing Martin Shulman, who called Neely in Pittsburgh. Although

Neely had spoken to the banker at least twice before, he failed to recognize the mimic.

By July, Neely still hadn't received any financial information from Goodman. On Thursday, July 2, he called Alan Batkin at Lehman to get his reaction to recent events at OPM. Neely mentioned the check-kiting incident, and Batkin said he was aware of the problems at OPM, but added that "nobody got hurt" and that it was all over with now and banks were making loans to OPM. Neely asked about OPM's financial condition, and Batkin—despite his earlier conversations with Zelbow and Clifton—suggested Neely speak with other Lehman representatives, Joel Peck and David Sacks, to learn more about that. He did say, however, that OPM was implementing controls recommended by Coopers.

That same day, Neely called Peck and Sacks—both lawyers—to learn more about OPM's financial position. Both men realized the importance of the phone call. Lehman had to be careful since it was slowly becoming aware of numerous problems with the leasing company, yet it could hardly afford to make matters worse by tipping off OPM's largest customer. To complicate matters, Lehman was also Rockwell's investment banker; hence two Lehman lawyers fielded Neely's questions. Neely, too, realized the importance of the call. He recorded the conversation. When he asked about the check-kiting, Sacks told him it was an isolated incident, that it had occurred over a year ago, and that it would not be repeated. Further, he said, "I know of no reason why anyone shouldn't do business with OPM."[19] Peck also told Neely that the OPM audit would be complete "in maybe another three weeks." But neither Lehman attorney mentioned the missing Rockwell files, Clifton's prediction of OPM's $3 million loss, or Zelbow's growing uneasiness with the leasing company.

Later that month, Robert Scheussler discovered that OPM had assigned a Rockwell lease to Tilden Commercial Alliance without first obtaining Rockwell's permission. Scheussler wrote Neely on July 18 stating: "I feel this adds a new dimension to the OPM issue."[20] Neely claimed he didn't know what Scheussler was talking about, but his actions belie that claim. Within a month he and Scheussler were planning another audit of Hasin's operation. Although Neely didn't recall any doubts about Hasin's integrity being expressed at this time,

Scheussler remembered that a number of people were concerned about Hasin—including Neely.

Apparently oblivious to the plans being made in Pittsburgh that August, Hasin proposed that OPM become the sole source lessor for Rockwell. The OPM loyalist argued that the company was a "de facto sole source" anyway. DePalma rejected Hasin's proposal.

On September 4, Scheussler completed his follow-up audit on Hasin's operation. Although noting improvements in the area of recordkeeping, the report cited a number of deficiencies in bidding procedures and in management of the SEA. The bid list varied; bid responses were "not adequately controlled"; OPM was granted extensions to respond; and so on. Moreover, Scheussler claimed that changes had been made in the SEA without adequate documentation. Finally, the report underscored concerns about OPM's financial viability and claimed that Rockwell's legal staff was investigating the "impact on Rockwell should OPM go out of business."[21] Following the audit, Hasin was relieved of his procurement duties, but, as one might expect, he continued to maintain control. Of the two people who relieved him, Hasin claimed:

> Neither one of them really knew what they were doing, and I was doing my best to help them understand the areas in which they were to function, since they were relatively complex.[22]

Hasin's superiors didn't see it that way. On December 1, Larry Manly, the ISC general manager of computing services, severely reprimanded Hasin for interfering with the procurement process. Manly wrote:

> I have had great difficulty in convincing you that there are areas in which you are exceeding the bounds of your responsibility. Notwithstanding the numerous discussions we have had in the area of appropriate practices in terms of equipment acquisition policies, you have persisted in filling each and every role ISC staff members are supposed to provide.
> . . .
> Your involvement in the acquisition cycle of equipment is important; however, past audits, internal procedures and specific meetings you and I have had have [sic] all pointed out that you have exceeded the authority of your office . . .[23]

"I expect a dramatic turnaround in your day-to-day activities," Manly continued. "As of this date, you are to cease initiating any *direct contacts* with Corporate Staffs regarding computer acquisitions."

His tail between his legs, resigned to follow Manly's directive, Hasin pursued his plans to manage OPM Data Services. Goodman incorporated the company in October and arranged to lease a building a few miles from Hasin's home. Although Hasin hated to lose control of his power base at Rockwell, he was satisfied with the deal he had worked out with Goodman. The employment contract he submitted to Goodman in September called for a salary of $125,000 a year and a sales commission of 1 percent of gross profits, which he estimated would provide another $125,000. In addition, OPM would provide Hasin with a Cadillac Seville. Hasin's projections showed that his sales commissions would provide him with $424,000 a year within five years. Not bad for a man who was earning considerably less than $50,000 a year at the time. The contract also provided for a fee of $800,000 to Graham and Madariaga, plus commissions on all future business.

The End of Bondage

LITTLE HAPPENED between Singer Hutner Levine & Seeman and OPM during the month of August since Joseph Hutner and Henry Peter Putzel were away on vacation. On Wednesday, August 27, 1980, however, Hutner learned that Lehman Brothers Kuhn Loeb insisted on an audit by a Big Eight accounting firm as a condition for its continuing involvement with OPM. Joseph Hutner, Eli Mattioli, Joseph S. McLaughlin, and Henry Peter Putzel and, possibly, Carl J. Rubino met that day to discuss what the law firm was permitted to disclose to an auditor if and when an engagement took place. Putzel and McLaughlin were also told about the Coopers & Lybrand resignation and the accounting firm's concern about the size of officers' loans. Putzel didn't remember being informed about growing cash flow problems at OPM or about bounced checks. Nor was he told that Coopers believed OPM was insolvent. Nor was he told that Andrew Reinhard attended the weekly Coopers meetings where many of OPM's cash flow difficulties were revealed. In fact, Putzel had the impression that "OPM was doing a very brisk business and making a fair amount of money."[1]

By the close of the Wednesday meeting, both Hutner and Putzel believed the retention of the auditors would bring the matter to a head.

They believed the auditors would discover the wrongdoing and either force Goodman to disclose to the authorities or blow the whistle themselves. No reputable accounting firm—and it appeared the Big Eight firm of Ernst & Whinney would be retained—would stand still for Goodman's charades. But to protect the auditors from being misled, Singer Hutner decided to again retain Marvin Weissman to monitor the audit.

Over the next several days, Hutner continued to have meetings and conversations with interested parties. On Thursday, August 28, he had an all-day meeting with Myron Goodman. On Friday evening, he spoke to Alan Batkin of Lehman and to Marvin Weissman. And on Monday, Hutner spoke to David Sacks of Lehman. Hutner didn't recall the substance of any of these conversations.

One would think that all the recent events would have heightened the Singer Hutner lawyers' concerns and their memories about OPM. Goodman had recently told Hutner that Fox & Company had ended its engagement with OPM; the firm had been informed by David Sacks of Lehman that Coopers suspended its engagement with OPM because it was concerned about the size of the loans made to Goodman and Weissman, and they also knew Lehman had recently imposed a set of conditions on OPM. But Hutner's testimony did not indicate any increase in concern about these events—he would claim he was always concerned. On September 4, however, he became alarmed.

On Thursday morning, September 4, Hutner and Marvin Weissman went to Ernst & Whinney's offices at the Citicorp building on Lexington Avenue in New York to meet with Harry Manchar, an Ernst & Whinney partner handling the proposed OPM audit engagement. Manchar said he was pleased with the prospects of this project and saw no reason why Ernst & Whinney wouldn't accept it. Hutner recalled there was a lot of chitchat about OPM, its background, and so forth. Before they ended the meeting, Manchar said he would like to meet Goodman and talk more about the company. They set a tentative appointment for the following day.

In the atrium of the Citicorp building, Hutner noticed Weissman was looking very distraught.

"What are we doing?" Weissman asked Hutner.

"What do you mean by what are we doing?"

Weissman was visibly upset. Marvin Weissman was disturbed

because of Hutner's apparent willingness to drag Ernst & Whinney and a man like Harry Manchar into the OPM affair. He felt sorry for Hutner.

"Well, this is terrible. Why are you getting Ernst & Whinney or Harry Manchar involved in this thing for? Why don't you quit? Why don't you get out?"

"I don't know what you are talking about. Tell me what you mean."

"Well, you know whatever it is that Myron has been holding back about?"

"What about it? Do you know about it?" Hutner asked.

"I have had a discussion with Steve Lichtman, and it's much worse than we thought."

"Lichtman knows about this?"

"What happened was, I was having a discussion with Lichtman, and Lichtman asked me to guess how much was involved, and I said ten million. Lichtman told me to keep going. Twenty million, I said and he said, 'Keep going.' Thirty million, and he said, 'More.' "

"Holy s . . t," Hutner blurted.

Hutner was shocked. He never expected the fraud to be that high. By the time he walked back to his office, however, his shock had turned to anger.

When Hutner reached his office, he spoke with several Singer Hutner attorneys and with Putzel before heading down to OPM for a previously scheduled meeting with Goodman. Hutner was angry, and he went into Goodman's office shouting. Goodman was apparently upset by Hutner's rage because, for the first time, he began to provide Hutner with bits and pieces of the underlying facts. Goodman talked in a very "discursive, almost drugged state," Hutner remembered, as Goodman confessed that he had committed substantial frauds.[2] Goodman's "stream of consciousness," in which he told Hutner how he committed the fraud and who the victims were, continued into the evening.

The following morning, before his meeting with Manchar and Goodman, Hutner called Putzel and told him he had something important to discuss. They agreed to meet at the Yale Club on Vanderbilt Avenue at one o'clock.

Before the meeting with Manchar, Hutner, distraught over recent events, told Goodman that the Ernst & Whinney engagement placed the law firm in a serious dilemma, and he wished the accounting firm would decline the engagement, thus sparing him the task of disclosure. Hutner claimed he said little during the meeting with Manchar and Goodman. He just listened and marveled at the way Goodman was able to carry on in light of what had happened.

Early that afternoon, Hutner met Putzel at the Yale Club and told him about Goodman's revelations. Putzel remembers Hutner saying that the fraud had been accomplished at the expense of the Singer Hutner lawyers since Goodman used the firm to disseminate false documents to lessees and creditors. Hutner "was very surprised at the simplicity and obviousness of the thing." "I can't image why we didn't see it," Putzel recalled Hutner saying.[3] Both attorneys realized the fraud was far worse than either of them had anticipated.

"Do we have to resign?" Putzel remembered Hutner asking. Putzel said he wasn't certain, but as they talked, they both reached the conclusion that it was appropriate to resign since the attorneys had been "the unwitting and innocent instrument of the fraud." Hutner said he wanted "to get the hell out," but Putzel was concerned that the law firm not drop OPM like a "sack of potatoes." "Withdrawal had to be accomplished in a manner least likely to cause injury to the client," Putzel told Hutner. "I believe that we agreed," Putzel later testified, "that if the firm simply resigned, OPM would not survive, and Mr. Hutner was sensitive, as was I, not to have the law firm be the proximate cause of the downfall of OPM."[4] Putzel was going to review the ABA's code of professional responsibility to determine whether Singer Hutner was permitted to withdraw from the OPM engagement. They also decided to speak with Joseph McLaughlin, Andrew Lawler, and other Singer Hutner attorneys before going much further.

But by the time he left, Hutner knew the law firm would be resigning. It was clear to him that "Myron Goodman was bad news" and that Myron had abused the trust Hutner had placed in him.

Later that afternoon, Hutner told Mattioli to send the *American Banker* articles describing OPM's check-kiting conviction to Manchar. After reading these articles, Manchar would think twice about getting involved with OPM, Hutner thought.

In the meantime, Marvin Weissman was so upset about the attempts by Hutner and Goodman to bring in Ernst & Whinney "blind" that he consulted his own firm's lawyers. He felt sorry for Hutner, but he was concerned about the law firm continuing to close OPM deals after June 12, still not knowing the details of the fraud. On top of that, Singer Hutner was now helping Goodman drag an innocent party into this mare's nest. On the following Monday, September 15, Marvin Weissman met with Arthur Schneck, Rashba & Pokart's outside legal counsel. Schneck advised Marvin Weissman to send a letter to Singer Hutner rescinding the engagement he had entered with the law firm a week earlier. They also decided to call on Manchar.

The following Wednesday, Weissman and Schneck had lunch with Manchar and two other Ernst & Whinney partners. Schneck had advised Marvin Weissman not to disclose the OPM fraud to Manchar since that information was confidential. They decided to do the next best thing: provide a warning, but spare the details. Schneck simply told the Ernst & Whinney partners that OPM had been Rashba & Pokart's largest billing client when it had resigned in April 1980. Marvin Weissman and Schneck never revealed the confidential information, but their message was unmistakable. Within the next day or so, Ernst & Whinney declined the OPM engagement.

It is unfortunate that Rashba & Pokart didn't choose a similar approach with Fox or Lehman. Apparently, to Marvin Weissman it was more important to protect the innocent; the others should have known by then whom they were dealing with. Weissman never told Hutner that he had met Manchar. In fact, Weissman had no further contact with anyone related to the OPM fraud until he met with Hutner in February 1981.

Another Confession

Following his meeting with Hutner, Putzel called Lawler to request a meeting with Goodman to obtain more specific information about the fraud. A meeting was set for Tuesday, September 9.

That Tuesday evening at about seven o'clock, Hutner, Reinhard, Rubino, and Mattioli met with Goodman in Reinhard's office. Lawler and Putzel didn't attend because everyone believed Goodman might be inhibited by their presence. Goodman began by saying that he had been short of cash in April or May 1979 when he initiated the fraud. He said there were two basic types of illegal financing techniques that he employed. "One involved a situation where there was a lease between OPM and a lessee," Mattioli remembered, "and the terms of that lease would be misrepresented to the lender on a financing, either by way of inflated monthly rental or inflated, exaggerated lease term, and that sometimes the equipment description would be enlarged to include equipment that wasn't part of the actual lease agreed to by the lessee."[5]

The other technique of fraudulent financing that Goodman described was the fictitious or "phantom" leases—the entire transaction was fraudulent. In these situations, Goodman said he used false IBM bills of sale, which he obtained some years before from a person who was able to get a large batch of the documents. Where signatures from Rockwell personnel were needed, Goodman forged them, something he had practiced before signing.

In either case, Goodman told the stunned lawyers, he would ask Singer Hutner to prepare an equipment schedule for a particular lessee —and, he added, all of the fraudulent leases involved Rockwell International. Goodman said Rockwell's general counsel's office was lax, not as diligent as it should be. Whenever Goodman needed signatures from Rockwell personnel, he would "walk the documents" through Rockwell's offices himself. After Singer Hutner prepared the equipment schedule, the law firm would send it to OPM, and Goodman would either forge the lessees' signature onto the schedule or, if there was a legitimate but much less lucrative lease with Rockwell, he would switch equipment schedules and forward the legitimate one to Rockwell for signature. Once it was signed by Rockwell, Goodman would again switch the signature pages of the legitimate and illegitimate schedules and forward the latter to Singer Hutner to await the closing. The lender financed the transaction based on the fraudulent schedules. Following the closings, none of which were attended by Rockwell's legal counsel, Singer Hutner would give OPM the closing documentation for dispersal to Rockwell. And, depending on the type of fraud being committed, Goodman would either again switch the documentation before forwarding it to Rockwell or not send anything to the aerospace company.

Hutner, who asked Goodman most of the questions during the

meeting, asked him how he was able to get Rockwell to pay more to lenders than they were required to. Goodman claimed Rockwell made payments to OPM, and OPM paid the lenders on Rockwell's behalf. OPM made up the difference between what Rockwell had paid OPM and what was owed the lenders.

Goodman said the fraud amounted to around $30 to $45 million, but since he had been making payments on the fraudulent financings, he owed only about $30 million. He believed it would take nine to fifteen months to pay it back entirely. Hutner said he doubted that. Goodman responded with some "jibberish" about big deals in the pipeline, Hutner remembered, and encouraged everyone to have faith.[6]

Rubino told Goodman that before anything else was done, he would like a spread sheet identifying the victim banks, the dates of the fraudulent transactions, the amounts, and so on. Goodman said he would get that to them in a couple of days, along with the John Clifton letter.

After Goodman left, several lawyers discussed the propriety of continuing to have OPM involved in the middle of its transactions. Wouldn't it be wiser to have the law firm forward unexecuted documents directly to the lessee and have the lessee return the copies directly to Singer Hutner, rather than interposing OPM in the middle? Hutner recalled such a discussion, but he didn't remember a decision to change the practice.

The following day, OPM, still in the middle, closed a loan with the Crocker National Bank for a little over $2.2 million. Singer Hutner represented OPM at the closing. The deal was fraudulent.[7]

One week after Goodman's disclosure, the Singer Hutner partners met with Putzel to discuss what to do next. Mattioli remembered there was an "open examination of the views." One partner, Howard Chase, wanted the firm to go to the authorities with the information it had. Another partner, Morton Levine, suggested that the law firm immediately stop representing OPM. Putzel told the assembled group that the information they had obtained was privileged and that the firm was bound not to disclose it. But he did say the firm should resign and encourage Goodman to make restitution. But resignation should be accomplished in a way that was least injurious to OPM, he added. In the interim, the partners decided to obtain verification from lessees of the terms of each OPM deal.

The following day, September 16, Putzel, Alan Jacobs, and Mattioli discussed the mechanics of the third-party verification. Jacobs, the most familiar with the lease transactions, said Sidney Hasin was the person at Rockwell who should be contacted to verify the deals. Mattioli called Goodman several times that day to explain the verification procedure. Goodman was told that unless he authorized the procedure, Singer Hutner would not close the deal. Goodman claimed that such a practice could raise all kinds of problems with Rockwell. The verification procedure might expose the earlier frauds, he said, and could hinder OPM's efforts to make restitution. Goodman said he would have to think about it. Goodman's balking did not raise any new concerns by Mattioli that the fraud might be continuing. Nor did Putzel or Rubino worry when Mattioli told them about Goodman's posturing.

On September 18, Goodman called Mattioli from Chicago and told him to go ahead with the verification procedure on the OPM-Rockwell deal. Goodman said he wanted the deal closed in the next few days, and he didn't want anything to hold it up. He complained that the deal was to have closed weeks ago, and now the verification would delay it more. Could Mattioli expedite the procedure? Goodman wanted to know—could he get the confirmation letter out to Rockwell and back in one day? Mattioli told Goodman that they could express mail the letter to Hasin but, in any case, that Reinhard would handle it.

On September 18, the verification letter was express mailed to Sidney Hasin. Goodman, who learned from Reinhard or from Reinhard's secretary—he did not remember who—when and how the letter would be sent, dispatched Stephen Lichtman and Mannes Friedman from Chicago to Seal Beach, California, to intercept the verification letter. With absolutely no idea how they would locate the document, let alone sign it and get it back to Singer Hutner, Lichtman and Friedman took a night flight to Los Angeles and arrived at Seal Beach early that Friday morning.

As they entered the lobby of Rockwell's Information Systems Center (ISC) headquarters in Seal Beach, the Rockwell security guard recognized the OPM team and waved them through. At the same time —unbelievably—Lichtman and Friedman noticed a courier with the verification package entering the lobby. More incredible still, Hasin's secretary had just arrived. The two couldn't have choreographed the players any better had they directed the scene themselves. Quick on their feet, Lichtman and Friedman explained to Hasin's secretary that they had Singer Hutner forward documents to them in care of Hasin since, at the time, they didn't know where they were going to be staying. The story sounded reasonable enough, and Hasin's secretary allowed the courier to give the letter to Friedman.

Their job still incomplete, Lichtman entered Hasin's office and kept him busy by talking about where they should go to lunch—one of Hasin's favorite topics—while Friedman forged Hasin's signature on the verification form and, as Reinhard instructed in the cover letter, telecopied it to the law firm from Rockwell's own telecopy room. Late that afternoon, following Reinhard's directive to Hasin, they mailed the original letter back to New York from the Los Angeles International Airport. They were beginning to worry that the fraud might be exposed, so the two decided to share responsibility for intercepting the letter. Each held a corner of the envelope and dropped it into the mail slot; should the crimes become known, they would each be guilty of mail fraud.

The following day, Singer Hutner received the verification letter signed by Hasin—or so it was thought. On September 19, a deal was closed on an OPM-Rockwell transaction relating to Equipment Schedule 0–52–80, the schedule that was the subject of the verification letter. Bankers Life Company of Des Moines provided over $6 million in financing for the deal. Of course, Singer Hutner represented OPM at the closing and, of course, the deal was fraudulent.[8]

On the day of the closing, Alan Jacobs showed a letter to Putzel and Mattioli that he had received the day before from Robert Clare, an attorney from the large New York City law firm of White & Case. White & Case represented an OPM creditor, Bankers Trust Company. Clare was concerned about payments coming from OPM to Bankers Trust rather than from Rockwell, as it was stipulated in the finance documents. Putzel and Mattioli told Jacobs to avoid contact with Clare and, if Clare reached him, Jacobs should simply say he could not discuss it.

The same day, Jacobs received a call from Joel Peck of Lehman, who was urging Jacobs to contact an attorney of another creditor who was making similar complaints. Putzel and Mattioli advised Jacobs to handle Peck the same way.

On Monday, September 22, the Singer Hutner partners talked about resigning from the OPM engagement. Resignation would not be an easy task. Although the firm was permitted to resign, it had an obligation to withdraw in a manner that would do the least harm to OPM, according to their advisors. "The only lawyers the firm ever had were about to dump him," Hutner later testified, "and that was not an easy thing to do."[9] The law firm's decision was not made any easier by economic considerations—its economic considerations, not OPM's. The firm was about to end the engagement of its largest client, by far. Since June, it had collected over $2 million in fees from OPM. And there was the disconcerting prospect of losing these fees to a bankruptcy trustee if OPM went bankrupt. Indeed, it was not an easy decision.

But most of the partners voted in favor of resignation. All but two —Andrew Reinhard and Alan Jacobs. Jacobs said he was troubled by the prospect of resigning, and he favored some alternative way of continuing to represent OPM. Reinhard really didn't offer a view; he merely suggested that the partnership might be better off thinking about it overnight and voting on the resignation in the morning. And that's what was decided.

The next morning, the partners voted to resign from the OPM engagement. At first, Reinhard abstained from the vote, but Hutner insisted that he cast his ballot, and he then voted in favor of resignation. While offering his vote, Reinhard suggested that OPM be given an adequate period of time to replace Singer Hutner and that, in the interim, the firm should continue to close OPM deals.

At about noon, Goodman arrived to meet with the partners and to hear their decision. He first met with Hutner, who told him the firm had decided to resign. Hutner said that OPM would be better served by legal counsel that did not have the knowledge Singer Hutner had; and, besides, the partners no longer felt comfortable representing OPM because of the massive size of Goodman's fraud. Hutner later testified, "that having decided that we wanted out, we wanted to get out as fast as possible. If the house of cards was going to collapse . . . we wanted as much distance between him and us as possible."[10]

After a short time, Reinhard and several other Singer Hutner partners joined Hutner and Goodman. Goodman began to read uninterrupted from a long typewritten memo he had prepared. Among other things, Goodman said the following:

> It appears to me the time is right for review with you, certain matters and problems which I feel either the firm or OPM must resolve so that we can move forward in a productive manner and maintain the relationship which commenced approximately ten years ago, when with a telephone call to my dear friend, Andrew B. Reinhard, I felt that the firm of Rappaport, Rubino and Pincus,* should represent my "tiny" company. If for reasons which you choose to discuss with me or, you choose not to, I expect that if you determine to resolve the matters and/or problems we can look forward to many, many more prosperous and successful years together. . . .
>
> As you know . . . I am a sincere and dedicated individual, whose only basic requirement . . . is that I be treated *fairly, professionally,* and that a *mutual personal relationship develops.* That is, most of you know me to be fair and generous with people I develop a close, personal bond with. However, that close, personal bonding can only remain solidified if both "ends of the bookends" feel that the bond is true, sincere, and not false. . . .
>
> However, if one part of the "bookend" does not sincerely want to continue being bounded to the other part, then, rather than either end of the bookends "fooling one another," I suggest that there should be a severance of the relationship.
>
> Before I go into the matters and problems, I would like to reiterate that in no way, shape, or form, do I want, nor expect, that the "bondage of the bookends" be kept intact in an immoral, illegal, or insincere manner.[11]

Goodman went on to say that he didn't like some of the things he had heard Singer Hutner attorneys had been saying about OPM. Most of all, Goodman said, he didn't like the way Singer Hutner was treating OPM employees. He said the firm had shown "a complete lack of professionalism and understanding" and, in a sense, it was undermining the relationship Goodman had with his own employees. He continued:

> if there is any asset that I cherish more than anything else, it is the loyalty of certain individuals at OPM to the company and to me as an individual. That loyalty, I can assure you will remain intact. . . .

*The predecessor law firm to Singer Hutner Levine & Seeman.

The last thing I want done, assuming that we remain as "attorney-client" is that dedicated individuals, who would not only give of their time and family lives, but with what I would venture to say, give their life, I will not tolerate imposing upon them any more fear or unsolicited representations. I truly feel right now that if the firm [Singer Hutner] wants to "protect its ass," there are many, many discrete ways in which that it can. However, I don't want to see another Hoby Shapiro or John Clifton or, Lehman Brothers. . . .

I do not need to remind you that we together have gone through many, many difficult times. We have also gone through many, many happy and joyous periods. However, in order for OPM to maintain its viability and survival, as long as I choose to keep the firm retained by OPM, you must work with me, around-the-clock, if necessary. . . .

On a personal note . . . I feel deep down with many, many hours of thought behind it, that an individual or individuals who never heard of OPM; who never heard of the leasing business; who did not even understand or try to understand the relationship which I believe exists between OPM and Singer Hutner; and, who obviously, are "white-shoed and ultra-Fascist attorneys" determined the future of OPM and Singer Hutner. There is no question in my mind that your counsel is representing you "by the book." Let me just say that I thought that "a little bending of the book" might be appropriate in this matter. However, as a number of my employees have noted, Singer Hutner is acting no different than those individuals or firms who decided to sever relationships because they were scared. Isn't an individual allowed his "day in court"? I would think that prior to a number of decisions which have been made between you and your counsel, it would have been discussed with me out of sheer courtesy. Most of you know me; if something is logical and proper, I will try to do it, but remember one thing, that is, part of the cause of the recent events is because I, Myron S. Goodman, felt that here was an exceptional bondage between the "bookends" and did what I did (if I did anything so terrible) because of other people. Singer Hutner was one of those persons or more appropriately, firms. Sometimes in one's life we must put aside the "book" and look deep down into each one of our soul's and determine what is proper in a given situation, irrespective of the "book." Maybe I made the mistake. That is, I should have looked out for myself, rather than the other people. I didn't. Whether that is good or bad, only God knows. However, God put us here to perform his precepts, and he did not put us here with the intent of telling us how to reach the end. The means to reaching the end are held in the individual. Whatever [in original] the end might be, and, I must reiterate that only God knows what the end is, then the means and ways to reach that end were put in our hands. I do not believe that I have to be subjected to an outside counsel who could care less about OPM or me as an individual when we have a problem before us which is resolvable. . . .

I think that we all have to resolve in our minds that we will either be kept "bonded" as bookends, or sever our relationship. It would be very, very sad for me, to have to ask Singer Hutner to resign. We have come a long, long way together. Through the ups and downs of the American business community. However, if we are to remain bonded (and indeed, I hope we will), we must resolve the above and a few other issues which can be discussed. Throughout the years, indeed, Singer Hutner has helped OPM in more ways than one. However, realistically, I believe that we have been grateful and certainly have helped Singer Hutner in many, many ways. To break the bond of the "bookends" now would be a disgrace and lead to a period of personal depression by, I am sure, the majority of the firm, and myself. Let us not allow that to happen.

About eight o'clock that evening, the same group convened for yet another meeting at the Singer Hutner offices. Hutner said he didn't want Goodman to think that the law firm wouldn't consider alternatives to a complete termination, but to continue working with OPM, Goodman would have to abide by certain conditions. Hutner added that Singer Hutner's involvement would also depend on what the spread sheets revealed. Before the meeting closed, Hutner told Goodman that the firm expected payment of the fees OPM owed them over the next week—$250,000 on Monday and another $250,000 on Wednesday.[12]

At the conclusion of the discussion, the group of lawyers and Goodman walked out of the room. Goodman stopped at the head of the staircase and spoke to the group, now several steps behind him. He was shaken with anger and told them, "If you do this and bring down the company, I will bring down this firm. You can't do this to my grandmother and parents, and I will bring down this firm."[13] Goodman then took the cane he held in his hand and heaved it, shattering it on the marble landing below. He then walked down the stairs into

Reinhard's office where, to everyone's surprise, waited Mordecai Weissman.[14] After ranting and raving for several more hours, Goodman and Weissman left.

The next day, Hutner received a message that David Sacks of Lehman called. After consulting with several Singer Hutner attorneys, Hutner decided not to return the call until late Monday—after the law firm had received its back payment from OPM. Howard Chase thought that if Goodman knew Singer Hutner was having discussions with Lehman, he might use the fees as leverage to influence what was said to Sacks. It would be better to wait until late Monday before calling him.[15]

That same day, September 24, Singer Hutner sent Goodman a copy of its letter of resignation. At Goodman's request, the law firm altered the language of the letter in a crucial way. The draft letter spoke of the law firm's "resignation"; the executed letter read "mutual termination." Hutner testified that the change was made to mitigate the effect of the split on OPM's future business. The law firm also agreed to describe the split to others, like Lehman, using those terms.

Following several days of lengthy meetings, Singer Hutner sent letters to Goodman on Saturday, September 27, requesting permission to verify the terms of a number of transactions OPM was contemplating. It also again requested the spread sheets itemizing the fraudulent deals OPM had entered into and the payment of back fees to the law firm.

That Monday, Goodman sent a confidential letter to Reinhard, authorizing verification on some, but not all, of the deals listed by the law firm. "I have not included the entire listing as outlined in your firm's letter of September 27, 1980," Goodman wrote, "[because] I want to thoroughly think through whatever ramifications there might be, as they relate to specific lessees."[16] No one at the Singer Hutner law firm realized that some of the Rockwell transactions listed in the September 27 letter but omitted from Goodman's letter had been closed over the summer; most of them turned out to be fraudulent. Nor did anyone become suspicious about Goodman's approving verification on some of the deals but not on others.

That same day, Goodman again met with the Singer Hutner partners. At the outset of the meeting, Goodman made some reference to the holiday season that had just passed, and for several minutes more, he read biblical passages to the assembled group. Mattioli recalled Goodman saying, in effect, "Sometimes the legitimate purposes of a man's activities are not apparent, or understandable by those about him, and in that event, the people about such an individual have to have some degree of faith in the legitimacy of his purposes."[17] Following his oration, Goodman once again tried to convince the Singer Hutner lawyers to stay on. He spoke positively about OPM's future. But all of this positive talk turned sour when Goodman was asked by Jay Seeman about the spread sheets. Goodman told the group that he would deliver the spread sheets the next day. He went on to say that the total amount of bad deals was about $100 million; the balance owed was in the range of $80 to $90 million. There was total silence. The amount Goodman had just given was twice as high as the amount he had previously offered. Could it be higher? several of them wondered; after a few moments, they repeatedly asked him that question. Goodman denied any such possibility.

The following day, Goodman delivered the spread sheets to Singer Hutner. It took the law firm a week to uncover the disturbing news that the fraud had continued throughout the summer of 1980. Virtually all the officers' certificates Goodman provided Singer Hutner were as false as the deals they certified. Singer Hutner had closed over $65 million in fraudulent deals since June 11, the day they had first learned something was wrong. Goodman had been lying to them, using them to perpetrate his massive fraud throughout the summer.

Of course, they were resigning; they were getting out. But since Goodman had lied to them, weren't they free to go to the authorities to put an end to the fraud? Again, they believed the frauds were over, and they also believed they were required by the ABA code of ethics to keep silent. As Hutner testified, he believed the fraud had ended because "it was inconsistent with sanity, and I believe Myron had a degree of sanity, at least in the way he conducted his business, to come in and confess in the full way that he did to the massive frauds that he had committed and at the same time intend to continue doing it."[18]

Since Goodman's confession dealt with past not ongoing frauds —the crucial condition on which the attorney-client privilege turns— the attorneys reasoned that the law firm was obligated to keep silent.

Putzel's November 12 letter to the law firm, summarizing his advice, stated the following:

> You are . . . obligated to respect the confidence of such disclosures, meaning that we were defrauded during the summer, and in spite of your understandable chagrin that the client had lied to you, to refrain from acting in a manner detrimental to its interests. We advised you specifically that precipitate withdrawal, even though prompted by disclosure of recent frauds perpetrated upon your firm, would be inconsistent with your firm's obligation to OPM.[19]

How many times would Goodman be allowed to commit frauds and confess to them before the law firm would consider the crimes ongoing? In other words, "How many bites at the apple would Myron get before past frauds became a continuing fraud for the purposes of professional responsibility?" Hutner was asked by Arthur Mathews of Wilmer, Cutler & Pickering. Hutner never gave a clear answer. At first he said Goodman had taken only two bites up until that point, but later he asked, somewhat sarcastically, "How large is the apple?"[20]

Over the next few months, Singer Hutner continued to represent OPM on transactions while the company looked for replacement counsel. It never sought to withdraw opinion letters that creditors had relied on in the past—opinion letters they now knew were false. Indeed, they were advised that doing so would also violate the attorney-client privilege. "Putzel made it clear to us, and it made good sense to me then and it makes good sense to me now," Hutner affirmed, "that the withdrawal of an opinion letter, especially after the firm's resignation, without explaining the reasons . . . would clearly be a violation of the attorney-client privilege."[21] The law firm did, however, alter the language in the opinion letters it used on OPM transactions during the months of October to December. They also refused to close any Rockwell deals.

Following the advice of Putzel, the Singer Hutner lawyers also took steps to prevent Goodman from permanently financing or "rolling over" certain bridge financings they knew were fraudulent. On about October 10, the law firm sent a letter to Goodman informing him of its intent to prevent this refinancing. It told him the firm would keep the files related to the bridge financings—files the firm mistakenly thought were necessary to obtain a new note—and it would be writing Lehman advising that "you [Goodman] do not intend to refinance these transactions."[22] Soon after sending Goodman the letter, Singer Hutner sent Goodman a second letter that was identical to the first, with one essential difference. The firm told *Goodman* to send a letter to Lehman telling the investment banker that he had no intention of refinancing the bridge loans.

By the middle of November, Goodman hadn't met Singer Hutner's demands. Mattioli drafted a letter on November 17, directing Goodman to comply "on or before November 20, 1980"—just one day before one of the bridge loans was to mature. Singer Hutner did not send the letter until November 26. To make matters worse, it prolonged the compliance date to December 3, 1980, which was two days beyond the maturity dates of four more bridge financings. Needless to say, the fraudulent bridge loans were rolled over.

While Goodman searched for another law firm, he bolstered his own in-house legal counsel, which had begun to assume a larger role in OPM's operations. This created another problem for the Singer Hutner lawyers: Should Gary Simon, OPM's general counsel, be told about the frauds? Singer Hutner wanted to inform Simon, but Goodman didn't want him told, so the lawyers said nothing. "Goodman personified the client," and he "was making it very clear, as the client, that he didn't want Simon to be told," Putzel later testified.[23] He further stated, "We had no right to ignore management's instructions . . . if we did," he continued, "we would be breaching the attorney-client privilege." Putzel didn't recall doing any legal research on the issue.

Instead of telling Simon about the frauds, the lawyers sent a letter specifying verification procedures that they advised him to follow on OPM transactions. Simon was outraged. He viewed the letter as a stumbling block, another attempt by Singer Hutner to obstruct the transition of law firms. Simon used the verification procedures, but through Myron Goodman. Singer Hutner didn't anticipate this, of course. Nor did the Singer Hutner attorneys know that Gary Simon had never before closed an OPM transaction. His instructor would be Myron S. Goodman.

Putzel felt that the verification memo was an adequate safeguard to protect Simon. He later said, "My expectation was that once Mr.

Simon saw this memorandum, that he would ask the questions that a prudent lawyer should ask once he receives a memorandum such as this."[24]

The New Lawyers

In mid-October, at the urging of Goodman, Mannes Friedman called his brother-in-law, Sidney Kwestel, a litigator with one of New York City's largest law firms—Kaye Scholer Fierman Hays and Handler—to solicit its interest in taking on OPM as a client. A meeting was scheduled for that afternoon.

Goodman, Friedman, Lichtman, and Simon arrived at Kaye Scholer's Park Avenue offices, and Goodman made his pitch to several senior people at the firm. Now quite skilled at such presentations, Goodman's performance was "superb," Kwestel said, as Goodman described OPM's business and projected growth, which he claimed was "going straight up."[25] The final hook was all he really needed. He told the lawyers that he had paid Singer Hutner $50,000 a week and estimated that OPM would be paying Kaye Scholer about $25,000 per week. Goodman told the group that Singer Hutner and OPM agreed to "mutually terminate"; no reason for the split was offered. Prior to the meeting, however, Goodman told Kwestel that Singer Hutner couldn't handle OPM's workload.

Shortly afterward, Peter Fishbein, a partner at Kaye Scholer and a longtime friend of Joseph Hutner's, called Hutner and asked "if there was anything he should be aware of" in considering OPM as a client. Hutner, who had previously consulted with Putzel about what he should say, told Fishbein, that "the decision to terminate was mutual and that there was mutual agreement that the circumstances of termination would not be discussed." When Fishbein told him the firm would probably accept the OPM engagement, Hutner said he had nothing to add.

At the second meeting with Goodman, Kaye Scholer agreed to accept the OPM engagement. The firm wasn't quite sure how it was going to staff the OPM account just yet, but the opportunity was too lucrative to pass up. Fishbein, knowing that Singer Hutner planned to fire some associates after losing its largest client, again called Hutner to see about the availability of the associates. Although several of the fired associates hadn't found work, Hutner said, none were available. The implication was strong enough, but Fishbein didn't pursue it.

Kwestel also did some checking of his own to learn how to staff the OPM account. He contacted his friend and neighbor, Andrew Reinhard. When Kwestel asked him about the termination, Reinhard told Kwestel not to press him.

Kaye Scholer went on to close—or assist OPM's attorneys in closing— more than $15 million in fraudulent deals from December 1980 until February 1981. Kaye Scholer received over $135,000 for three months' work. It never suspected fraud, and Singer Hutner never told anyone in the firm. Nor did Singer Hutner tell anyone else.

Lehman Decides to Terminate

By mid-September, OPM had not retained a Big Eight accounting firm, though Lehman had imposed a September 29 deadline to do so. Even before September 29 had passed, however, Lehman decided to resign. Alan Batkin, Lewis Glucksman, and David Sacks all claimed the resignation was unrelated to Goodman's failure to retain one of the Big Eight. Nor did Lehman say its resignation was related to any suspicions it may have had. Lehman claimed it had none. The resignation wasn't related to anything Hutner may have said to his friend, Sacks, either. Nor was it related to Coopers' resignation. Instead, Lehman's resignation came about because OPM's deals were getting smaller and smaller, the investment banker claimed. The company was simply too much trouble, according to the testimony given by the underwriters.

On the day Lehman resigned, Sacks called Hutner as a matter of courtesy—after all, Hutner had brought OPM to Lehman. Sacks remembered Hutner saying, "I'm very happy that you called me because I was trying to find a way to tell you . . . [we too] have terminated our engagement."

"Why?" Sacks asked.

"I have a deal with Myron in which neither of us will comment other than [to say] that the engagement has been terminated," Hutner responded.[26] Sacks, also a lawyer, knew not to push it.

On October 2, Robert Clare, unable to get satisfaction from Singer Hutner, called Alan Batkin about his client's payment problems with OPM. This time, one of OPM's checks had bounced. Clare also found out from Alan Jacobs about the OPM-Singer Hutner split. Jacobs told Clare he couldn't discuss the reason for the split. Clare asked if Batkin knew anything about it. Batkin didn't but suggested that perhaps White & Case might want to take on the OPM engagement. Clare said he would discuss it with several partners and get back to him. Batkin never mentioned that Lehman, too, had quit OPM. Fortunately for White & Case, it declined Batkin's offer to take the OPM account.

At about this time, Glucksman called his friend, Clarence Frame, at the First National Bank of St. Paul (FNBSP), and told him Lehman was resigning from the OPM account. Glucksman said that although Lehman was leaving, it had lined up a former Lehman partner, Warren Goeltz, to help place OPM debt. Since the FNBSP knew Goeltz, Glucksman thought he would be helpful to them.

On October 6, Batkin called Jeffrey Werner to tell him about Lehman's resignation. Batkin explained that OPM's deals had changed and that the fees were getting smaller and smaller and that Lehman had decided it just wasn't worth the effort any longer. Werner was shocked. He had no idea that Lehman was even considering resignation. But to mitigate the effect of this latest development, Batkin told Werner about the Goeltz arrangement. Goeltz would use a Lehman office, Batkin said, but would act independently of the firm. Batkin also told Werner that the First National Bank of Jefferson Parish (FNJ) stock had been sold at a profit and that OPM's financial statements for 1979 had been completed, showing a positive net worth. OPM had also decided to sever its relationships with its legal counsel—Singer Hutner—Batkin explained. Goodman apparently had been dissatisfied with the law firm for some time. Lehman recommended the New York City firm of Cleary, Gottlieb, Steen & Hamilton to replace Singer Hutner; Goodman was considering it. Batkin didn't recall much of this conversation.

Notwithstanding Batkin's mixing optimism with bad news,

Werner thought that, under the circumstances, the FNBSP should stop making loans to OPM, but the subject never came up at the bank until the middle of October. What Werner didn't know was that the bank stock had not been sold and that the draft financial statements submitted by Fox showed that OPM had a negative net worth of $21 million, not a positive net worth, as Batkin had said.

Three days later, Batkin called Andrew Reinhard to see if he could find out why Singer Hutner was terminating its relationship with OPM. Reinhard said he could not reveal the firm's reason for resigning but told Batkin that the law firm would continue to represent OPM and issue opinion letters until a new law firm was brought on board. Despite the contention by Batkin, Glucksman, and Sacks that Lehman terminated its relationship with OPM because OPM deals were getting too small, Batkin was clearly trying to gain some assurance from Reinhard that there were no improprieties to be concerned about. Batkin later testified:

> I felt that I could take a certain degree of comfort if a law firm indicated that they were going to continue to represent the client and issue opinions at a closing, and if there was some reason, some problem that they might have known about which led to their resignation, if such [a] problem existed, presumably it was not sufficiently serious to interfere with them issuing their opinion and continuing to represent the company.[27]

On October 17, Werner met with Batkin and Goeltz to discuss the OPM situation. The resignation by Lehman was going to make it difficult for the FNBSP Bank to continue financing OPM transactions, Werner said, since they believed they had a primary relationship with Lehman, not with OPM. Further, Werner said the lack of OPM financial statements since 1978 violated one of the bank's basic lending policies. To induce the St. Paul bank to continue financing OPM deals, Lehman would have to continue to act as OPM's financial advisor or, as Goodman later put it, as an "off-the-record consultant."[28]

On October 23, Werner met with the bank's senior vice-president, Andrew Sall. Both Werner and Sall decided that the FNBSP would no longer provide financing on OPM transactions. Werner called Batkin and told him of the bank's decision.

The Fall of the House of Cards

O N THURSDAY, September 18, 1980, Robert Clare, an attorney for White & Case, wrote Alan Jacobs complaining that a client of his —Bankers Trust Company—had been receiving payments from OPM rather than from Rockwell; several installments were delinquent as well. Jacobs, who had heard Myron Goodman's confession to the massive Rockwell fraud a week earlier, knew that OPM's control over the flow of payments was one of the ways Goodman was able to carry out his crimes, but he had been advised by Henry Peter Putzel to avoid discussing the issue with Clare. He decided not to respond to Clare's inquiry.

In October, Clare called Alan Batkin with the same complaint. Batkin said he'd look into the matter, but he failed to mention that Lehman Brothers Kuhn Loeb had terminated its relationship with OPM at the end of September. That same month, Clare again contacted Jacobs, who told him about the OPM-Singer Hutner Levine & Seeman split but added that Clare shouldn't be concerned about it.

On November 3, the matter still unresolved, Clare tried another approach that broke one of Goodman's unwritten rules. He made direct contact with Rockwell International. Clare called Daniel Byrnes, a Rockwell attorney, and complained about the payment problems. Clare read a list of equipment schedules to Byrnes for which payments either were lagging or were coming from the wrong source. The list included three phantom leases, Equipment Schedule 79–26, Equipment Schedule 80–1, and Equipment Schedule 80–2. Two days later, Clare again spoke to Byrnes and, this time, with Sidney Hasin. Neither Rockwell official noticed the fictitious equipment schedules on Clare's list. A month later, Clare mailed to Byrnes copies of the consent and agreements on the problem transactions. Still there was no reaction to the phony leases.

At that point—in early December—John Hayes, who had assumed Hasin's responsibilities for lease documentation, searched the disorganized Rockwell files for the leases listed in Clare's letter. He found all the leases except the phantoms, which was not too surprising since they didn't exist as far as Rockwell was concerned. When Hayes asked for an explanation, Hasin suggested that perhaps Clare had mixed up his numbers. Hasin's suggestion was not seriously considered by Hayes, who continued his search.

Robert Clare had received no reply from Rockwell for nearly two months. Bankers Trust was receiving payments during that period— it apparently didn't matter that those payments were made by OPM. But on January 23, Clare again called Byrnes on behalf of a different White & Case client who had also experienced late payments on OPM-Rockwell deals. The following week, Clare forwarded copies of the consent and agreements on the most recent problem transactions, including a phantom and two altered leases. Once more, Byrnes didn't notice the fraudulent documents or the phony equipment schedule numbers. Meanwhile, Hayes was still hunting for the missing documents that Clare had notified Rockwell about in November. In late January, Rockwell's bookkeeping department asked OPM to deliver copies of the missing documents.

Knowing that they could never present the lender version of the missing equipment schedules to Rockwell officials, the fraud team was forced to create a new set, a set that would appear so inconsequential, they reasoned, that the large aerospace company could easily have misplaced or overlooked the documents. A meeting with Samuel Ganz and Mannes Friedman was scheduled for Wednesday, February 11, in California.

Ganz and Friedman arrived at the Information Systems Center (ISC) in Seal Beach early that Wednesday morning. Armed with newly created equipment schedules they believed could easily be passed off as insignificant Rockwell leases, the two OPM couriers were nervous but confident that the fraud team's handiwork would pass the test. Unbeknownst to them, however, the diligent Hayes had obtained from Bankers Trust the lender version of the missing documents, which had arrived the evening before.

Into the ISC conference room walked Friedman and Ganz with OPM's version of the missing leases. Hayes had his own version. Comparisons of the two sets of documents were shocking. The lender's copy of Equipment Schedule 80–1 revealed a monthly rent of $25,566, OPM's $231. The discrepancy in the monthly rental for Equipment Schedule 80–2 amounted to nearly $32,000. Friedman, who was becoming adept at the fraud game, never missed a beat, however, and offered an explanation that seemed somewhat plausible to Hayes, but not quite right. Several calls from Friedman to Goodman produced more of the same. To Hayes, something just didn't add up. Moreover, Friedman's explanation and behavior bothered him.

After Friedman's departure, Hayes returned to his office and examined more closely the two sets of documents. It was then that he noticed the "rather poor forgeries,"[1] of Robert Petersen's signature. If the signature didn't give the bogus leases away, Petersen's title would have—it was wrong.

Hayes immediately notified Rockwell officials, who called Clare in New York. A meeting was scheduled for Wednesday, February 18, at the Bankers Trust offices at 280 Park Avenue.

On Wednesday morning, attorneys for Rockwell and for Bankers Trust met and compared documents on several leases. It became quite apparent that significant discrepancies existed on a number of leases. That afternoon a call was made to John Martin, the U.S. attorney for the Southern District of New York, and an appointment was scheduled for later that day.

Highs and Lows in the Life of Myron Goodman

At the same time the Rockwell attorneys were meeting at Bankers Trust, Sidney Hasin was with Myron Goodman at Goodman's hotel room in the Hyatt near the Los Angeles International Airport. Hasin, who had recently submitted a letter to Rockwell announcing his early retirement, but coincidentally neglected to say that he was going to work for OPM since "they didn't ask," claimed he and Goodman were discussing the future of OPM Data Services.[2] At about 11 A.M., Mary Kyle, Hasin's secretary, called Hasin at the Hyatt. Sounding quite upset, Kyle told Hasin that the locks on his office door had been changed and that his files had been taken to the eighth floor at the ISC.

Hasin, confused and angry about what had taken place, said he had no idea why his files would have been impounded. He told Goodman what had happened, and although the implication was obvious to Goodman, his demeanor was unchanged. He placated Hasin, telling him, "Well, you have so many important contracts, files and so forth, I'm sure they wanted control over all of these before you left."[3] Hasin returned to Seal Beach to find out more about the impoundment. Goodman left for a previously scheduled luncheon engagement with Maury Dahn, Hasin's boss, and Dalton Davis, the ISC controller.

At lunch, Dahn and Davis told Goodman that the B–1 bomber and space shuttle projects would require an increase in Rockwell's computer capacity, implying that OPM stood to do very well once Rockwell was given the green light. Knowing about the problems that beset OPM, Rockwell was trying to obtain a release of an IBM mainframe that OPM had on sublease from Rockwell. Goodman, one minute believing the jig was up, the next, being offered more Rockwell business, relaxed. The Rockwell representatives had him where they wanted him. They obtained Goodman's signature.

On his return to Seal Beach, Hasin was told by Linda Holman, Dahn's secretary, that Dahn wanted to tell him personally what was going on. Some time later, Dahn called Holman and told her that lunch was taking longer than anticipated and that Hasin should meet him at 8 A.M. the following morning.

At eight the next morning, Hasin met with Dahn, who told him that there were possible "improper deals regarding OPM" and that he wanted Hasin to meet on Friday morning with Charles Hart, Rockwell's chief legal counsel. Later that day, Goodman called Hasin to find out whether he knew anything more. Hasin told him that the problems were related to OPM, but he didn't know anything else. Now realizing that the end was near, Goodman asked Hasin if he could be of any assistance—should he stay in town? No, he might just as well go back to New York, Hasin replied.

Before Goodman's flight lifted off the ground that afternoon, he learned that subpoenas had been delivered to the OPM offices.

The Grand Jury Subpoenas Arrive and the Cover-up Begins

On the afternoon of February 19, 1981, Bruce Woods, a U.S. postal inspector, served a subpoena to OPM and individual subpoenas to OPM officers, Joel Klein, Allen Ganz, Peter Cimino, and Hoby Shapiro. Gary Simon accepted their subpoena on behalf of the company. The others, with the exception of Shapiro, who had left OPM a year earlier, accepted their subpoenas in person. Simon then met with Michael Weinberg, and they both decided Goodman and Weissman should be contacted in California; they were scheduled to return to New York that afternoon. Simon asked Ruth Holloway, Goodman's secretary, to reach him in California.

Simon spoke to Goodman for only a few minutes. He said Goodman seemed sullen. Goodman told him to stay at the office, and he would get back to him.

About fifteen minutes later, Simon received a phone call from Andrew Lawler, who said that he represented the company and that he wanted a copy of the subpoenas. Simon told Lawler that he had never heard of him and that he needed confirmation that Lawler did represent OPM. Goodman called Simon again and confirmed that Lawler did represent OPM and had represented it since the summer of 1980. Several more calls were exchanged. Goodman told Simon that "he didn't know what this was about,"[4] but it was clear to Simon that he was upset about something. Goodman asked Simon to make arrangements for them to charter a flight from California and have Goodman's chauffeur pick them up at the airport.

Back in New York, Goodman met with other OPM officers involved in the Rockwell fraud—Allen Ganz, Stephen Lichtman, Mannes Friedman, and Jeffry Resnick. They were told they were going to have a "hang tough" attitude. They then proceeded to destroy and remove OPM documents relating to Rockwell. Margo Carrao, one of the secretaries in the OPM executive area, reported that the paper-shredding machine was working overtime that day; Goodman even opened the machine to mix up the paper so that no one would try to piece the shreds together. Ganz told Resnick to destroy a Vydec disk that had contained Rockwell equipment schedules financed since the fall of 1980. Resnick cut up the disk and "flushed it down the toilet."[5]

Resnick and others removed documents from Goodman's office closet and took them to Goodman's home on Long Island. Some time later, Ganz and Resnick moved five files from Ganz's office; Ganz then transported them to his home and hid them under his house. Lichtman suggested that he burn the documents in his fireplace, but Ganz was worried that he'd be discovered by his wife. He was also uncomfortable with the image of himself crouched next to the fireplace, burning incriminating material. Although he told the others he had burned the documents, he actually dumped them into trash cans behind his house.[6]

Gary Simon met Goodman and Weissman in Goodman's office at about 7:00 A.M., February 20. Goodman pointed to six or seven files of documents and told Simon that they contained all the material he needed to respond to the subpoena. Simon didn't learn until some time later that Goodman and others kept or destroyed the "hot documents," as they came to be called.

More evidence was destroyed in the weeks that followed as the group met and planned their cover story. Their imaginations apparently tiring at this point, the team concocted an implausible story that the fraud was carried out by Goodman alone. Each player planned to deny any knowledge of fraudulent activity, and each believed the tale would work. Call it wishful thinking or logic at this point, Ganz argued, "[Goodman] had Singer Hutner duped. He had Lehman duped. Why couldn't he have OPM people duped?"

Goodman even planned to spare Weissman from prosecution.

Over the years, Goodman had accumulated a briefcase full of documents that he kept in a closet at his home, documents that implicated Weissman in the early frauds. In late February or early March, he took the briefcase to Weissman's house less than a mile away, and together they burned the documents in a fireplace.

The Aftermath

On Sunday, February 22, Sidney Hasin called Goodman at home. He wanted to hear from Goodman's lips about the improprieties that Rockwell's attorneys had told him about on Friday morning. "I have to see my lawyer," Goodman replied and hung up.[7] That was the last time Hasin ever spoke to Goodman.

Investigations ensued everywhere. At Rockwell, Hasin was asked to postpone his retirement to examine documents relating to the fraud. While aiding the Rockwell investigation, Hasin recalled a set of documents that Lichtman had sent him the summer before. He remembered asking Lichtman to update some of the Rockwell files. Lichtman had sent Hasin a set of three-ring binders full of documents during the summer of 1980. Inadvertently, Lichtman sent a chart, what the OPM trustee called the "smoking gun," listing twelve phantom leases and two other altered leases. The chart included the equipment schedule numbers, the types of equipment, the length of leases, and the rental. Hasin claimed he didn't open the binder until October, and he didn't notice the smoking gun. Again, in January, while cleaning his office, Hasin opened the binder. He discarded the entire contents of the binder *except* for the smoking gun and took the notebook to his home because he thought "he would like to look at it at some point later in time."[8] The events in February and March triggered Hasin's return to the smoking gun, and when he examined it carefully—he claimed for the first time—its significance was unmistakable. He wrote at the top of the page, "Not reviewed until 3/23/81."[9]

On Friday, February 26, Myron Goodman resigned. On March 11, OPM filed for court protection from creditors under Chapter 11 of the federal bankruptcy laws. At the time of the bankruptcy, a subsequent audit revealed that OPM had a negative net worth of $412 million; yet several days before filing for bankruptcy, Stephen Kutz told Goodman he had a way "to make OPM look good on its financial statements."[10] Two weeks later, Irving Picard, the U.S. trustee, appointed James P. Hassett as the OPM trustee. Hassett and the trustee's counsel, the Washington law firm of Wilmer, Cutler & Pickering, conducted an investigation of the fraud and activities of OPM's officers for over two years, at a cost of more than $2.5 million. On April 25, 1983, the trustee submitted a 600-page report documenting the investigation.

A dozen blocks from OPM, Audrey Strauss, an assistant U.S. attorney, conducted a parallel but isolated investigation that led to criminal convictions of Myron Goodman, Mordecai Weissman, Allen Ganz, Stephen Lichtman, Martin Shulman, Mannes Friedman, and Jeffry Resnick. All except Resnick served time at the Allenwood Federal Prison Camp in Montgomery, Pennsylvania.

U.S. Attorney Strauss was able to crack the cover story when Allen Ganz learned that certain testimony given in the trustee's investigation linked him to the fraud. Ganz met with Lichtman and Friedman in a parking lot and told them he planned to confess his role in the frauds to the authorities. Several days later, Lichtman and Friedman agreed to come clean as well, and all three went to the U.S. attorney's office shortly afterward. Allen Ganz was able to exchange his cooperation for the U.S. attorney's agreement not to seek an indictment of his father, Sam.

Both Shulman and Resnick continued to hang tough. Sticking to the cover story and unaware that their partners had confessed to federal authorities, both Shulman and Resnick committed perjury in testimony they provided in the bankruptcy hearings. Following Resnick's false testimony, Ganz lured the unsuspecting Resnick into a conversation in which he admitted his involvement in the fraud and its cover-up. The U.S. attorney recorded that conversation. Federal prosecutors also convicted Richard Monks, Josef Verner, Henry Weiss, and Harold Farkas of income tax evasion stemming from payoffs made by Goodman and Weissman. Monks was the only one of this group who received a prison term. John Clifton and Marvin Weissman were granted immunity from prosecution in exchange for their cooperation in the federal investigation. Andrew Reinhard was not prosecuted, nor was anyone else at Singer Hutner, at Lehman Brothers Kuhn Loeb, or at Fox & Company. The Singer Hutner lawyers, however, are being investigated by a New York City Bar committee on legal ethics. Sidney Hasin wasn't prosecuted and quietly retired from Rockwell at the age of fifty-seven. George Prussin was not prosecuted either.

The public exposure of fraud at OPM led to a rash of finger-pointing and scores of civil suits charging Rockwell, Lehman, Singer Hutner, Rashba & Pokart, and Fox with complicity. Many suits were settled in March 1983 when the defendants agreed to pay creditors $65 million. They will lose millions more in other suits. The creditors were represented by lawyers from forty-seven law firms, who were paid nearly $15 million in legal fees.

Several people tried to cover their tracks to avoid being implicated in the scandal. On March 3, a week after Goodman resigned, Joseph Hutner had lunch with Marvin Weissman. It was the first time in months they had been in contact. Hutner told him he wished that Singer Hutner had resigned when Rashba & Pokart had and that he believed he would have problems with the U.S. attorney. At the end of their meeting, Hutner said that he hoped Weissman would forget the conversations they had in June through September.

Andrew Reinhard met with Goodman three times following OPM's collapse. According to Goodman, at the first two meetings, one on the street near OPM in mid-March and the other in Goodman's hospital room in May, Goodman assured Reinhard that he would be protected from being implicated in the fraud. The third meeting occurred in August 1981, after Ganz had confessed to the U.S. attorney. Goodman called Reinhard and asked to meet him on the corner of Madison Avenue and 65th Street in Manhattan. They met and walked through Central Park, and Goodman told Reinhard about the disclosure by Ganz to the authorities, but Goodman reiterated his promise to keep Reinhard out of it.

Moreover, the OPM fraud touched off a number of organizational and personal changes. Careers have been altered, lost, and in some cases, temporarily set back. Singer Hutner, now called Singer & Chase, was forced to lay off a number of associates in 1980 and 1981, and many partners have since left the firm. The firm also closed its offices in New Orleans and in Los Angeles. By 1983, the firm was comprised of just three partners, and much of the office space they occupied on 59th

Street is now rented to other attorneys. Joseph L. Hutner became "Of Counsel" to the firm. Andrew Reinhard and Alan Jacobs are now practicing law at another New York law firm as is Eli Mattioli. Henry Peter Putzel continues to practice law in Manhattan and still teaches at Fordham. Joseph McLaughlin is now a federal district court judge in the Eastern District of New York. He was one of several candidates considered for the State Court of Appeals, New York State's highest court.

At OPM, the trustee was compelled to release a number of OPM employees; dozens left voluntarily during the two years the firm was being investigated. John Clifton was rehired by the trustee after the bankruptcy and continued to work for OPM for about a year. He now works for a leasing company in New Jersey. Lou Dibari and Ed Hracs, the two OPM accountants who helped Clifton document the frauds, still work for OPM.

The trustee's investigation revealed that most of the money obtained in the frauds was used to keep OPM in business and to support the luxurious lifestyles of Goodman and his team. To recoup some of the stolen funds, the trustee took possession of Goodman's home, automobiles owned by the company, and other items. In 1981, the trustee sold the FNJ bank stock for over $16 million, one of the few investments made by Goodman and Weissman that actually turned a profit. The trustee also moved OPM from 71 Broadway in Manhattan to Greenwich, Connecticut, in January 1984.

In 1984, Trustee Hassett brought suit against Myron Goodman, his wife Lydia, his attorneys Emmerich Handler, Martin C. Sukenik, Jehoshua Graff, and David Segal, and a stockbroker, Barry Pomerantz, for, according to Hassett's claim, their "conspiracy to defraud" the OPM trustee. In a complicated stock swap from Lydia to Pomerantz and back to Lydia, which Hassett called "a spurious and sham sale," Lydia attempted to conceal approximately $500,000 to $1 million of stock in the Genetic Systems Corporation, stock that was purchased with OPM funds, the suit charged. In March 1983, Lydia sold the Genetic stock for approximately $1.2 million and, according to Hassett, used the proceeds to pay $700,000 to attorneys Handler, Sukenik, Graff, and Segal, and the other $500,000 was loaned by Lydia to Chartin 14 Realty Corporation (a firm controlled by Handler, Sukenik, Graff, and Segal). The trustee's suit was settled out of court and about $750,000 was returned by the defendants to the trustee.

In late May 1985, the OPM trustee, following four years of cleaning up after Goodman and Weissman, executed a purchase agreement to sell OPM to the Chicago-based Pritzker family—owners of Braniff and Hyatt—for $17 million. The sale is subject to the ultimate approval of the bankruptcy court.

At Rockwell, Sidney Hasin retired, as did William Neely, the Rockwell treasurer. Robert Scheussler, the auditor who first investigated Hasin's operation in 1979, now holds Hasin's job. And in mid-1983, Rockwell settled a derivative shareholder suit by agreeing to adopt new leasing rules. The suit charged that poor supervision by Rockwell managers allowed the aerospace company to become a victim of the OPM frauds and that management then participated in a cover-up. Rockwell denied the charges but agreed to settle by adopting the rules and by paying $125,000 in legal fees to the attorneys for the plaintiff, Harry Lewis. In 1984, Rockwell submitted a claim to the Air Force for losses related to the OPM fraud. Since the fraud involved computers used for defense work, Rockwell was looking to the government to absorb some of these costs. This claim is being negotiated.

In 1984, Lehman was acquired by American Express, another company with ties to OPM. David Sacks is now "Of Counsel" to Simpson Thacher & Bartlett, and Lewis Glucksman has occupied and vacated Lehman's chief executive officer slot. He later headed the financial insurance group for Fireman's Fund Insurance Company, also a subsidiary of American Express for about six months. He now runs his own consulting firm in Princeton, New Jersey. Alan Batkin and Joel Peck are still with the company. Jeffrey Werner left the First National Bank of St. Paul for a better position with another midwest bank. Stephen Kutz left Fox to begin a new venture, the accounting firm of Garen Kutz and Rogovin, which broke up following public disclosures of the OPM frauds. Kutz now works for one of his former clients. Morton Berger is still with the embattled Fox and is knee-deep in litigation stemming from the Saxon Paper debacle. Fox was Saxon's auditor, and preliminary investigations suggest that a certain amount of "book cooking" occurred there as well. On June 8, 1983, the Securities and Exchange Commission charged Fox with careless and improper auditing of three Fox clients: Saxon Industries, Flight Transportation, and Alpex Computer Corporation.[11] The SEC charged that the Fox auditors working on Saxon's books ignored "red flags" of trouble and "recklessly" disregarded standard auditing procedures. In June 1983, Fox signed a consent decree with the SEC that restricts them from accepting new business from publicly traded companies while a special committee reviews its procedures. And, finally, George Prussin is still running Sha-Li Leasing despite having to return $850,000 to the OPM trustee, but he has found new competition in the computer leasing business. Mordecai Weissman's wife, Carol, now works for a computer leasing company on Long Island.

Toward an Explanation of Blindness and Paralysis

Other People's Mistakes

In the aftermath of OPM, numerous people sifted through the evidence and discovered "retrospective errors" and unheeded warnings on the part of particular players associated with the incident. Signs of trouble were present but were simply missed by the persons involved. In his report to the bankruptcy court, for instance, the OPM trustee, James P. Hassett, claimed that the OPM fraud was possible because of "other people's mistakes." A "variety of simple measures" by those associated with OPM "could have or should have detected fraud or prevented its continuation," the report concluded. "Instead, in an 'after you, Alphonse' routine, all stood by in the mistaken belief that others were checking to verify that things were really as they seemed or proceeded on the unfounded assumption that others who knew about the fraud would act to stop it."[1]

Why didn't OPM's bankers, lawyers, and accountants discover the crimes committed by Goodman and Weissman? And when questionable conduct was uncovered, what were the conditions that allowed it to continue? Why didn't people take steps to stop the fraud?

It is difficult to provide a single answer to these questions. There is none. Of course, some would say such conduct continued without interference because too many people and the organizations they worked for were reaping substantial rewards from OPM; in short, there were strong incentives to look the other way. Avarice is certainly part of the answer; there is little question that personal and corporate self-interest played a major role in allowing OPM's crimes to continue for so long. But money alone has rarely proven the motivator that people believe it to be.

In the OPM scandal, two conditions were prominent that made the fraud possible and difficult to stop. First, and most obviously, OPM appeared legitimate. OPM had real or exaggerated ties to elites, whether they were prestigious institutions or well-known individuals in the financial community. Goodman and Weissman surrounded themselves with accouterments of success: stylish and expensive clothes, limousines and corporate aircraft, lavish homes and offices, and an entourage of attendants that catered to their needs. They took exotic vacations and kept busy schedules, frequently traveling throughout the world. They provided themselves with other evidence of their apparent success, such as financial statements showing growth and profit as well as newspaper and magazine articles commenting on their achievements. And they shielded or quickly covered up anything that discredited their manufactured image. They also carefully structured deals so that they appeared risk-free and profitable. All of this had two effects: one, the front attracted victims, it disarmed them, and it caused them to let their guard down; and two, the positive character made it easy for outsiders to dismiss suspicious behavior—it was difficult to believe wrongful conduct could be going on under the collective noses of such an elite group. Even when suspicions were strong, it was hard for anyone to raise questions without feeling foolish. I have termed this the "organizational weapon," a term borrowed from Philip Selznick and, later, Stanton Wheeler and Mitchell Rothman.[2]

Second, victims were relatively easy targets for a number of reasons. Often victims sought quick, easy, and lucrative returns from OPM. Once they realized these returns—even for a short time—they became hooked and, in some cases, dependent on their relationship with the leasing company. Once individuals began looking good in the eyes of their superiors, it was hard for them to take steps that may have jeopardized their performance record. These "golden shackles," as I have called them, led to disastrous consequences. Frequently, victims were neophytes in the transactions in which they were defrauded. For instance, many victims had moved quickly into OPM's grasp, all too eager to reap the rewards and benefits of the apparently booming business. Victim organizations were typically spread too thin or were too inexperienced to have adequate controls to protect themselves; for protection they tended to rely on the presence of OPM's elite associates. There were times, too, when victims themselves were marginal, perhaps having committed certain infractions on their own. Not wanting to call attention to these violations, they were reluctant to blow the whistle.

In addition to these two conditions, there were systemic factors, conditions "out there" that made it difficult to discover and blow the whistle on Goodman's and Weissman's conduct. Information about OPM was diffused among many individuals and organizations, few of which had verifiable evidence of wrongdoing. Even with such evidence in hand, however, individuals looked around and saw others appearing calm, and it became easier for them to dismiss the evidence as insignificant or to pass off the responsibility for doing something to others; it became easy for individuals to make themselves not know. In addition, certain social norms made it difficult to disclose information about the wrongdoing. From a very early age in our society, we are discouraged from "squealing" or "tattling" or "butting into other people's business." It is especially difficult to blow the whistle on those we are loyal and indebted to.

None of these factors alone explains what occurred in the OPM affair. But interactively they provide a context for understanding what happens in OPM-like situations. This is not meant to serve as an apology for those who acted negligently in their dealing with OPM nor in any way to diminish their culpability; the behavior of many players involved in the OPM debacle surely deserves condemnation. But the purpose of this book is to address a more fundamental question. What were the conditions that led to such mistakes?

The Organizational Weapon

As described in chapter 1 and elsewhere in this book, Goodman and Weissman picked their associates carefully, knowing full well they could snowball their connections into greater and greater success. They knew, too, that such associations inhibited the diligent pursuit of information about the company and its deals. Most people were comforted by the presence of OPM's investment bankers, auditors, lawyers, bankers, and accountants. Moreover, OPM structured its deals so that they appeared safe to participants; virtually everyone felt they couldn't lose. Further, Goodman and Weissman deceived victims and unwitting accomplices by carefully controlling the information they revealed about themselves and OPM, thereby shaping the impressions others formed of them.

In all frauds, the con must create the appearance of legitimacy so nothing appears out of the ordinary to the mark. Writing about organizational frauds, Erving Goffman, the sociologist, wrote that

> since a con merchant must swindle his clients under those circumstances where clients appreciate that a confidence game could be employed, the con man must carefully forestall the immediate impression that he might be what in fact he is, just as the legitimate merchant, under the same circumstances, would have to forestall carefully the immediate impression that he might be what he is not.[3]

When individuals are deciding whether or not they want to do business together, they seek information about each other and their respective organizations. They glean clues from the representative's dress, mannerisms, speech, and so on. They may be interested in the other's socioeconomic status and affiliations, attitudes and values, abilities and trustworthiness, among other things. They examine the organization in much the same way—they make judgments about the firm's operation on the basis of how it presents itself to the outside world. The organization's facilities, its public relations material, its financial statements, and its associations with elite customers and clients, lawyers, bankers, and accountants all form an image, an impression that helps outsiders—and many times insiders, too—to define the situation, to make a determination about what sort of business associate the other will be.

It is in the interest of each organization to influence the judgment of the other, to manage the impression formed to attain the outcome it desires. In making the situation appear attractive, each party tries to influence the actions of the other, to sell a product, retain a client, obtain a loan, or negotiate a merger or acquisition. The con knows this all too well. To operate, organizations involved in improprieties must subscribe to the same type of behavioral norms found in straight organizations—at least on the surface. Fraudulent operators create organizational structures and incorporate procedures that mirror the myths of their institutionalized environments, thereby shaping the impressions others form of them. Copying such organizations, the con proceeds as if he were beyond reproach, retaining lawyers, auditors, investment bankers, and whomever else he needs to deflect suspicious concern and build legitimacy. Establishing such connections, the fraudulent organization is like a weapon and becomes "what the gun or knife is for the common criminal—a tool to obtain money from victims."[4]

One's perception, of course, is influenced also by other circumstances, such as the experience and economic needs of potential prey. Persons who fully understand the business in which the con operates and are relatively secure financially are less likely to be duped by frauds.

Impression management, however, not only involves a positive affirmation of corporate character and the accredited values of society, but a concealment or shielding of information that is incompatible with the fostered image. Erving Goffman wrote that

> when one's activity occurs in the presence of other persons, some aspects of the activity are expressively accentuated and other aspects which might discredit the fostered impression, are suppressed. It is clear that accentuated facts make their appearance in what I have called a front region; it should be just as clear that there may be another region—a "back region" or "backstage"—where the suppressed facts make an appearance.[5]

It is to OPM's backstage that we now turn.

Shielding. To sustain the definition of the situation, executives embellish and overcommunicate certain facts and hide others; information discrediting the circumstances represented to both outsiders and insiders alike is hidden or disguised. Marginal operators "cook the books," withhold or alter information, employ diversionary tactics, and change locations or personnel when their scheme is uncovered to maintain their image. Goodman and Weissman did all of these things and more to shield their fraudulent scheme.

Two critical tasks were faced by OPM: (1) it had to present an image of growth and profit in the face of mounting losses and a bleak future and (2) it had to conceal evidence of illicit activity.

Goodman and Weissman routinely submitted bogus financials to impress outsiders. Altered financial statements were presented to the Chase Manhattan Bank in 1974, to equity brokers Kent Klineman and Joel Mallin on several occasions in the 1970s, to Goldman, Sachs & Company in late 1975, and to Rockwell International officials in 1979. Moreover, financials produced by Fox & Company may not have been fraudulent but, they did violate generally acceptable auditing procedures and attained the same end. Lenders and other sponsors who relied on OPM's financial reports were led astray: they believed OPM had more growth and greater profits than was actually the case. Both Lehman Brothers Kuhn Loeb and the First National Bank of St. Paul (FNBSP), in part, relied on such statements in reaching a decision to do business with OPM. "Had they refused to deal with OPM," the trustee concluded, "it is doubtful whether Goodman could have carried off the Rockwell fraud."[6]

A more difficult task for Goodman and his collaborators was making the illegitimate transactions appear legitimate. Official papers had to be procured from IBM, Rockwell, and the Bank of New York; this material and other documents had to be altered; and all of the paper had to be juggled and distributed in a way that prevented outsiders from uncovering the swindle. And although Goodman and his team were not especially careful with their alterations, few errors were ever detected.

Many organizations come "to believe in their routine pieces of paper," Harold Wilensky wrote in his analysis of another fraud, the Great Salad Oil swindle.[7] Representatives develop a checklist of documents that must be presented and procedures adhered to for a deal to close. As long as everything *appears* in order, few questions are ever raised. Most participants in OPM transactions "didn't consider it necessary," as one banker testified, to verify each of the transactions.[8] One lawyer said, "If there was any concern about protecting a client against fraud, we wouldn't be at the closing in the first place."[9] No one was sure who verified the deals, or as one witness put it, who "went out and kicked the tires,"[10] but as long as things *appeared* legitimate, the transactions closed without a hitch. Anesthetized by the apparent routine, everyone involved in these fraudulent transactions missed the obvious irregularities.

Like other criminal acts that go unnoticed, the OPM swindle was fraught with behavioral and procedural ambiguities, several of which have since been interpreted as unheeded flags of fraud. Goodman's obsessive control over the Rockwell account and his mail rule are two examples. Conduct such as his was part of the "noise" that made it difficult to decipher clues of criminal activity from Goodman's unusual procedures. Such policies might arouse suspicions, yet excessive control of this kind is not unusual in the world of business, particularly in young companies operated by eccentric entrepreneurs. Owners of growing corporations often maintain total dominance over operations, especially those involving a large and important client. Goodman's purpose for restricting communication with Rockwell is now obvious, but, at the time, did not seem extraordinary.

Goodman's delaying tactics, which kept people in the dark for long periods of time, were also ambiguous forms of avoidance that did not trigger concern. For instance, Goodman put off responding to Rockwell's requests for financial statements in 1980; he ignored Martin Zelbow's pleas for Rockwell and American Express documents; and he refused to provide Singer Hutner with full disclosure of his fraudulent activities. For a time, the delaying tactics worked.

On a number of occasions, slipups in the scheme nearly triggered an end to the fraud and called forth from the fraud team what the OPM trustee termed "crisis response techniques." Retrieval of information destructive to the fostered image, for example, was necessary in several instances. In other situations, members of Goodman's team impersonated officials in different organizations to reassure a suspicious party. By doing so, OPM's front was preserved.

There were times, however, that information out of character with the fostered impression became known to outsiders. Such "unmeant gestures,"[11] as Goffman called them, had to be neutralized by Goodman and others in order to save the show.

Neutralization.   Many contra-normative behaviors are defined in a way that lessens their seriousness; they are, in effect, neutralized. Alcoholics are said to have a "stress-related dependency"; embezzlers claim they were simply "borrowing"; Nixon's "plumbers" called acts of theft, forgery, and libel, "dirty tricks" or "pranks." Myron Goodman referred to fraud as "double-discounts" and "double-hocking," to corporate bribery as "commission payments," and to check-kiting as the "check matter" and "technical violations." Verbalizations of this kind allow subjects to adjust to two contradictory roles—that of normal, upstanding citizens and that of criminals. Such use of language also allows associates to accept the contradictions in another's behavior.

Wrongful conduct may also be explained away by the deviant actor or by the valuable allies who come to their defense, thereby attaining the same end as the verbalization. An effective accounting for illicit conduct may restore the individual's image to its original state "if the actor convinces others that the conduct and surrounding circumstances were unique."[12] Accounts—whether they combine elements of excuse, justification, or apology—represent one of the few tools offenders have available to repair their image in the eyes of those who judge them; they provide a context in which to view the questionable conduct and to salvage self-respect. When used effectively, accounts bring the malefactor back into the fold.

Myron Goodman's first serious brush with discovery occurred when Rashba & Pokart uncovered the early fraudulent loans in 1975. Confronted by Marvin Weissman, Goodman justified the improper loans claiming they were necessary because of the company's cash flow difficulties. "It's no big deal," he said. "I'll pay it off," thereby implying no one was hurt by the crimes.[13]

When the check-kiting scheme unraveled, Goodman's account to executives at Lehman was one of his most effective. Correctly perceiving higher stakes, he admitted he was wrong and swore it would never happen again. He was "extremely apologetic," "very contrite," and "emotional"—he even cried at the meeting. His performance had restored his image in the eyes of those at Lehman. "It seemed they [OPM] were involved in a situation that wasn't going to be repeated," Lewis Glucksman recalled. "A mistake was made by a young man." A similar story was repeated at the FNBSP.

Once they are convinced the act was an aberration or was less serious than at first glance, loyal associates often become defenders of the wrongdoer. Hasin, for instance, justified the activity of Goodman and OPM to skeptics at Rockwell. Batkin did the same to Werner at the FNBSP. Reinhard and others did the same at Singer Hutner.

Goodman's confessions to Marvin Weissman and, he alleged, Andrew Reinhard, also provided elements of apology, excuse, and justification. In substance, Goodman admitted that double-hocking was wrong, that he wouldn't do it again. He also asked their help in repaying the bad loans. His revelation, in effect, drew a distinction between Myron Goodman, the person who committed the frauds, and Myron Goodman, the repenter. He wanted their help in restoring the normative image he held for himself. When a confessor "stands up and tells to those who are present things he would ordinarily attempt to conceal or rationalize away," Goffman wrote, "he sacrifices his secrets and his self-protective distance from others, and this sacrifice tends to induce a backstage solidarity among all present."[14] Goodman's confessions had similar effects.

Both of these techniques allowed Goodman and others to maintain a positive character, to create and uphold a facade that lulled victims into believing their investments were safe and that Goodman was sincere and trustworthy. But quite apart from these things that Goodman and others did to mislead, a number of factors made victims relatively easy targets, all too willing to accept Goodman's charades and accounts.

Organizational Vulnerabilities and Golden Shackles

The 1970s, the decade in which OPM operated, was the most turbulent economic period this nation has faced since the depression. Personal and corporate bankruptcies occurred at record levels. Several important banks, one of the Big Three automakers, and some of the country's largest municipalities were forced into bankruptcy or came perilously close to doing so. Inflation rose to double-digit levels, while unemployment, at 3.5 percent in 1969, climbed to 11 percent in the early 1980s. The profit rate for nonfinancial organizations was not much better. Further, the Dow-Jones Industrial Average plummeted from 2,604 in 1965 to around 1,000 in 1982. Productivity rates also declined. The private business economy was growing at 3.3 percent a year from 1948 to 1966; the rate dropped to 2.1 percent from 1966 to 1973, and to just over 1 percent between 1973 and 1978. In 1979, the productivity rate decreased—American workers were only 98 percent as efficient as they had been when the year began.[15]

The firms in OPM's orbit were greatly affected by the troubled economy, and their growing dependence on the leasing firm caused them to interpret events favorably, neutrally, or even to look the other way.

Traditional sources of revenue for investment bankers, for instance, evaporated as small investors had fewer and fewer dollars for speculation, and large investors sought safer havens in other markets, such as real estate. Competitive pressures from foreign and domestic banks recently freed from regulation added to the difficulties of the investment banks. To counter these trends, many underwriters began to broaden their services and expand their focus in the areas of leasing, mergers and acquisitions, private placements, and international financings.

Even the gentlemanly investment houses like Lehman felt the pinch and were forced to take a more aggressive posture. Following the death of the patriarchal Robert Lehman in August 1969, the firm was saddled with mounting losses and power struggles. In the early 1970s, Lehman's capital reserves dipped to $15 million.* In 1973, Lehman lost $18 million and was on the brink of bankruptcy. The firm was kept afloat by a $7 million investment by Banca Commerciale Italiana. That same year, Peter G. Peterson was appointed vice-chairman, and within months he was named chairman of the 123-year-old investment banking firm.

The scrappiness of Lehman's new chairman and his number two man, Lewis L. Glucksman, quickly brought Lehman back into prominence. By 1976, the underwriter netted $20 million—quite impressive considering the flagging business conditions. A decade after Peterson and Glucksman took command, Lehman's capital exceeded $225 mil-

---

*An investment banker's capital is an important indicator of the firm's strength.

lion. Profits before taxes for the 1981 fiscal year were about $120 million and over $140 million for 1982. Before Lehman became part of American Express in 1984, the firm employed over 3,000 people and had become one of Wall Street's largest investment bankers.

Such a rapid turnaround, however, does not occur without costs, and OPM may be one of them. Organizations that achieve such success must often trade security and relative stability for growth and profit. Employees are encouraged—pushed—to generate more and more business, to expand markets, and to test untested waters. Lehman was quite experienced at placing corporate debt, for instance, but most of that work was with long-term debt. During the 1970s, when interest rates were rising rapidly, many lenders were looking to invest in short-term notes, and OPM was thought to be a good opportunity for Lehman to expand this growing area.

Recessions also often force corporations to trim away excess fat, but doing so reduces support functions, making it difficult to carefully scrutinize transactions and business relationships. Shortly after Peterson took command of Lehman, he laid off 200 of the firm's 1,200 employees. Moreover, while all organizations search for stable revenue streams—steady business from several large customers like OPM—it is particularly important for investment banks to do so since much of their revenue comes in unpredictable ways that are difficult to anticipate and plan for. And, of course, stable customers become even more important in a recession.

All of these things undoubtedly placed pressure, perhaps subconscious pressure, on Lehman representatives who dealt with OPM.

For instance, Alan Batkin of Lehman was dependent on and loyal to Goodman. OPM was a very lucrative client for Lehman and for Batkin in particular. Batkin had also become friendly with Goodman, not in a social way, but certainly in a less formal way than many business relationships. Goodman had even donated money to a charitable foundation controlled by Batkin's uncle. On September 2, 1980, just prior to Lehman's resignation, Goodman donated $25,000 to the David Yellon Teacher's College in Jerusalem. The check was sent to Sanford Batkin, a fund-raiser for the college and Allan Batkin's uncle, who had been introduced to Goodman by his nephew.

Although Batkin enjoyed the success that the OPM engagement brought him, he did not yield to Goodman's pressure as others had done. Batkin asked difficult questions about OPM's financial statements in 1979, he and his superiors berated Goodman about the check-kiting that same year, and, when OPM's financial reporting procedures appeared hopelessly inadequate, Batkin insisted that OPM retain a consultant.

But even Batkin and others at Lehman did certain things that seem questionable. In 1979 and 1980, for instance, they failed to inform certain lenders about OPM's check-kiting. In early 1980, Batkin appeared to ignore certain signals, such as John Clifton's resignation and his telling Batkin that OPM was probably insolvent. Also in 1980, as the reports from Coopers & Lybrand were becoming more and more bleak, Batkin seemed to discount them and tried to bolster OPM to outsiders and perhaps even to his own superiors. Jeffrey Werner of the FNBSP was surprised when Coopers resigned in August since Batkin's reports were sounding more positive in the weeks preceding the split. But Batkin emphasized the personality clashes and played down the looting when explaining the breakup. In September 1980, when Lehman resigned, Batkin encouraged Werner to maintain the OPM relationship, and he even arranged an investment banker to handle the transactions. And, finally, like other organizations and individuals that eventually quit OPM, the stated reason for Lehman's resignation was somewhat deceptive. Lehman claimed it terminated the OPM relationship because OPM no longer generated the business they once had. There was never any hint of the series of troubles that Lehman had experienced in the previous six months.

Lenders or the "other people" in OPM transactions also felt severe economic and competitive pressures in the 1970s. Indeed, for the past two decades, the banking industry has undergone volatile and rapid changes. During the inflationary periods in the late 1960s and 1970s, market interest rates climbed to record levels, but deposit rates did not—financial intermediation* did not occur. In fact, savers shifted their dollars from banks and into more interest-sensitive securities, creating a condition called "disintermediation." Interest rates paid to depositors couldn't be raised to compete with money markets because the rates were controlled by Federal Reserve regulatory ceilings. And bankers were unable to adjust the interest rates borrowers paid on loans because, in many cases, the rates were fixed.

Pressure came from other sources as well. In the mid- to late-

---

*The difference between what banks paid in interest to depositors and what they received in interest on borrowed money; also known as the "spread."

1970s, commercial and industrial loans began to dwindle. Although economic conditions limited corporate capital investment in the post-recession period, real fixed investment actually rose at a 3 percent annual rate from 1975 to 1979. But banks didn't benefit from this modest growth: Commercial loans at New York banks, for example, dropped by 5 percent per year in real terms.[16] Whatever business expansion was going on, it was being financed primarily through the sale of securities, not loans. Thus, not only was there a shift of dollars out of the banks, but their ability to lend profitably was also stymied.

And, although changes in the regulatory environment permitted substantial product and geographical diversification for banks, deregulation also opened the gates for a flood of competition from nonbanks and foreign lenders. For the first time in decades, bank officers were shaken from their bankerly somnolence and forced to become more aggressive and speculative. But some didn't, and others won't, survive. Because of the number of weak institutions, regulators arranged more bank mergers (between strong and shaky banks) in the last decade than they had since the 1940s. Despite such efforts, there were more bank failures in the 1970s than at any time since the depression.[17]

To survive, bank officers steered their institutions into unfamiliar territory, providing rewards for lending officers for loans made in these new and apparently lucrative areas. Many of the nation's largest banks, for example, lent billions of dollars to communist and underdeveloped nations in the mistaken belief, perhaps, that nations don't go bankrupt. It is now believed by some that most of those funds will not be recovered. Some of these same banks moved into other markets as well, bringing them into contact with companies like OPM. Many of the bankers who lent money to OPM had little experience with the leasing industry; they, too, had moved into new markets.

The Philadelphia Savings Fund Society (PSFS), the nation's largest mutual savings bank and the largest lender to OPM, for instance, underwent unprecedented growth in many new markets in the mid-1970s, but as is often the case when businesses move too fast, the bank's aggressive strategies came back to haunt it. Competition was severe, inflation was spiraling, and operating costs were on the rise. In 1975, the year the bank made its first loan to OPM, deposits at PSFS increased by 15 percent over the previous year, to $3.6 billion. Assets grew by $500 million to nearly $4 billion. The bank opened six new offices, bringing the total number of branches to fifty-three throughout a seven-county area. By 1978, the bank's assets and deposits jumped to $5.9 billion and $5.4 billion respectively, and net income skyrocketed to $44.7 million, a 35.6 percent gain over the previous year and almost two and a half times as great as in 1975.

Over the course of the next year, however, the tide began to change. By 1980, net income was $21.4 million, less than half what it had been just two years before[18] and, according to the *Wall Street Journal,* the bank posted a $61.1 million loss in 1981.[19] During the late 1970s, PSFS had faced the growing problem of disintermediation, and the bank's management, aware that stability and profits increasingly depended on interest-sensitive assets rather than on mortgages, began investing in securities with shorter maturities—which included private placements on OPM deals. From 1975 until March 1980, when PSFS stopped making loans on OPM transactions, the bank provided $279 million in loans to OPM.

Nearly all of the creditor victims on OPM transactions had to expand their markets, both in terms of geography and service, during the 1970s. All but one of the victim lenders on the fraudulent Rockwell deals were based outside New York City. Because of their inexperience in these new areas and the greater risk involved, we can assume they relied more heavily on the representations made by others than they might have otherwise. In a survey of victim lenders on OPM transactions, the trustee's attorneys found that representations made by Lehman and by Singer Hutner were important in the decision to participate in OPM transactions.[20] Of course, this was part of the defense strategy for most of the lenders. Trying to recoup their losses, the lenders naturally shifted the responsibility for their victimization from themselves to Lehman, to Singer Hutner, and to others. Notwithstanding the obviousness of the strategy, under the circumstances, there is undoubtedly truth to the claim. OPM's other associations, such as with Rockwell, also carried considerable weight. OPM was an unfamiliar name, but Lehman and Rockwell were not.[21]

Inflation and the recessionary periods in the 1970s also squeezed the profits of accounting firms. Expansion of new audit work slowed since fewer and fewer companies were formed, a smaller number of firms went public, and corporations issued less stock. Although most of the Big Eight firms increased revenues by 15 percent a year during the decade, much of this increase was due to price inflation. All of the big accounting firms were forced to extend their services and expand their markets both here and abroad to maintain even modest growth.[22] Consulting or management advisory services, as the accounting industry refers to it, became increasingly important, overseas operations grew, and engagements by small businesses—once ignored by the Big Eight—generated intense competition, placing considerable strain on medium- and small-sized accounting firms.

Fee-cutting became more and more widespread as auditors fought harder and harder to win engagements. Such practices drew the attention of a prestigious commission established by the American Institute of Certified Public Accountants in the mid-1970s. The Commission on Auditors' Responsibilities, or the Cohen Commission, as it came to be called, in honor of its chairman, the late Manuel F. Cohen, noted that unrealistic time and budget pressures frequently caused substandard audits. A survey of auditors conducted by the commission found that 58 percent of the respondents had signed off on an audit step without completing the work or noting that the audit step was omitted; time and budget pressures were the main reasons cited for not performing the work.[23]

It is difficult to say with any certainty whether these general trends affected the audit work on OPM. We do know that Marvin Weissman's firm, Rashba & Pokart, continued to do bookkeeping work for OPM long after it learned about the frauds in 1975. Since Rashba & Pokart was no longer the company's auditor, however, it had less responsibility for discovering irregularities and disclosing them, if and when they were found. In 1976, that responsibility fell on Fox. Fox had no experience with auditing leasing companies when it took on the OPM engagement in 1976. Several generally accepted auditing procedures were violated on Fox audits, which stemmed from the complexity of lease accounting and from the constant pressure of Goodman. Stephen Kutz, who headed the Fox audit team and who was no doubt fully aware of the consequences if he resisted Goodman's demands, acceded to the owner's wishes. Given the overall environment, losing the OPM account was something neither Kutz nor Fox could afford.

Although many consider the 1970s the salad days for law firms, they, too, faced inflationary and competitive pressures. Salaries for the best and the brightest young lawyers jumped from an average of $15,-

ooo in 1968 to $43,000 in 1980 at big New York firms. Inflated expenses such as these took a considerable chunk out of the profits at the leading firms. According to a confidential annual study by Price Waterhouse of twelve leading New York City law firms,[24] gross fees, after adjusting for inflation, increased by only 12 percent between 1975 and 1980, while operating costs were growing at three times that rate. A decade before, partners expected to receive more than half of the gross revenues; in 1980, they received just over 36 percent. If discounted for inflation, net income per partner increased only seven-tenths of a percent from 1975 to 1980.

Inflated costs have forced lawyers to fight intensely for legal business. To expand their markets, many law firms have opened branch offices both here and abroad; firms routinely raid another's talents and, with increasing frequency, merge entire practices to remain competitive. Adding to the difficulty, cost-conscious corporations have expanded their own in-house legal staffs to handle routine matters.

The competition among law firms no doubt added to the dilemma confronting the Singer Hutner lawyers. Although Singer Hutner had grown rapidly throughout the decade, much of its growth was due to OPM. Over 60 percent of its annual revenues came from a single client; it was virtually a captured law firm. And, in 1980, when Singer Hutner learned about the Rockwell fraud, the economy was undergoing its second recession in six years. Moreover, competition between law firms was at its zenith—hardly the time to begin drumming up new business.

As described in earlier chapters, Rockwell, too, was going through a difficult period in the mid-1970s. Several acquisitions increased their long-term debt, and the effects of the recession and the ups and downs of the B-1 bomber did not make matters any easier. Under such circumstances, Rockwell and other lessees found that leasing to be more attractive than purchasing expensive computer equipment. In their rush to lease, however, a number of companies—Rockwell in particular—were ill-equipped to identify and to monitor the many pitfalls associated with leasing.

Controls at Rockwell were extremely poor, making the company a perfect vehicle for fraud. For instance, as part of the lease-financing documentation on OPM transactions, Rockwell was required to sign a "consent and agreements" that obligated it to make payments directly to the financial institution. The consent and agreements was one of the ways lenders protected themselves from fraud and from the commingling of funds. But no one informed the accounting department at the Information Systems Center (ISC) (Rockwell) of this direct payment provision; the bookkeeper responsible for making the installments on computer leases never heard of the consent and agreements and made payments according to OPM's directives. On all fraudulent deals, she paid OPM; on all others, she paid the lenders directly.

Rockwell also placed responsibility for computer leasing in the hands of one person, Sidney Hasin. No one at Rockwell had any experience with or knowledge of leasing, except Hasin. And no one who supervised Hasin had as much knowledge about the computer industry as he did. Rockwell was truly ill-prepared to have made such heavy use of a type of financing they knew little or nothing about. And Hasin made a series of decisions that made him increasingly dependent on OPM. In the mid-1970s, Hasin arranged a number of long-term lease contracts on mainframes that saved Rockwell millions of dollars. But when these machines became obsolete, OPM came forward as the only lessor willing to extricate Hasin—and Rockwell—from their predicament. Goodman agreed to take the equipment and sublease it at above-market rates. Another time, Hasin caused OPM to provide leases on three mainframes (referred to as the "swing machines"), which Hasin knew cost OPM millions of dollars. On both deals, Hasin depended on OPM to bail him out; he relied on OPM to salvage his career. But by doing so, Rockwell became dependent on OPM for more than $40 million. An OPM default on these obligations would have jeopardized Hasin's career and that prospect—according to the OPM trustee—gave him substantial reason for his silent complicity in OPM's questionable activities.[25]

Hasin violated Rockwell's bidding procedures to benefit OPM (and himself), allowed Goodman and his team free rein at Rockwell, including control over sensitive financial documents, and, on at least one occasion, knowingly participated in a fraudulent transaction. Hasin also filtered the information he passed upward to his superiors to favor OPM; he frequently defended OPM against charges made by others. Moreover, he distorted and misinterpreted directives he received, such as the freeze on OPM business in 1980, to benefit OPM. Hasin had no legal obligation to discover or even report the crimes (no one did), but his lax procedures and his failure to question certain practices—stemming from his own ambitions—allowed the frauds to go on.

It is not unusual for organizations in troubled markets to expand their reach. But when they do so, they do so at a much higher risk. Employees are often stretched too thin, controls are lacking, in-house supervision and monitoring are poor, and problems are not anticipated. Moreover, in difficult times, the signals emanating from the top of the organizations stress the need to generate more business and to do so quickly. Employees are recognized for revenue they bring in and for dollars they save—not for being careful; hence, less time is spent scrutinizing the long-term implications of transactions, and more time is spent figuring out ways to drum up new business and to keep the business they have.

Under these circumstances, employees—indeed, entire organizations—can easily become dependent on apparently stable, rather lucrative business relationships. For instance, suppose you were responsible for bringing in a client who provided $1 million a year in revenue to your firm. Notwithstanding unusual circumstances, that $1 million becomes expected, it is your normal performance; any deviation is a reflection on you. Or, to examine another situation, suppose you were responsible for negotiating several multimillion dollar deals that saved your company hundreds of thousands of dollars. It is quite likely that should any of these deals later backfire, you would be held responsible.

The implications of such dependencies are clear. Individuals are quick to look the other way in order to avoid pushing hard for compliance. Some individuals may even become involved in wrongful conduct.

Situations such as these are especially dangerous when individuals are loyal and dedicated to, in addition to being dependent on, the malefactor, a common situation in the OPM affair. In these circumstances, people are less likely to question irregular behavior for fear of offending the other party. Moreover, they are more likely to accept justifications offered by the wrongdoer; people feel obligated to reciprocate past favors either through cooperation, silence, or quiet withdrawal.

Entire organizations need not be dependent on and loyal to another to become a pawn in the other's game. All it takes is one individual. And it may not be that the person knows about illicit behavior; he may suspect, but fearing what would happen should the truth be known, he fails to follow up, to check carefully; he simply closes his eyes. He knows but makes himself not know.

There are also systemic reasons that make it easier for people to practice this conscious avoidance.

Segmentation

Because of confidentiality norms between professionals and their clients, Goodman's own restrictions on communications, and individuals realizing that disclosing certain facts would not be in their interest, many people involved with OPM were prevented from learning all there was to know about Goodman and his company. Information was diffused across and within organizations; Rashba & Pokart, and John Clifton, for instance, knew about the early frauds committed by Goodman and Weissman, but few others did. Stephen Kutz of Fox knew that Goodman maintained control of the confirmation letters associated with financial audits, letters that could have easily uncovered fraudulent transactions, but few others had this knowledge. In 1979, after learning about OPM's check-kiting, representatives from Lehman kept quiet about the infraction. They failed to disclose the facts to financial institutions that they were soliciting to place OPM debt, all except the First National Bank of St. Paul.

In 1980, LeRoy McClellan chose not to reveal OPM's delinquencies to lenders checking on OPM because he feared a possible libel suit by the leasing company. Also in 1980, Marvin Weissman again kept silent about the Rockwell frauds following Goodman's confession to him. In 1980, Coopers & Lybrand was silent about Goodman's and Weissman's looting of the company during a period it believed OPM was insolvent (Coopers did inform Lehman, however). And, in 1980, the Singer Hutner attorneys kept quiet about the Rockwell frauds.

All of these individuals and organizations were concerned about their own exposure. As they learned more about OPM's misdeeds, they moved to protect themselves, not the other potential victims who dealt with the leasing company. For instance, following its discovery of fraud in 1975, Rashba & Pokart became OPM's bookkeepers. No longer the company's auditors, the firm was not required to disclose its knowledge of OPM's frauds. In 1980, when Clifton resigned, although he tried to inform Singer Hutner of Rockwell frauds, he misled others by saying he quit OPM because he wanted to get back into public accounting.

The withdrawals of Rashba & Pokart, of Lehman, and of Singer Hutner were done in a similar way. All withdrew either because of their growing suspicion of improper behavior or because of their knowledge of fraud, yet their messages to outsiders were ambiguous. Lehman told the St. Paul bank that it was withdrawing from OPM because its deals were getting smaller, but Lehman was willing to make available to St. Paul an independent investment banker to assist with the bank's relationship with OPM. By informing people of their "mutual termination," Singer Hutner negated what would have been a strong warning signal to others.

The most damaging aspect of this nondisclosure from a system's point of view is that these specialists acted as though they didn't know of or even suspect that anything was wrong when in fact they did know. Actors in a system or group often gauge their reactions to each other by examining the behavior of others. If everyone appears calm, all members may be led (or misled) to react with less urgency than if they were alone.[26] The FNBSP, for example, depended on Lehman's involvement in the OPM "system." As Lehman reacted with relative calm to crisis after crisis, the FNBSP, although concerned about events, followed suit. Things couldn't be all that bad if Lehman was staying on. The same could be said for other lenders and even for Rockwell. As institutional representatives became concerned about their firm's involvement with OPM, they frequently checked the responses of others like Lehman or Singer Hutner. If the important actors in OPM's network weren't abandoning ship, others were also less likely to do so. When they finally did quit OPM, others were quick to follow; within months of each other, Rashba & Pokart, Clifton, Coopers & Lybrand, Lehman, and Singer Hutner all terminated their relationships with OPM.

These social psychological processes may be much more subtle, too. Suppose an individual bank officer, a Singer Hutner associate, or a Lehman employee heard or saw something that was not quite right about an OPM transaction. Without checking with others, he may have convinced himself that everything must be okay or else someone in the network would have caught the errors. Indeed, John Clifton testified about having such feelings.

Against the backdrop of competitive and economic difficulty described earlier stands the individual bank officer pressed to lend at rates that improve the bank's profitability; the investment banker, the accountant, and the lawyer driven to increase revenue; and those responsible for purchasing capital equipment at firms like Rockwell, trying to reduce the cost of such machines. Threatened by unstable markets and, undoubtedly, growing pressure to maximize performance, representatives found OPM attractive and able to reduce the uncertainties they faced. Early experiences proved favorable, and many people who handled the OPM account for their respective firms enjoyed the concomitant rewards and recognition for handling the lucrative association. But, as time passed, individuals became dependent on OPM's business, and they feared falling from their perch. In many cases, some people had also become loyal to Myron Goodman and to OPM. As OPM's troubles began to surface, rather than seeing OPM for what it really was, they misinterpreted and ignored certain facts and otherwise found reasons for their continued involvement with the leasing company— they had too much to lose by exiting, and they had become dependent.

To be sure, much of the evidence of fraud available to these representatives was equivocal, and only a handful of people had actual knowledge of the crimes. Moreover, a number of people, sensing something wrong, initially acted responsibly. Lehman, for instance, believed OPM needed assistance with financial matters and insisted that Goodman retain Coopers & Lybrand. When John Clifton discovered fraud for a second time, he retained an attorney, documented the crimes, and attempted to inform OPM's legal counsel. Singer Hutner, too, acted responsibly by retaining Putzel and McLaughlin. But in each instance, representatives of various institutions acted slowly in response to further warnings coming from OPM, and they frequently interpreted such signals in a favorable or, at least, neutral way. By doing so, they lulled others—including their own superiors—into thinking things were all right. Moreover, when OPM's performance became so poor or they realized the frauds were too large for Goodman to make restitution, and when they finally did exit, they still failed to warn others, and the OPM frauds continued.

Modern businesses necessarily depend on many organizations to survive. Operating in a complex economy such as ours can be treacherous going without the aid of professionals and specialist firms to navigate a course past complicated regulations, tax laws, financial and technological matters, accounting and reporting procedures, and so on. Organizations are under considerable pressure to be more rational, to hire specialists, to form alliances to reduce risk and error, and to develop structures to maximize efficiency and effectiveness; few things are left to chance, at least nothing that really matters.[27] By interlocking a network of experts, all the bases are covered; tax lawyers examine our tax shelters and write-offs, computer specialists appraise the value of equipment and advise us on our purchases, investment bankers tell how to finance capital goods and corporate expansion, auditors suggest how best to present our financial picture, and attorneys try to keep us within the bounds of the law. We rely on the expert judgment of a myriad of professionals to reduce risk; suppliers, customers, employees, on the other hand, depend on the presence of such specialists as a sign of their approval of the focal organization and its business practices. From afar, it is difficult for outsiders to distinguish legitimate organizations from illegitimate ones. They come to believe in the soundness of the endeavor and the apparent controls that are in place.

To function smoothly, such organizations develop shared understandings regarding the tasks each is to perform and when it is to perform them. Standards for the quality of products and services must be agreed on and adhered to, performance schedules maintained, and so forth. Further, it is generally believed that fiduciaries, like auditors and lawyers, monitor transactions and businesses in accordance with the standards of their respective professions; such beliefs are the underpinnings of the trusting relations on which our economy depends. If individuals could not believe the lawyer's opinion letter, the auditor's certificate, and the representations made by those without fiducial responsibility, the entire system would slow to a halt.

Every organization is surrounded by a unique constellation of such entities, which some have termed "control agents," which maintain an interest in ensuring the organization's compliance with norms and certain standards of performance.[28] Some agents are held more responsible for an organization's conduct than others: fiduciaries, like lawyers and auditors, for instance. Other agents include law enforcement and regulatory bodies, bankers, clients, and professional associations.[29] Although in many cases such agents are retained by the focal organization, because of their fiduciary role, we trust them to do what is proper for everyone involved.

This is the classic view of differentiated systems, the "myth system" that allows commerce to proceed unhindered by doubt and by too much caution. But this view is fraught with paradoxes and inconsistencies; under the veneer of efficiency and effectiveness are numerous opportunities for misunderstanding, conflict, and conscious avoidance, as well as the potential to conceal illicit acts.

The "experts" we are so quick to rely on often do not "know," as the OPM story illustrates so well. Or if they do know, they may not tell us because it is not in their interest to do so. Or the norms of their profession may preclude disclosure.

Division of labor is a necessary part of organizational life, but all too often the divided units do not work together. They may work on the same deals for the same client, and they may rely on each other, but they frequently have very different interests. They are more segmented than they are an integrated whole.[30]

Companies that come together for a particular project, transaction, or series of transactions, as we have seen in the OPM case, generally have specific—often narrow—concerns. Within each organization, the aspects of the deal that occupy an individual's time are further differentiated. This narrow focus can make it difficult for anyone to discover illicit activity by making it possible for evidence to slip or, in some cases, be pushed through the cracks; indeed, segmentation creates cracks. And, because there are multiple actors, each is quick to assume that others are responsible for certain aspects of the deal; when trouble appears, it is relatively easy to shift responsibility for acting to someone else.

Epilogue

IT IS DIFFICULT to say with any certainty whether such "mistakes" are on the rise. We cannot be sure. But it seems as if reports of such debacles and the apparent negligence associated with them appear more and more regularly in the business press. The National Student Marketing, Equity Funding, Home Stake, and the Great Salad Oil swindles are just a few of the substantial frauds that have occurred in recent years. Each of these crimes was committed by the principals of seemingly profitable, growing enterprises. In each case, like OPM, major institutions, lawyers, and accountants were involved. And in each of these cases, like OPM, numerous red flags signaled trouble long before the eventual discovery of fraud; most of the signals went unheeded.

In the past several years, we have also read reports of serious and costly mistakes made by some of the nation's largest banks, reports that appear shockingly similar in character to OPM and the above-mentioned frauds. In the late 1970s, for instance, the Chase Manhattan Bank, the third largest bank in the United States, decided to expand its securities lending business; by doing so, Chase Manhattan hoped to increase revenue in fee-generating activities rather than relying so heavily on loans. (Chase had lost a great deal of money on real estate loans during the recessions in the 1970s.) The small group of Chase Manhattan bankers who headed the operation occupied a part of the basement of Chase Manhattan's Wall Street headquarters. Before long, they became involved with Drysdale Government Securities, a small New York firm that dealt with the obscure practice of buying and selling government securities.

Although Drysdale, an aggressive, four-month-old firm, was turned away by other New York banks (even other departments within Chase Manhattan had shunned Drysdale), Chase's cellar operation grabbed as much of Drysdale's business as it could get its hands on. Its inexperience and its drive to maximize volume to reap the rewards that Chase Manhattan had established for the group—bonuses were tied to the business that the bankers generated—led to heavy trading with the small, undercapitalized Drysdale firm. The Chase Manhattan entrepreneurs wrongly believed they were acting only as brokers, and therefore they were under the mistaken impression that they were not responsible for a customer's failure to meet its commitments; credit checks were sloppy, if done at all. When Drysdale defaulted on its obligations in 1982, Chase Manhattan was left with a $285 million loss.

During the same period, the Penn Square Bank of Oklahoma City, whose headquarters was a small, windowless office in a residential shopping center, was selling $2 billion in loans on gas and oil projects "upstream" to big banks like Chase Manhattan, Chicago's Continental Illinois Bank, and the Seattle First National Bank. At the time, the booming oil business was attractive, and several big banks—particularly those from depressed regions like Chicago's Great Lakes and the Pacific Northwest—were quick to buy into the Penn Square deals. While loan syndications of this sort are fairly common in businesses where large amounts of capital are required, prudent bankers carefully check the borrower's credentials and collateral.

But Penn Square was shaky. Anyone who walked into Penn Square's modest shopping mall office would have been surprised at its dealings with the New York and Chicago banks. The man in charge of Penn Square's oil and gas loans was thirty-four-year-old William G. Patterson, who was known to wear Micky Mouse ears in the office and drink beer from his boot. He was also known to make loans to a number of risky credits. Yet Chase Manhattan and Continental Illinois believed the inexperienced Patterson and his staff had checked on the collateral of the loans they purchased and kept their eyes—and ears—on the borrowers. Seattle First National "looked at Continental and Chase and thought it was in good company," said one high-ranking official at that bank.[1] All of this sounds much too familiar.

Apparently, few people at Chase Manhattan, Continental Illinois, or Seattle First National carefully checked the paperwork provided on the Penn Square loans. If they had, they would have found it wanting. On many of the loans, the only items in the records were the borrowers' names and addresses. Routine credit checks were missing, as were formal lending agreements and legal papers needed to secure the collateral. Nor had any of these big banks thought to check Penn Square's rating with the comptroller of the currency. If they had done so, they would have learned that Penn Square was on the comptroller's "problem list," a fact the comptroller's office failed to pass on to affected banks.

On the Fourth of July weekend in 1982, Penn Square was closed by federal regulators. The biggest loser on the Penn Square deals was Continental Illinois, once the nation's sixth largest bank, which lost $200 million. The Penn Square debacle, coupled with substantial loans to troubled companies such as International Harvester, Braniff, Chrysler, Charter Company, and AM International, brought the Chicago bank to the brink of collapse. In mid-1984, the Federal Deposit Insurance Corporation (FDIC) rescued Continental Illinois with $4.5 billion.

We are continually surprised by such reports. After all, fraudulent operators and poor credits always leave trails. The residue of fraud—altered documents, lies, and missing assets—is there to be found. In each of these cases, warning signals had appeared long before the eventual discovery of misconduct. But the crimes and suspect behavior had occurred for years.

Following incidents of this sort and the publicity they engender, there is often a cry for reform. Many people push for more rules and policies to prevent such crimes from occurring or at least allowing them to continue for so long. In the case of OPM, a congressional committee and the American Bar Association continue to debate the ethical standards for lawyers who learn about a client's illegal conduct. Bankers have stiffened loan requirements on OPM-like deals and, in some cases, now require on-site inspection of the computer equipment used as collateral. Many lessees and lessors have also been forced to alter traditional ways of doing business. All of these changes stem, in part, from the OPM fraud. Are such changes likely to prevent future occurrences of fraud? Can we really do anything to reduce the risk of such crimes?

Perhaps. But there are no simple solutions. If our studies of organizations have taught us anything, it is that there is no such thing as an optimal policy for a situation of great complexity. If we try to reduce the risks of one thing, we frequently surrender something else; we become caught in a network of "interlocking dilemmas."[2] Controls protecting against fraud and similar misconduct must be balanced against the probability and costs of future occurrences. In other words, the costs of compliance should not exceed the expected potential loss due to the behavior we are trying to prevent. If procedures for granting loans become too restrictive, for instance, loan officers may bypass even the most crude credit checks to avoid the hassles. Or, worse yet, the business of business may become so bogged down with rules and regulations that nothing gets done; Max Weber's "iron cage" of bureaucracy may come to fruition.

I have noted several times throughout this book that crimes of this magnitude are rare events. Indeed, one of the reasons people associated with OPM may have initially ignored the signs of fraud is that the possibility of criminal activity never occurred to them; there was little in their experiences that told them to be on the lookout for such crime. Their feelings were probably well-grounded. It is undoubtedly true that most transactions are without fraud and deception, although we really don't know for certain. Nor do we know whether such crimes are on the rise, although they seem to be. Nonetheless, it would be a mistake to radically alter traditional ways of doing things on the basis of several cases. But are there lessons to be learned from OPM that go beyond the prevention of fraud?

I believe so. Many managers and professionals face similar difficult decisions that were faced by the people associated with OPM and, it appears, increasingly so. For instance, a test engineer learns his boss is withholding damaging information on a new product. Should the engineer report the matter to more senior managers? In another instance, an accountant is asked—pressured—by an important client to disguise certain liabilities that are material to a client's financial statement. The accountant has already been told his firm will be fired if it persists in reporting the liabilities or in qualifying the statement. Should the accountant persist? Wouldn't it be easier to find some "partially" legitimate way to disguise the liabilities? Who would know?

A manager is present when a colleague and friend discuss a kickback with one of the company's suppliers. Should the manager confront the friend? Suppose the friend agrees not to take the kickback, but later the manager learns that he did? Should the matter be reported? Whom should it be reported to?

A very senior level executive in a well-paying job in a small- to medium-sized manufacturing firm has a suspicion that the CEO of his company is embezzling money. Should the executive look into the matter? How can this be done without arousing the suspicions of the CEO? What if the executive uncovers evidence that the CEO is, in fact, embezzling money—should it be reported to the board of directors? What if it turns out that there was a reasonable, legitimate explanation for the missing funds, yet the CEO now knows the executive suspected him of foul play?

A young partner in a medium-sized law firm learns that one of his most important clients, and one that he had become quite friendly with, is about to obtain a loan through fraudulent means. Should the lawyer confront his client? What if the client insists that it is a "minor misrepresentation," that no one will be the wiser, and, in any case, no one will get hurt? Should the lawyer resign if the client proceeds with his fraud? Should the lawyer warn the victim? Wouldn't it be easier for the lawyer to look the other way, particularly since he is not directly involved in the transaction?

These are not uncommon experiences. Managers and professionals everywhere are torn between the need to trust associates, allowing them the freedom to operate unrestricted by too many controls, but knowing full well that this trust leaves them vulnerable to fraud and to other forms of misconduct. All persons in the position of monitoring the activities of others, whether they are accountants, bankers, lawyers, consultants, or managers, must balance the need to maintain a relationship with those they monitor, to be friendly, cordial, and cooperative to get the information and business they need, against the possibility of becoming blind to what goes on around them or becoming co-opted by the wrongdoers.

People in business today must also maintain the sometimes difficult balance of one's own personal and professional ethical standards against those of the corporations they work with. And, often, individuals simply don't know whether certain conduct is "right" or "wrong," legal or illegal, and since others around them appear unconcerned, they, too, are inclined to ignore the matter. Many questions about suspicious activity are never asked for this very reason. Managers and professionals feel pressure to act self-assured, to be "in the know." Those who are cautious and too reflective move too slowly and miss out on the big deals. No one wants to appear foolish in the eyes of his superiors or clients; it is often best to leave certain questions that are troublesome in the hands of specialists—asking the "obvious" question may give him away.

There are other reasons people do not act, of course. As mentioned earlier, personal and corporate self-interest frequently serves as a disincentive for detecting and reporting corporate misconduct. The accountant who is too thorough or the lawyer who is too careful may not be invited back by the client. And lawyers or accountants can quite easily convince themselves to bend the rules if the matter is not their primary responsibility or if the rule-bending is insignificant or if they really don't know, in the legal sense, that the rule was being violated.

In the OPM case, we have seen how situational pressures, both financial and personal loyalty and friendship, led people to look the other way in the face of mounting evidence of fraudulent activity. The loose structure of accountability, both within and between organizations, diffused knowledge and personal responsibility for acting on the fraudulent signals, making it easier for people to claim they had no knowledge of Goodman's and Weissman's criminal ways.

These conditions exist elsewhere in American society, and they are conditions that encourage bystander apathy, where there is no responsibility or incentive to take the steps necessary to control corporate misconduct. What can and should be done?

It is difficult if not impossible to offer prescriptions on such complex matters, but it is possible to suggest several directions that will prevent or, at least, lower the probability of future OPM-like frauds.

First, we need to examine carefully the laws and codes of ethics that govern the behavior of professionals engaged in business practice. Laws and codes of ethics communicate normative information—acceptable and unacceptable patterns of behavior—and legal standards could help delineate responsibilities among corporate actors. But, all too often, ethical codes are pretensions, written by persons within the same profession and designed to protect members from criminal and civil action. And because rules of conduct must be approved by the profession's legislative body, they are frequently ambiguous, offering little real guidance to the practitioner.

Further, the confidentiality norms of the professions need to be reexamined in light of the increasing interdependence of organizations. More and more in society today, professionals are granting confidentiality to their clients, thereby closing off a major opportunity for outsiders to learn about improprieties being committed by companies they do business with. Lawyers, bankers, auditors, and other consultants are among the corporate advisors who are being asked to keep silent about the information they obtain from their clients.[3] There are often sound reasons for granting these confidences. Lawyers, for instance, would be severely handicapped as advocates for their clients if the clients were uncomfortable about revealing certain information; the confidentiality between an attorney and client provides a confidence that the facts revealed will be protected. While this protection is critical, it is just as critical that attorneys, as officers of the courts, do not use confidentiality as a cloak for criminal activity.

Moreover, for laws and ethical standards to have the necessary deterrent effect, they must be enforced and enforced swiftly. This is especially difficult in cases involving corporate misconduct. Unlike street crime, where there are usually an identifiable perpetrator and victim, white-collar crimes may involve a number of victims and offenders with varying degrees of culpability. Sorting all of this out takes time. And the accused in white-collar crimes can often afford high-powered attorneys whose legal maneuvering also stretches the period from indictment to sentencing. Notwithstanding these difficulties, some of the delay seems excessive. For instance, it took over two years for the U.S. attorney to investigate, negotiate a plea, and bring Goodman and his team before Judge Charles S. Haight for sentencing. As of December 1984, nearly four years after an investigation ensued, neither the American Bar Association nor the American Institute of Certified Public Accountants has ruled on the conduct of the lawyers or accountants involved with OPM.

But rules and codes only come into effect after a problem is perceived—or to put it another way, when a certain amount of damage has already occurred. And every institution will sooner or later come up against a situation that cannot be solved by following the rules— there may not be any. Further, rules and laws only establish outer limits: what we are not allowed to do. But there are many gray areas in which individuals are left on their own and where inconsistent and competing norms only encourage inaction. What about the circumstances where there are no rules?

The second area of attention would include more clarification of appropriate conduct in these gray areas and more guidance in resolving some of these dilemmas. This effort can be led by business and professional schools, which can devote more effort to teaching ethical and moral responsibilities. Professional associations can do more to publicize cases and red flags of misconduct. John Clifton, for instance, stopped rationalizing Goodman's conduct only after he had read an article on the flags of fraud in an accounting journal.

Professional groups may want to create hotlines where members can call in anonymously to resolve ethical issues. Committees and study groups in all professions may also help to shed new light on some of these difficult issues.

Corporations and professional firms can do more, too. Many leading corporations are developing guiding principles or corporate philosophies that serve as public statements of the organizations' approach to business. They help direct the actions of employees where rules and procedures don't exist. These mission statements help shape a consistent corporate culture that more and more business analysts say is critical to a company's success.

In some cases, these corporate philosophies need to be broadened to address ethical issues. Most important, they need to be living, breathing statements of how an organization actually operates. They have to help individuals decide what is right. Senior managers can exemplify their organization's values through their decisions, and incentives can be provided for conduct that upholds these values. Seminars, training, and educational programs can be established to communicate the message and alert employees to red flags of fraud, other forms of misconduct, and appropriate responses to each.

On a broader scale, the business and legal communities have an obligation to do more to do away with the get-away-with-what-you-can climate that seems to predominate in some circles today. More needs to be done to identify and eradicate euphemisms that neutralize the seriousness of business crimes. Phrases like "business is business" or "business as usual" reduce the seriousness of the crime to all those who hear such remarks. Substituting "double-hocking" for fraud or "commissions" for bribery or "fudging" or "creative accounting" for fraud and misrepresentation—have the same effects.

We can simplify the way transactions are handled. And we can change the laws and ethical rules to provide clearer accountability and, hopefully, more communication between these interdependent actors. But laws and rules alone cannot carry the burden of controlling corporate crime. Members of the business community have the ultimate responsibility to communicate their unwillingness to accept or tolerate the kind of conduct exhibited by so many in the OPM affair and others like it.

APPENDIX

Listing of Witnesses and Organizational Affiliations

NAME	ORGANIZATION
Aiello, Frank	American Express
Alexander, Klaren Keith	Fox & Company
Alpert, Charles	OPM
Baptist, Preston	OPM
Barany, Craig B.	OPM
Batkin, Alan Richard	Lehman Brothers Kuhn Loeb
Berger, Morton	Fox & Company
Byrnes, Dan	Rockwell International
Carrao, Frank	OPM
Carrao, Margo	OPM
Childs, Rogers C.	Philadelphia Savings Fund Society
Clare, Robert	White & Case
Clifton, John	OPM
Clover, Ralph	Drinker, Biddle & Reath
Dahn, Maury	Rockwell International
Davis, William	Shulman Berlin & Davis
Dillion, Gerald P.	Bank of New York
Driscoll, Emmett	Bank of New York
DuVall, Theresa A.	Bank of New York
Evans, Michael	Chemical Bank
Feinerman, Judah	Judd Associates
Friedmann, Mannes	OPM
Ganz, Allen	OPM
Ganz, Samuel	OPM
Gauthier, G.	Rockwell International
Glucksman, Lewis	Lehman

Goodman, Myron S.	OPM
Greenberg, Max	Lehman Brothers Kuhn Loeb; OPM
Haggerty, William	Fox & Company
Hasin, Sidney	Rockwell International
Holloway, Ruth	OPM
Hutner, Joseph	Singer Hutner Levine & Seeman
Jacobs, Alan	Singer Hutner Levine & Seeman
Kearney, Michael	Frank B. Hall & Company, Inc.
Klapperman, Rabbi Gilbert	Beth Shalom Synagogue
Klineman, Kent	Klineman Associates
Kutz, Stephen	Fox & Company
Kyle, Mary	Rockwell International
Lamm, Norman	Yeshiva University
Laskin, Burton	Rashba & Pokart
Lesnick, David H.	OPM
Lichtman, Stephen M.	OPM
McClellan, LeRoy	Philadelphia Savings Fund Society
McLaughlin, Dean Joseph	Former Dean of Fordham Law, now Federal District Court Judge
Malinowski, Timothy	Simpson Thacher & Bartlett
Mattioli, Eli	Singer Hutner Levine & Seeman
Moscarello, Louis	Coopers & Lybrand
Neeley, William	Rockwell International
Orlinsky, David	Counsel to Sha-Li Leasing, Prussin
Peck, Joel	Lehman Brothers Kuhn Loeb
Petersen, Robert E.	Rockwell International
Phillips, Alan	Fox & Company; OPM; Sha-Li Leasing
Pierce, Jack	Rockwell International
Pierre, Antoinnette Marie	OPM
Plotch, Walter	Yeshiva University
Prussin, George	Electronic Memories and Magnetics Corporation; OPM; Sha-Li Leasing
Putzel, Henry Peter III	Attorney
Rabinowitz, Shlomo	OPM
Reinhard, Andrew	Singer Hutner Levine & Seeman
Resnick, Jeffry	OPM
Sacks, David	Lehman Brothers Kuhn Loeb
Santulli, Richard Thomas	Goldman Sachs & Company; RTS Capital Corporation
Scheussler, Robert W.	Rockwell International

Schulhof, Jacob	Jess E. Gross Inc.
Shapiro, Hoby	OPM
Shulman, Martin	American Express; OPM
Simon, Gary S.	OPM
Spindel, Paul	Oppenheim, Appel, Dixon & Company
Vande Woude, Theodore	Merrill Lynch Fenner & Pierce
Weinberg, Michael B.	OPM
Weissman, Marvin	Rashba & Pokart
Weissman, Mordecai	OPM
Werner, Jeffrey	First National Bank of St. Paul
Wilner, Bernard	Rockwell International
Zelbow, Martin	Coopers & Lybrand
Zieses, Marshall	Rashba & Pokart
Zimmerman, Richard	Richard Zimmerman Designs

A NOTE ON THE DATA

In March 1981, OPM filed for protection from its creditors under Chapter 11 of the Federal Bankruptcy Act. In the same month, the United States trustee, Irving Picard, appointed James P. Hassett as the trustee to the OPM estate. From that time until March 1983, Mr. Hassett conducted an investigation of OPM and its principals pursuant to his responsibilities as the OPM trustee under rule 205 of the Federal Bankruptcy Act. Attorneys for the trustee, the respected law firm of Wilmer, Cutler & Pickering, examined witnesses from May 1981 until February 1983 to determine major events, the extent of the fraud, participants, victims, and so forth. The trustee's counsel interviewed, at length, over seventy-five witnesses (a listing of witnesses and their organizational affiliations appears in the appendix), which produced more than 60,000 pages of testimony in 281 days. In addition, over one million pages of documents were produced in the trustee's investigation. Their findings have been recorded in the trustee's report to Bankruptcy Judge Burton Lifland (United States Bankruptcy Court, Southern District of New York in re. OPM Leasing Services, Inc., reorganization no. 81–B–10533 [BRL], the *Report of the Trustee Concerning Fraud and Other Misconduct in the Management of the Affairs of the Debtor*, April 25, 1983, herein referred to as the Hassett Report). I attended the depositions of most of the witnesses. I also attended the sentencing of each of the criminals. These examinations, the sentencing hearings, the transcripts and accompanying exhibits, and the Hassett Report were my primary data sources. In addition, I have interviewed several witnesses on my own as well as OPM employees who were not called to testify, but were working for the leasing company when the frauds occurred. Moreover, I have interviewed James P. Hassett, and Stephen Black and Arthur Matthews of Wilmer, Cutler & Pickering on numerous occasions, each of whom have provided invaluable background information and insight on the leasing industry and the behavior of those involved with OPM. Talks with lawyers for witnesses have also helped make clear the roles of their clients. I have also spoken to a number of people outside of OPM who are familiar with the industry, the legal issues, investment banking, and accounting principles. Articles, reports, books, and memoranda were also used to supplement the interviews and testimony. Specific references to certain parts of the narrative are noted in the following citations. All cited testimony refer to depositions given in the OPM trustee's investigation.

NOTES

Chapter 1

1. Statement made by federal district court Judge Charles S. Haight, Jr., in sentencing Goodman and Weissman on December 20, 1982.

2. Letter from OPM Trustee James P. Hassett to Judge Charles S. Haight, Jr., 29 November 1982.

3. Statement made by Judge Charles S. Haight in sentencing Goodman and Weissman on December 20, 1982.

4. Stuart Taylor, Jr., "Two Get Prison in Computer Case," *The New York Times*, 21 December 1982, p. D1; Paul Blustein, "Two are Sentenced to Prison Terms in OPM Fraud," *The Wall Street Journal*, 21 December 1982, p. 16.

5. Letter Hassett to Haight, 29 November 1982.

6. Testimony provided by Myron S. Goodman for Chapter 11 proceedings Under the Bankruptcy Reform Act, U.S. District Court, Southern District of New York, Docket No. 81–B–10533 (BL), pp. 93–94.

7. Sissela Bok, *Secrets: On the Ethics of Concealment and Revelation* (New York: Pantheon, 1982).

8. Lawrence W. Sherman, *Scandal and Reform: Controlling Police Corruption* (Berkeley, Ca.: University of California Press, 1978).

9. Following the Kitty Genovese murder in Kew Gardens, Queens, in 1964, several social psychologists conducted a series of experiments in which subjects under varying circumstances were fooled into thinking a stranger was in distress. When the naive subject was alone, he or she would rush to the aid of the victim, but if others were present, naive subjects were much less likely to act. The presence of others diffused responsibility. John M. Darley and Bibb Latane, "Bystander Intervention in Emergencies: Diffusion of Responsibility," *Journal of Personality and Social Psychology*, vol. 8, 1968, pp. 377–383; see also C. Mynatt and S.J. Sherman, "Personality Attribution in Groups and Individuals: A Direct Test of the Diffusion of Responsibility Hypothesis," *Journal of Personality and Social Psychology*, vol. 32, 1975, pp. 1111–1118.

Chapter 2

1. Testimony provided by Allen Ganz (closed session) for Chapter 11 Proceedings Under the Bankruptcy Reform Act, U.S. District Court, Southern District of New York, Docket No. 81–B–10533 (BL). See also Hassett Report, p. 57.

2. Letter from Goodman to the Commissioner of Young Israel Softball League, 13 June 1977.

3. Hassett Report, pp. 57–58.

4. Hassett Report, p. 194.

5. Hassett Report, pp. 189–194.

6. Hassett Report, p. 21.

7. Author interviews with former OPM employees, 1982–1983.

8. Statement made by John Clifton to the author, February 2, 1982.

9. Testimony provided by Myron S. Goodman, November 10, 1982.

10. Two Big Eight firms had audited OPM's books in previous years; Peat, Marwick, Mitchell and Company conducted an audit of OPM's books for the 1972 fiscal year and Touche Ross & Company for the 1973 fiscal year.

11. Testimony provided by Myron S. Goodman, November 10, 1982.

12. Horne Nadler & Company did not conduct a full-fledged audit. The report was based on financial records submitted to them by OPM. See the Hassett Report, pp 219–220.

13. Testimony provided by Marshall Zieses, January 9, 1982.

14. Testimony provided by John Clifton, January 26, 1982.

15. Hassett Report, pp. 192–194.

16. Hassett Report, pp. 47–48.

17. Hassett Report, p. 111, fn. 65.

18. Testimony provided by Marshall Zieses, January 9, 1982.

19. Goodman testified that he has confided in Marvin Weissman about the frauds a year before the discovery made by Zieses. The trustee's investigation found little support for Goodman's claim.

Chapter 3

1. Testimony provided by Richard T. Santulli on March 5, 1982 for Chapter 11 Proceedings Under the Bankruptcy Reform Act, U.S. District Court, Southern District of New York, Docket No. 81–B–10533 (BL).

2. Hassett Report, p. 425, fn. 2.

3. Testimony provided by Myron S. Goodman on November 18, 1982.

4. Testimony provided by John Clifton on January 26, 1982.

5. Testimony provided by John Clifton on January 26, 1982.

6. Testimony provided by John Clifton on January 28, 1982; see also Hassett Report, p. 235.

7. Testimony provided by Morton Berger on August 25, 1981.

8. Testimony provided by Marvin Weissman on March 17, 1983.

9. Testimony provided by Morton Berger on August 25, 1981; testimony provided by Stephen Kutz on July 23–24, 27, 29 and August 4–5, 1981.

10. Testimony provided by Marvin Weissman on March 17, 1983.

11. Testimony provided by Morton Berger on August 25, 1981 and testimony provided by John Clifton on January 28, 1982.

12. Testimony provided by Morton Berger on August 25, 1981.

13. Kutz Exhibit 12, OPM Bankruptcy Proceedings.

14. Fox was retained only after passing the Myron Goodman test. Goodman told Fox that he preferred that OPM's leases be classified as operating leases as opposed to finance leases. Coincidentally, classifying leases as operating leases improves the lessor's balance sheet picture. Before engaging Fox, Goodman gave the firm a sample of leases to classify; Fox classified most of the sample leases as operating leases.

15. Testimony provided by Stephen Kutz on July 27, 1981.

16. Testimony provided by Marshall Zieses on January 9, 1982.

17. Hassett Report, p. 240.

18. On several occasions in late 1975 and 1976, Goodman and Weissman stuffed cash in an envelope and gave it to Danny Asher, one of OPM's chauffeurs, to take to IBM's White Plains office. Asher would drive to IBM's office at 360 Hamilton Avenue and, as is customary at an IBM

facility, he would sign it, identifying his organizational affiliation as OPM, for which Goodman later chastised him, and was ushered to Monks's office. Monks and Asher would exchange packages and Asher would drive back to New York.

19. Rockwell's procurement policy stated that all items over $500 in value were to be obtained through competitive bidding. Hasin thought the bidding policy was "misguided" and didn't apply to leasing.

20. Hassett Report, p. 493.

21. John Conti, "Substantial profit decline is seen for Rockwell in fiscal 1975; Dividend may face pressure," *The Wall Street Journal*, 21 March 1975, p. 29.

22. For equipment under $500,000, only Dahn's approval was required. Equipment valued between $500,000 and $1,000,000 required approval from DePalma and the vice-president of operations. And equipment over $1 million had to be approved by Rockwell's management committee. See Hassett Report, p. 492.

23. Rockwell's importance in the area of national defense provided the company priority in the purchase of the most advanced equipment as it became available. Moreover, IBM often used Rockwell as a test site for its new equipment. But being a sophisticated user did not mean it was sophisticated in acquiring the equipment.

24. Hasin Exhibit 49, OPM Bankruptcy Proceedings.

25. Testimony provided by Sidney Hasin on September 11, 1981.

26. "Leasing's New IBM Jitters," *Business Week*, 27 February 1978, p. 70.

Chapter 4

1. Hassett Report, pp. 55, 195.

2. Testimony provided by Richard T. Santulli on August 7, 1982 for Chapter 11 Proceedings Under the Bankruptcy Reform Act, U.S. District Court, Southern District of New York, Docket No. 81–B–10533 (BL).

3. Batkin Exhibit 7–1, OPM Bankruptcy Proceedings.

4. Joseph Weschberg, *The Merchant Bankers* (Boston: Little, Brown, 1966), pp. 219–261.

5. Lehman Brothers Kuhn Loeb, Descriptive Memoranda, 1980, p. 6.

6. Weschberg, *The Merchant Bankers*, p. 252.

7. Weschberg, *The Merchant Bankers*, p. 252.

8. Weschberg, *The Merchant Bankers*, p. 227.

9. In July 1983, Petersen announced his resignation; he turned the reins over to Lewis L. Glucksman at the end of the year. In April 1984, Lehman was acquired by Shearson/American Express, an acquisition that was initiated by several Lehman partners who were tired of the infighting within the firm—battles often caused by Glucksman. Glucksman is no longer the head of Lehman.

10. Weschberg, *The Merchant Bankers*, pp. 248–249.

11. Weschberg, *The Merchant Bankers*, p. 249.

12. Weschberg, *The Merchant Bankers*, p. 251.

13. Michael C. Jensen, *The World of the Great Wall Street Investment Banking Houses* (New York: Weybright and Talley, 1976).

14. Tim Carrington, "Lehman Brothers' Peterson plans to quit as co-chief Glucksman gets full control," *The Wall Street Journal*, 27 July 1983, p. 5.

15. Testimony provided by David Sacks on August 26, 1982.

16. Testimony provided by David Sacks on August 26, 1982.

17. Testimony provided by Lewis L. Glucksman on August 17, 1982.

18. "The 500,"*Fortune*, 30 April 1984, pp. 274–322.

19. Testimony provided by Alan Batkin on August 27, 1981.

20. It is interesting that Lehman succeeded Goldman, Sachs as OPM's investment bankers.

The relationship between Lehman and Goldman, Sachs goes back to the early 1900s. Philip Lehman and Henry Goldman were friends, and their two firms jointly underwrote securities, including securities for a Goldman cousin, Julius Rosenwald, who owned Sears, Roebuck. By the 1920s, however, a bitter feud started and lasted some thirty years, until a permanent truce was established in 1956 when, once again, Sears needed money to establish its sales acceptance subsidiary. Perhaps the OPM fraud will start another feud.

21. SEC v. First Securities Co. 463 F. 2d 981, 988 (7th Cir.), cert. denied, sub nom. McKy v. Hochfelder et al. 409 U.S.880 (1972). Lower courts ruled that the auditor was negligent for its failure to conduct proper audits of First Securities Company, a small brokerage firm, thereby failing to detect internal practices and procedures that prevented an effective audit. One such practice was the defendant's "mail rule." The U.S. Court of Appeals for the Seventh Circuit subsequently overruled the lower court.

22. Testimony provided by Myron S. Goodman on November 11, 1982.

23. Hassett Report, p. 248.

24. Testimony provided by John Clifton on January 4, 1982.

25. Testimony provided by Marvin Weissman on September 23, 1981.

26. It wasn't exactly Kutz's method. Kutz did discover a precedent for the technique described. Alanthus, another computer leasing company, also recognized certain income immediately rather than amortizing it over the life of the lease. But when the Financial Accounting Standards Board (FASB) issued its Standards No. 13—accounting for leases—in late 1976, Alanthus restated its financials bringing them in line with FASB 13. By doing so, the company's earnings declined. Fox continued to use the "Kutz method" in spite of FASB 13 and never amended the 1976 financials.

27. Hassett Report, pp. 80, 255; appendix 20, affadavit of Phillip E. Lint.

Chapter 5

1. Testimony provided by Sidney Hasin on January 13, 1982 for Chapter 11 Proceedings Under the Bankruptcy Reform Act, U.S. District Court, Southern District of New York, Docket No. 81–B–10533 (BL).

2. Hassett Report, pp. 503–530; see also testimony provided by Sidney Hasin on October 11, 1981.

3. Testimony provided by Sidney Hasin on January 8, 1982.

4. Testimony provided by Sidney Hasin on January 8, 1982.

5. Testimony provided by Sidney Hasin on January 8, 1982.

6. Testimony provided by Sidney Hasin on January 8, 1982.

7. Testimony provided by Sidney Hasin on January 13, 1982.

8. Testimony provided by Sidney Hasin on January 14, 1982.

9. Testimony provided by Myron S. Goodman on November 17, 1982.

10. Howard E. Aldrich, *Organizations and Environment* (Englewood Cliffs, N.J.: Prentice-Hall, Inc., 1979); Jeffrey Pfeffer and Gerald Salancik, *The External Control of Organizations* (New York: Harper & Row, 1978).

11. Goodman claimed Weissman taught him the art of kiting, but Weissman denies doing so. See Hassett Report, p. 116.

12. Testimony provided by Lewis L. Glucksman on August 17, 1982.

13. Testimony provided by Alan Batkin on September 1, 1981.

14. Testimony provided by Lewis L. Glucksman on August 17, 1982.

15. Testimony provided by Alan Batkin on September 1, 1981.

16. Goodman remembered Sacks telling him that OPM was a substantial client—somewhere in Lehman's "top five percent."

17. Testimony provided by Lewis L. Glucksman on August 17, 1982.

18. Testimony provided by Jeffrey Werner on February 24, 1982.

19. OPM was one of the first, if not the first, equipment leasing company for which the FNBSP provided credit for.

20. The "normality" that Glucksman describes did not occur in the OPM debacle. Indeed, Lehman portrayed OPM's financial picture in favorable terms to the St. Paul bank in 1980 when it had reason to believe the company was on the verge of collapse.

21. Testimony provided by Lewis L. Glucksman on August 17, 1982.

22. Testimony provided by Jeffrey Werner on February 23, 1982.

23. At one point, Goodman testified: "Anytime you give financials to banks they usually cause more problems," something he learned from his experience with Chase Manhattan Bank in 1974.

24. The Hassett report concluded: "The obvious explanation for the 'unexplainable' was that OPM was receiving back large amounts of equipment under early termination provisions and was unable to re-lease the equipment at rentals even approximating the original rentals. As a result, while OPM's equipment-related debt remained fixed and OPM became obligated to reimburse the lessees for their payments to the financing institutions, OPM's lease receivables declined from the original rental amount to the much lower amount it was receiving on the re-lease of the equipment. The part of the footnote 2/footnote 4 discrepancy that was truly 'unexplainable' was how Weissman and Goodman could possibly obtain funds by legitimate means to fill the $76 million gap." See Hassett Report, p. 280.

25. Testimony provided by Jeffrey Werner on February 23, 1982; see also Werner Exhibit 31.

26. Batkin Exhibit 25, OPM Bankruptcy Proceedings.

27. Prussin pleaded his fifth amendment rights during the bankruptcy proceeding, but through his lawyers, he claimed he did not believe OPM was on the verge of bankruptcy. Moreover, the payments were merely money owed him for the commission agreement he had with OPM. The OPM trustee filed suit against Prussin and Sha-Li Leasing (Prussin's leasing company) to recoup the money paid to Sha-Li. Prussin filed a counter suit against the trustee for libel. During the summer of 1984, the OPM trustee settled his claims against Prussin. Prussin paid OPM $850,000.

28. Testimony provided by Myron S. Goodman on November 11, 1982.

29. Weissman didn't recall this being discussed on January 1. He did recall a meeting between the two on February 1, however.

30. According to Goodman, an *explicit* discussion about him taking the rap did not occur until July 29, 1980.

31. Hassett Report, p. 24.

32. Testimony provided by Myron S. Goodman on November 11, 1982.

33. Hassett Report, p. 126.

34. Hassett Report, pp. 123–129.

35. Testimony provided by Myron S. Goodman on November 17, 1982.

36. Hassett Report, p. 127.

37. Testimony provided by Myron S. Goodman on November 17, 1982.

38. Testimony provided by Myron S. Goodman on November 17, 1982.

39. See Hassett Report, pp. 190–191. The OPM trustee brought suits against Ganz, Lichtman, Shulman, and Friedman for breaching their fiduciary responsibilities as officers of the company with their participation in the Rockwell fraud. The actions against the former officers are to recover salary and loans made to participants in the fraud. The trustee has settled the claim with Allen Ganz.

40. Goodman testified that Reinhard was aware that the February 9 Rockwell transaction was a fraud. Indeed, Reinhard was aware of OPM's crimes all along, Goodman said, and he often relied on the attorney to assist in the fraud or its coverup. Although the trustee concluded that there is a "ring of truth" to Goodman's testimony about Reinhard, there are many inconsistencies.

41. Singer Hutner attorneys denied ever requesting original documentation according to the Hassett Report, p. 370.

42. Hassett Report, p. 500.

43. Hassett Report, p. 145.

44. The Hassett Report referred to such carelessness as "other people's mistakes."

45. Testimony provided by Myron S. Goodman on November 17, 1982.

Chapter 6

1. "Computer Firm Indicted for Kiting," *American Banker*, 10 March 1980, p. 16. In June 1982, the U.S. Supreme Court ruled that check-kiting does not involve a false statement to a bank (Williams v. United States 102 s. ct. 308 [1982]) and thus does not violate the federal false statements statute, 18 U. S. C. 1001.

2. "Computer Firm is Indicted for Check-kiting," *American Banker*, 15 April 1980, p. 3; see also fn. 1, this chapter.

3. Goodman and Weissman had obvious reasons to fear a long investigation and trial that undoubtedly would delve into their financial affairs. Rather than risk the discovery of their earlier crimes, they were forced to plead guilty.

4. Carl J. Rubino of Singer Hutner was OPM's primary contact with the prosecutor's office. Rubino directed his efforts at trying to save Goodman from a jail sentence because of Goodman's excessive fear of incarceration. Rubino was able to do so by claiming that Goodman's physical ailments impaired his judgment, that he really had no intention of committing fraud.

5. Batkin Exhibit 58–3E, Chapter 11 Proceedings Under the Bankruptcy Reform Act, U.S. District Court, Southern District of New York, Docket No. 81–B–10533 (BL).

6. Lehman contends it neither requested nor used the guide.

7. Testimony provided by LeRoy McClellan on March 8, 1982.

8. Batkin Exhibit 48–2, OPM Bankruptcy Proceedings.

9. Batkin Exhibit 48–46, OPM Bankruptcy Proceedings.

10. Actually, Fox had been doing consulting services for OPM between November 1976 and December 1979 in addition to its audit work.

11. Batkin Exhibit 37–B, OPM Bankruptcy Proceedings.

12. According to Krause, "If a dealer [like OPM] sends in payment for one or more of his accounts this must be questioned. Dealer payments are regarded as a 'red flag' which could signify any one of a number of situations injurious to the financier's interests. It could mean . . . that the transaction is actually fraudulent." Robert C. Krause, "Financing Industrial Time Sales," in *Commercial Financing*, edited by Monroe R. Lazere (New York: The Roland Press, 1968), p. 177.

13. Testimony provided by Alan Batkin on November 3, 1981, and Myron S. Goodman on November 18, 1982.

14. Testimony provided by Alan Batkin on November 7, 1981.

15. Zelbow was not fresh from business school, however. Previously, he had worked as a consultant, corporate planner, and investment banker. And although he was a CPA, he had never done audit work.

16. Zelbow Exhibit 2, OPM Bankruptcy Proceedings.

17. Zelbow Exhibit 14, OPM Bankruptcy Proceedings.

18. Testimony provided by Louis Moscarello on November 23, 1981.

19. Testimony provided by John Clifton on April 29, 1982, and Martin Zelbow on September 15, 1981.

20. Hassett Report, p. 318.

21. Testimony provided by Martin Zelbow on September 15, 1981.

22. Testimony provided by Martin Zelbow on September 15, 1981.

23. Testimony provided by Martin Zelbow on September 24, 1981.

24. Testimony provided by Martin Zelbow on September 15, 1981.

25. Testimony provided by Myron S. Goodman on November 18, 1982, and Martin Zelbow on September 16, 1981.

26. Testimony provided by Martin Zelbow on September 16, 1981.

27. Zelbow Exhibit 40, OPM Bankruptcy Proceedings.

28. John Clifton, conversation with author, 2 February 1982.

29. Klineman, a Harvard Law School graduate, had previously been under indictment for conspiracy in the Home Stake Fraud. Charges were dropped on February 7, 1977, but Klineman was later sued by the Home Stake trustee and settled out of court for $100,000. Between December 1972 and January 1981, Klineman and Klineman Associates received about $5.3 million in fees from OPM. Hassett Report, p. 483.

30. Testimony provided by Myron S. Goodman on November 10, 1982.

31. Testimony provided by John Clifton on April 29, 1982.

32. Testimony provided by John Clifton on April 29, 1982.

33. Hassett Report, p. 297.

34. Goodman's motivation to confess at that time is unclear. He testified that he wanted Marvin Weissman's help in devising a plan or strategy to pay back the fraudulent loans as he had done previously. Marvin Weissman claimed that Goodman was concerned about the confirmations Fox wanted to send out in connection with the 1979 audit. See Hassett Report, pp. 300–301.

35. Testimony provided by Myron S. Goodman on November 30, 1982, and Marvin Weissman on March 17, 1983.

36. Goodman claimed Reinhard was unaware of Marvin Weissman being present when he called.

37. Goodman testified that Reinhard knew about OPM's frauds for some time and even helped carry them out. See chapter 5, fn. 40.

38. Hassett Report, p. 55.

39. Hassett Report, pp. 341–353.

40. Hassett Report, p. 302.

41. Testimony provided by Morton Berger on September 3, 1981.

42. The *accountant* has no duty to disclose an illegal act to the Board of Directors, but an *auditor* does. The Statement on Auditing Standards No. 17 states that:

> when an illegal act, including one that does not have a material effect on the financial statements comes to the auditor's attention, he should consider the nature of the act and management's consideration once the matter is brought to their attention. If the client's board of directors, its audit committee, or other appropriate levels within the organization do not give appropriate consideration . . . to the illegal act, the auditor should consider withdrawing from the current engagement or dissociating himself from any future relationship with the client.

Since Rashba & Pokart were not OPM's auditors at the time, there was no *obligation* to inform Reinhard and Mordecai Weissman.

43. Testimony provided by John Clifton on April 29, 1982.

44. Testimony provided by John Clifton on April 29, 1982.

45. Testimony provided by John Clifton on April 29, 1982.

46. Testimony provided by William Davis on August 24, 1982.

47. Clifton Exhibit 310, OPM Bankruptcy Proceedings.

48. Testimony provided by Preston Baptist on June 30, 1981.

49. Testimony provided by Myron S. Goodman on November 2, 1982; see also the Hassett Report.

50. Testimony provided by John Clifton on April 29, 1982.

51. There are two versions of the meetings: Davis's view, which is presented in this chapter, and Hutner's, which is presented in chapter 8. The two versions are rarely in agreement. I should note, however, that much of Davis's testimony coincided with two memos he wrote shortly after his meetings with Hutner. See Hutner Exhibits 5 and 6, OPM Bankruptcy Proceedings.

52. Testimony provided by William Davis on August 24, 1982; see also Hutner Exhibit 5.

53. Goodman testified that he instructed Hutner not to inquire about the facts. Hutner denies Goodman gave such an order.

54. Testimony provided by William Davis on August 24, 1982.

55. The two cases Davis received from Mattiolo were United States v. Johnson 546 F. 2d 1225, Fifth Circuit (1977) and United States v. Gravitt 590 F. 2d 123, Fifth Circuit (1979).

56. Testimony provided by William Davis on August 24, 1982.

57. Gresham M. Sykes and David Matza, "Techniques of Neutralization: A Theory of Delinquency," *American Sociological Review*, 1957, vol. 22, pp. 664–670.

58. Leon Festinger, Henry W. Reicken, and Stanley Schacter, *When Prophecy Fails* (Minneapolis, MN: University of Minnesota Press, 1956); Leon Festinger, *A Theory of Cognitive Dissonance* (Stanford, CA: Stanford University Press, 1957).

59. John C. Coffee, "Beyond the Shut-eyed Sentry: Toward a Theoretical View of Corporate Misconduct and an Effective Legal Response," *Virginia Law Review*, 1977, vol. 63, pp. 1099–1278.

60. Albert Speer, *Inside the Third Reich* (New York: Avon, 1970), p. 379.

Chapter 7

1. Hassett Report, p. 456.

2. Zelbow Exhibit 46, Chapter 11 Proceedings Under the Bankruptcy Reform Act, U.S. District Court, Southern District of New York, Docket No. 81–B–10533 (BL).

3. Testimony provided by Martin Zelbow on September 24, 1981.

4. Testimony provided by Martin Zelbow on September 24, 1981.

5. Testimony provided by Louis Moscarello on November 23, 1981.

6. Moscarello testified, "The fact that a company has cash flow problems is no reason for not doing work for them, as long as you're sure you're going to get paid for it."

7. Testimony provided by Myron S. Goodman on December 9, 1982.

8. Marvin Weissman wanted Goodman to call Hutner rather than Andrew Reinhard because he assumed Reinhard already knew about the frauds.

9. Testimony provided by Joseph L. Hutner on June 14, 1982.

10. Testimony provided by Joseph L. Hutner on June 14, 1982.

11. Testimony provided by Joseph L. Hutner on June 14, 1982.

12. Eli Mattioli, who was not present during this meeting, testified that he was told Reinhard and Goodman left Hutner's room together. Asked whether Goodman and Reinhard left his office together, Hutner testified, "I don't recall, they may have."

13. Reinhard told Eli Mattioli that he was in his office with the Clifton letter in one hand and a letter opener in the other hand, and Goodman approached him and took the letter out of his hand. Goodman provided yet another version. He said he saw Reinhard reading the letter, and he took the letter from him. He said he and Reinhard together made up the "interception" story to protect Reinhard. Testimony provided by Myron S. Goodman on December 9, 1982, and Eli Mattioli on April 26, 1982.

14. Hassett Report, appendices 21–25.

15. Henry Singer denies being a party to these discussions. But Joseph Hutner's testimony seems to corroborate Weissman's. Hutner remembers Singer telling him that Goodman had "double-hocked" certain microcomputer leases, but Goodman claimed to have paid off the bad loans. Moreover, Hutner said that Goodman had insisted that Singer and Reinhard, who also knew, not tell anyone, not even the other Singer Hutner lawyers.

16. Although Goodman and Weissman didn't know it, they weren't the only ones committing fraud on this transaction; the vendor representative forged the lessee's signature. See Hassett Report, p. 361, fn. 91.

17. Hassett Report, p. 362.

18. The OPM trustee stated that one of the "most difficult issues encountered" in their investigation "was whether Reinhard knowingly participated in any fraudulent activities at OPM." The U.S. attorney investigated Reinhard's conduct and decided not to seek a grand jury indictment against him, but the OPM trustee wrote that the prosecutor's decision "is not dispositive." Much of what is written here is drawn from the testimony of Myron Goodman and from the OPM trustee's report. Reinhard asserted his Fifth Amendment privilege. Although the trustee concluded that Goodman's testimony had "a ring of truth" to it and, in some instances, was corroborated by other testimony, the trustee also commented that "the credibility of Goodman as a witness is undermined by his history of deceit and dishonesty and a number of anomalies in his testimony." See Hassett Report, p. 342.

19. Hassett Report, p. 338.

20. Testimony provided by Myron S. Goodman on November 3, 1982.

21. Letters written to the U.S. attorney in 1981 on Reinhard's behalf spoke of his "spirit of generosity," "integrity," and "fairness." One person wrote: "Andy was always available to Myron. Andy . . . could not say 'no' to anyone's request for help—be it small or large." See Hassett Report, 353.

22. A review of Reinhard's calendar indicates he was not on the West Coast on that date. Goodman also testified he told Weissman about the proposed Rockwell fraud on this flight. Goodman may be confused about who was told when.

23. Testimony provided by Myron S. Goodman on November 23, 1982.

24. Hutner Exhibit 8, OPM Bankruptcy Proceedings.

25. Testimony provided by Joseph L. Hutner on July 29, 1982.

26. Mattioli was also about to suggest McLaughlin when Rubino spoke. Both Rubino and Mattioli were Fordham Law School graduates and knew the dean from their association with the school. Rubino, somewhat older than Mattioli, knew McLaughlin from various alumni functions he had attended in the past; Mattioli had taken an evidence course taught by the dean. Both had a great deal of respect for his legal acumen and high integrity. They thought his expertise on the attorney-client privilege would be particularly helpful in addressing the problems facing Singer Hutner. Testimony provided by Joseph L. Hutner on July 30, 1982.

27. Testimony provided by Joseph L. Hutner on July 30, 1982.

28. Testimony provided by Joseph L. Hutner on July 30, 1982.

29. Hutner did not remember McLaughlin saying he had no expertise in professional responsibility or on legal ethics. He also did not recall any discussion about the alleged division of labor between Putzel and McLaughlin. Hutner further stated, "We perceived ourselves as having a problem and we believed, based on his reputation . . . he was the man to guide us through all the problems presented by it." See Hutner transcript of testimony, pp. 700–701.

Chapter 8

1. Testimony provided by Henry Peter Putzel III on May 26, 1982 for Chapter 11 Proceedings Under the Bankruptcy Reform Act, U.S. District Court, Southern District of New York, Docket No. 81–B–10533 (BL).

2. Mattioli Exhibit 3, OPM Bankruptcy Proceedings.

3. Putzel's notes of the June 20 meeting have the notations "bill/month $1.5 mil debt service (paying early terminations on computers) Debt service @ 50 mil/yc"—Putzel doesn't recall what he was told about the amount of OPM's debt, but if either of these figures is an indication, the amount was substantial.

4. McLaughlin and Putzel relied on the American Bar Association's Code of Professional Responsibility. Disciplinary Rule 2–110 (c) (1) and (2) reads, in part that, "a lawyer may not request permission to withdraw in matters pending before a tribunal, and may not withdraw in other matters, unless such a request or such withdrawal is because:

(1) His client:
    (a) Insists upon presenting a claim or defense that is not warranted under existing law and cannot be supported by good faith argument for an extension, modification, or reversal of existing law.
    (b) Personally seeks to pursue an illegal course of conduct.
    (c) Insists that the lawyer pursue a course of conduct that is illegal or that is prohibited under the Disciplinary Rules.
    (d) By other conduct renders it unreasonably difficult for the lawyer to carry out his employment effectively.
    (e) Insists, in a matter not pending before a tribunal, that the lawyer engage in conduct that is contrary to the judgment and advice of the lawyer but not prohibited under the Disciplinary Rules.
    (f) Deliberately disregards an agreement or obligation to the lawyer as to expenses and fees.
(2) His continued employment is likely to result in a violation of a Disciplinary Rule."

5. Testimony provided by Henry Peter Putzel III on May 26, 1982.

6. Hassett Report, appendices 21–25.

7. Testimony provided by Joseph L. Hutner on July 29, 1982, and Henry Peter Putzel III on May 26, 1982.

8. Irving Janis, *Groupthink: Psychological Studies of Policy Decisions and Fiascos*, 2nd edition (Boston: Houghton Mifflin, 1982), p. 9.

9. Irving Janis, *Groupthink*, p. 38.

10. Irving Janis, *Groupthink*, p. 38.

11. Testimony provided by Henry Peter Putzel III on May 26, 1982.

12. Testimony provided by Eli Mattioli on April 27, 1982. No one considered contacting equipment manufacturers such as IBM to determine whether OPM had actually purchased the equipment it was financing, which would have had a less deleterious effect on OPM's reputation.

13. Testimony provided by Joseph L. Hutner on July 30, 1982.

14. Hassett Report, p. 387.

15. Testimony provided by Henry Peter Putzel III on May 26, 1982.

16. Testimony provided by Henry Peter Putzel III on May 26, 1982.

17. Testimony provided by Joseph L. Hutner on July 30, 1982.

18. Hassett Report, appendices 21–25.

19. This is in spite of Davis's warning that the frauds involved submitting false documents to the law firm. Putzel later testified that, at the time, he was just beginning to understand these transactions and that he relied heavily on Singer Hutner to analyze the financing documentation since that was not his area of expertise and that was not what he was retained for.

20. Hassett Report, appendices 21–25.

21. Mattioli Exhibit 20, OPM Bankruptcy Proceedings.

22. Testimony provided by Joseph S. McLaughlin on August 30, 1982. Although Putzel and McLaughlin took this position, they continued to look to Goodman as OPM's representative. Indeed, Putzel testified that Goodman "personified" OPM. None of the attorneys did any research on the question of whether an officer who admits using the corporation for criminal activity can be trusted to speak for the company.

23. Testimony provided by Henry Peter Putzel III on May 26, 1982.

24. The Singer Hutner attorneys raised questions about the reliability of the information Davis provided them. Hutner said he didn't trust Davis and found him "sleazy." When they considered how much the law firm actually knew, such statements about Davis probably had some effect on McLaughlin and Putzel. Nonetheless, since Davis was an attorney, Putzel said, according to Mattioli, he "warranted more respect for his statements than would be the case if he was a non-attorney."

25. There is little question about Goodman's partial confession being a privileged communi-

cation, but the information obtained from Davis is less clear. Hutner's and Mattioli's second conversation with Davis occurred on June 16, three days after Clifton's resignation. Clifton was no longer an employee of OPM and, therefore, conversations between him or his attorney and counsel for his former employer would not have been subject to the privilege.

26. Many of Singer Hutner's opinion letters stated, in part, that OPM was not in "default with respect to any obligation under applicable law, judgment, order, writ, injunction, decree, rule or regulation of any court, administrative agency or other governmental authority to which it is subject." Some attorneys would have advised the law firm to alter their opinions in addition to retracting earlier ones that they then had reason to believe were false.

27. Testimony provided by Henry Peter Putzel III on May 27, 1982.

28. Testimony provided by Joseph S. McLaughlin on August 30, 1982.

29. Testimony provided by Joseph L. Hutner on August 2, 1982.

30. Testimony provided by Henry Peter Putzel III on May 27, 1982.

31. Mattioli didn't recall any discussion about whether it was permissible for Singer Hutner to contact the vendor for an explanation. Nor did it occur to Mattioli—nor, apparently, to Jacobs and Putzel—that if the fraud had been ongoing, it might not have been an adequate safeguard to check with an OPM employee about the problem.

32. Testimony provided by Henry Peter Putzel III on May 27, 1982.

33. Testimony provided by Joseph L. Hutner on August 3, 1982, and Henry Peter Putzel III on May 27, 1982.

34. During this phone conversation, Stephen Lichtman was called to the executive suite by Goodman's secretary to stop Goodman from committing suicide. Lichtman listened from the conference room adjacent to Goodman's office and he heard some animated conversation. He peeked into Goodman's office through the crack in the door and saw Goodman sitting comfortably in his chair, arms flailing away, but otherwise not visibly upset, yet he was threatening suicide. According to the U.S. attorney's sentencing memorandum to Judge Charles S. Haight, Goodman said "he had put on the performance just to keep the lawyers in their place." Goodman didn't recall the incident.

35. Before the scheduled meeting on August 6, Hutner asked Putzel for a written confirmation of the advice he and Dean McLaughlin had provided the law firm. Putzel said that Hutner was anxious to have something in writing before the forthcoming meeting with Goodman on August 6. Putzel drafted the letter and discussed it with Hutner and McLaughlin before he and the dean signed it. The early handwritten draft states "We advised you that you would be obligated to keep such disclosures confidential if they related to past conduct." The executed letter, typed on Dean McLaughlin's stationery, contains no reference to "past fraudulent conduct." No one recalled who suggested omitting that phrase.

36. Testimony provided by Joseph L. Hutner on August 3, 1982.

37. Testimony provided by Henry Peter Putzel III on May 27, 1982.

Chapter 9

1. Zelbow Exhibit 49, Chapter 11 Proceedings Under the Bankruptcy Reform Act, U.S. District Court, Southern District of New York, Docket No. 81–B–10533 (BL).

2. Testimony provided by Louis Moscarello on December 22, 1981.

3. Coopers's general counsel also told Moscarello it was under no obligation to tell anyone else.

4. See Zelbow Exhibit 66, OPM Bankruptcy Proceedings; Moscarello testimony on December 22, 1981.

5. See Batkin Exhibit 5A, OPM Bankruptcy Proceedings; Moscarello testimony on December 22, 1981.

6. In 1969, three accountants from the accounting firm Lybrand, Ross Brothers and Mont-

gomery, the predecessor firm to Coopers & Lybrand, were convicted of knowingly drawing up and certifying falsely misleading financial statements for Continental Vending Machines Corporation. The accountants certified a receivable—loans made to Harold Roth, president of Continental Vending—whose collectability was essential but collateralized only by securities of the very company whose solvency was at issue. In addition, the accountants failed to reveal a known increase in the receivable (United States v. Simon, 425 F. 2d 796 [2d cir. 1969]). Both Batkin and Moscarello were working for Coopers at the time, and they well remembered the impact it had on the firm.

7. Rule 301 of the code reads: "A member shall not disclose any confidential information obtained in the course of a professional engagement except with the consent of the client."

8. Section 391 of the AICPA's *Professional Standards* includes the following ethics ruling.

3. Information to Successor Accountant About Tax Return Irregularities .005 Question— A member withdrew from an engagement on discovering irregularities in his client's tax return. May he reveal to the successor accountant why the relationship was terminated?

.006 Answer—Rule 301 is not intended to help an unscrupulous client cover up illegal acts or otherwise hide information by changing CPAs. If the member was contacted by the successor he should, at a minimum, suggest that the successor ask the client to permit the member to discuss all matters freely with the successor. The successor is then on notice of some conflict. Because of the serious legal implications, the member should seek legal advice as to his status and obligations in the matter.

9. Testimony provided by Michael Weinberg on July 8, 1981.

10. Hassett Report, p. 171.

11. Testimony provided by Sidney Hasin on October 15, 1981.

12. The agreement was referred to as the sublease extension agreement because it extended certain OPM subleases and provided for future subleases.

13. About the same time, Hasin helped Goodman with Equipment Schedule 81 and the "Bridges to Nowhere."

14. "Computer Firm Indicted for Check-Kiting," *American Banker*, 10 March 1980, pp. 1, 16.

15. Testimony provided by Sidney Hasin on October 15, 1981.

16. See Neely Exhibit 28, OPM Bankruptcy Proceedings. Reference to the *Computer and Communications Buyer*, an industry weekly, published by Hesh Weiner. Weiner wrote an article critical of OPM's business practices and the check-kiting conviction, and the article came to DePalma's attention.

17. Testimony provided by Sidney Hasin on October 15, 1981.

18. McClellan and others at PSFS were apparently unconcerned that payment came from OPM rather than from Rockwell.

19. Neely Exhibit 19, OPM Bankruptcy Proceedings.

20. Neely Exhibit 42, OPM Bankruptcy Proceedings.

21. Hasin Exhibit 120, OPM Bankruptcy Proceedings.

22. Testimony provided by Sidney Hasin on December 7, 1981.

23. Hasin Exhibit 130, OPM Bankruptcy Proceedings.

Chapter 10

1. Testimony provided by Henry Peter Putzel III on May 27, 1982 for Chapter 11 Proceedings Under the Bankruptcy Reform Act, U.S. District Court, Southern District of New York, Docket No. 81–B–10533 (BL). Several Singer Hutner attorneys were very aware of potential financial problems at OPM. While preparing the complex materials for the purchase of the FNJ

stock, Joseph Hutner and Henry Singer met numerous times with Marvin Weissman and Myron Goodman to discuss OPM's financial condition. In a meeting at Goodman's home in June 1978, Singer noted that if all the lessees with early termination rights exercised those rights, OPM would have faced a shortfall of $80 to $90 million.

2. Testimony provided by Joseph L. Hutner on August 4, 1982.

3. Testimony provided by Joseph L. Hutner on August 4, 1982, and Henry Peter Putzel III on May 28, 1982.

4. Putzel was relying on another ABA rule for his position. Disciplinary Rule 2–110 (A) (2) reads:

> [A] lawyer shall not withdraw from employment until he has taken reasonable steps to avoid prejudice to the rights of his client, including giving due notice to his client, allowing time for employment of other counsel, delivering to the client all papers and property to which the client is entitled, and complying with applicable laws and rules.

5. Testimony provided by Eli Mattioli on May 11, 1982.

6. Testimony provided by Joseph L. Hutner on August 4, 1982.

7. Hassett Report, appendices 21–25.

8. Hassett Report, appendices 21–25.

9. Testimony provided by Joseph L. Hutner on August 4, 1982.

10. Hassett Report, p. 398.

11. Mattioli Exhibit 55, OPM Bankruptcy Proceedings.

12. Hutner claimed he was only "placating" Goodman; the law firm never seriously considered continuing the engagement. Perhaps this was Hutner's way of posturing to ensure that OPM paid Singer Hutner the fees it owed them, sort of "conning the con."

13. Testimony provided by Eli Mattioli on May 21, 1982.

14. Stephen Lichtman was also waiting for Goodman that evening. Hearing the commotion and Goodman's screaming, he couldn't get out of Singer Hutner's offices fast enough. Lichtman came running out of the building and said to Goodman's chauffeur, Frank Carrao, "I'm getting the hell out of here."
"What's wrong?"
"He's going crazy up there. He's screaming and carrying on and he's smashing his cane against the floor," Lichtman told him. Instead of waiting for Goodman, Lichtman took a cab home. When Goodman came out several hours later, Carrao purposely asked Goodman where his cane was, and he replied, "I broke it over somebody's head."
Testimony provided by Frank Carrao on December 9, 1981.

15. The law firm was quite concerned about getting its back fees. It even thought about demanding payment in writing, but Carl Rubino rejected that idea because it might inspire "irrationality" from Goodman.

16. Hassett Report, p. 400.

17. Testimony provided by Eli Mattioli on June 1, 1982.

18. Testimony provided by Joseph L. Hutner on September 15, 1982.

19. Mattioli Exhibit 103, OPM Bankruptcy Proceedings. On the question of whether the frauds were past or future crimes, Hutner contacted a former law school classmate of his, Professor Arthur Miller of the Harvard Law School. Miller didn't have an answer, so he referred Hutner to the vice-dean and now dean of the Harvard Law School, James Vorenberg. Vorenberg didn't know either, so he suggested Hutner speak to Andrew Kaufman of the same law school. The substance of the conversation between Kaufman and Hutner is being withheld on grounds that the conversation was a privileged communication between the two attorneys.

20. Testimony provided by Joseph L. Hutner on September 15, 1982.

21. Testimony provided by Joseph L. Hutner on September 15, 1982.

22. Mattioli Exhibit 79, OPM Bankruptcy Proceedings.

23. Hassett Report, p. 405.

24. Testimony provided by Henry Peter Putzel III, see transcript p. 544.

25. Hassett Report, pp. 416–421.

26. Testimony provided by David Sacks on August 26, 1982.

27. Testimony provided by Alan Batkin on November 5, 1981.

28. Batkin Exhibit 88 and 91, OPM Bankruptcy Proceedings.

Chapter 11

1. Hassett Report, pp. 199–204.

2. Testimony provided by Sidney Hasin for Chapter 11 Proceedings Under the Bankruptcy Reform Act, U.S. District Court, Southern District of New York, Docket No. 81–B–10533 (BL), see transcript p. 1471.

3. Testimony provided by Sidney Hasin, see transcript p. 1476.

4. Testimony provided by Gary R. Simon on June 15, 1981.

5. Testimony provided by Jeffry Resnick on January 20, 1982.

6. Hassett Report, pp. 206–207.

7. Testimony provided by Sidney Hasin, see transcript p. 1481.

8. Testimony provided by Sidney Hasin, see transcript p. 496.

9. Hassett Report, pp. 520–521.

10. Hassett Report, p. 295.

11. Eric N. Berg, "S.E.C. Files Suit Against Fox & Co.," *The New York Times,* 9 June 1983, p. D4.

Chapter 12

1. Hassett Report, pp. 44–45.

2. Philip Selznick, *The Organizational Weapon* (Glencoe, Ill.: The Free Press, 1960); Stanton Wheeler and Mitchell Lewis Rothman, "The Organization as Weapon in White Collar Crime," *University of Michigan Law Review,* 1982, pp. 1403–1426.

3. Erving Goffman, *The Presentation of Self in Everyday Life* (Garden City, N.Y.: Doubleday, 1959), p. 225.

4. Wheeler and Rothman, "The Organization as Weapon in White Collar Crime," p. 1406.

5. Goffman, *The Presentation of Self in Everyday Life,* pp. 111–112.

6. Hassett Report, p. 29.

7. Harold L. Wilensky, *Organizational Intelligence: Knowledge and Policy in Government and Industry* (New York: Basic Books, 1967).

8. Testimony provided by LeRoy McClellan on March 2, 1982 for Chapter 11 Proceedings Under the Bankruptcy Reform Act, U.S. District Court, Southern District of New York, Docket No. 81–B–10533 (BL).

9. Hassett Report, p. 594.

10. Testimony provided by LeRoy McClellan on March 2, 1982.

11. Goffman, *The Presentation of Self in Everyday Life,* p. 204.

12. Mitchell Lewis Rothman and Robert P. Gandossy, "Sad Tales: The Accounts of White Collar Defendants and the Decision to Sanction," *Pacific Sociological Review*, vol. 25, 1982, pp. 449–473.

13. Testimony provided by John Clifton on January 26 and 28, 1982, and Marvin Weissman on September 23, 1981.

14. Goffman, *The Presentation of Self in Everyday Life,* p. 204.

15. *Economic Report of the President* (Washington, D.C.: U.S. Government Printing Office, 1977, 1978, 1979, 1980); Robert B. Reich, *The Next American Frontier* (New York: Times

Books, 1983), pp. 117–139; Lester C. Thurow, *The Zero-Sum Society* (New York: Basic Books, 1980).

16. Sanford Rose, "Dark Days Ahead for Banks," *Fortune*, 30 June 1980, pp. 86–90.

17. Thomas Mayer, James S. Dusenberry, and Robert Z. Aliber, *Banking and the Economy* (New York: W.W. Norton, 1981).

18. Philadelphia Savings Fund Society Annual Report, 1975, 1978–1980.

19. John Helyar, "Western Savings, Philadelphia Savings Merge with $294 Million in FDIC Help," *Wall Street Journal*, 5 April 1982, p. 6.

20. Survey conducted by the OPM trustee's attorneys.

21. We can speculate as to why New York City banks, for the most part, rejected OPM business in the late 1970s. Throughout the mid-1970s, OPM had a number of New York banks handle its accounts, but the bankers constantly confronted bounced checks and other difficulties on OPM accounts. The bankers eventually asked OPM to find another bank. Indeed, one OPM officer referred to this period as "OPM's march through the New York banking community." With OPM's kind of reputation, the local banks were understandably reluctant to lend OPM any money; lenders outside of the New York region weren't privy to the rumors. Why the New York-based Lehman was not aware of the rumors is not clear.

22. Peter W. Bernstein, "Competition Comes to Accounting," *Fortune*, 17 July 1978, pp. 88–96.

23. *Commission on Auditor's Responsibilities: Report, Conclusions and Recommendations* (New York: The Commission on Auditor's Responsibilities, 1978), p. 110.

24. Peter W. Bernstein, "Profit Pressures on the Big Law Firms," *Fortune*, 19 April 1982, pp. 84–91, 94, 98, 100; Tamar Lewin, "Business and the Law," *The New York Times*, 15 November 1983, p. D2.

25. Hassett Report, p. 524.

26. Bibb Latane and John M. Darley, "Bystander Apathy," in *Current Perspectives in Social Psychology*, 4th ed., eds. Edwin P. Hollander and Raymond G. Hunt (New York: Oxford University Press, 1976), pp. 140–152.

27. Fred H. Goldner, "The Division of Labor: Process and Power," in *Power in Organizations*, ed. Mayer Zald (Nashville: Vanderbilt University Press, 1970), pp. 97–143.

28. Mayer N. Zald, "On the Social Control of Industries," *Social Forces*, September 1978, pp. 79–102.

29. Such organizations make up what Dill referred to as the organization's "task environment." William R. Dill, "Environment as an Influence on Managerial Autonomy," *Administrative Science Quarterly*, 1958, pp. 409–443.

30. Rosabeth Moss Kanter, *The Change Masters: Innovation for Productivity in the American Corporation* (New York: Simon & Schuster, 1982).

Epilogue

1. Penny Lernoux, *In Banks We Trust* (Garden City, New York: Doubleday, 1984).

2. Randall Collins, *Sociological Insight: An Introduction to Non-obvious Sociology* (New York: Oxford University Press, 1982).

3. Sissela Bok, *Secrets: On the Ethics of Concealment and Revelation* (New York: Pantheon, 1982).

INDEX